201.72
COR   24.99

Corsi, Jerome R. PhD

BAD SAMARITANS

DATE DUE

Praise for *BAD SAMARITANS*

Dr. Corsi has written powerfully and breathtakingly on numerous major topics for years. Now he has taken on a persistent foe of the American public—the (so-called) American Civil Liberties Union and its campaign to deny the public their religious civil liberties. This book is a clarion call for action that should be heard far and wide.

CARL OLSON, CHAIRMAN,
STATE DEPARTMENT WATCH

Jerome Corsi authoritatively details the many ways in which the ACLU undermines the Judeo-Christian foundation of American society. He also shows how this objective serves the political interests of the Left. The ACLU won't like it, but that's all the more reason why those who truly value freedom will embrace it.

BILL DONOHUE, AUTHOR, *THE POLITICS OF THE
AMERICAN CIVIL LIBERTIES UNION* AND *TWILIGHT OF
LIBERTY: THE LEGACY OF THE ACLU*, PRESIDENT OF THE
CATHOLIC LEAGUE FOR RELIGIOUS AND CIVIL RIGHTS

Our first civil liberty is the freedom of religion. Ironically it's the right the American Civil Liberties Union works most doggedly to undermine. In *Bad Samaritans* Jerry Corsi rips the mask off of the ACLU and its agenda for a godless world once and for all.

MICHAEL CENTANNI, CHAIRMAN,
FREEDOM'S DEFENSE FUND

Jerome Corsi has done a masterful job of detailing the ACLUs ongoing campaign against God and Christianity, a campaign that perfectly set the stage for Barack Obama's effort to secularize America and proclaim to the world that "we do not consider ourselves a Christian nation." Corsi's Bad Samaritans should be required reading for every pastor so he can educate his flock about the threat to religious freedom in America.

PHYLLIS SCHLAFLY,
PRESIDENT, EAGLE FORUM

In *Bad Samaritans* Jerry Corsi correctly identifies the ACLU as both an organization seeking a collectivist world order based on flawed liberal magic think and money grabbing commercial enterprise. His appraisal of the ACLU move into social issues to bring about radical societal change is accurate and documented. Corsi's analysis of the case in which my atheist mother, Madalyn Murray O'Hair, was involved in to remove prayer from the schools is precise and demonstrates the use of American courts to destroy America's civil foundations. This is a must read book for those seeking knowledge of the origins and objectives of the ACLU.

WILLIAM J. MURRAY, CHAIRMAN,
RELIGIOUS FREEDOM COALITION

bad

SAMARITANS

bad
SAMARITANS

THE ACLU'S RELENTLESS CAMPAIGN TO ERASE
FAITH *from* THE PUBLIC SQUARE

JEROME R. CORSI, PhD

THOMAS NELSON
Since 1798

NASHVILLE   DALLAS   MEXICO CITY   RIO DE JANEIRO

Published in Nashville, Tennessee, by Thomas Nelson. Thomas Nelson is a registered trademark of Thomas Nelson, Inc.

Thomas Nelson, Inc., titles may be purchased in bulk for educational, business, fund-raising, or sales promotional use. For information, please e-mail SpecialMarkets@ ThomasNelson.com.

Scripture quotations are taken from the Holy Bible, New International Version®, NIV®. Copyright © 1973, 1978, 1984, 2011 by Biblica, Inc.™ Used by permission of Zondervan. All rights reserved worldwide. www.zondervan.com

Library of Congress Control Number: 2012955445

ISBN: 9781595554741

Printed in the United States of America

13 14 15 16 17 RRD 6 5 4 3 2 1

*For William J. Murray, William A. Donohue, Joseph Farah,
and Phyllis Schlafly, four Good Samaritan warriors in Jesus
Christ, who have led the battle against the ACLU's War on God*

. . . one nation under God, with liberty and justice for all.

—Pledge of Allegiance to
the United States of America

CONTENTS

Preface

PROTECTING FAITH, PRESERVING LIBERTY

Without religion the government of a free people cannot be maintained.

—W. CLEON SKOUSEN[1]

G od did not inspire our Founding Fathers to create the United States as a land of religious freedom only to see subsequent generations squander that precious religious freedom because a group of politically motivated lawyers funded by the American Civil Liberties Union (ACLU) fought, nearly unopposed, a sophisticated, ideological War on God.

Since its founding, the ACLU has set out to pervert the First Amendment, written to *preserve* religious freedom, into a twisted interpretation where "freedom *of* religion" is now read to mean "freedom *from* religion," a reinterpretation made necessary if the ACLU is to accomplish its long-standing goal of removing God from America's public square.

The ACLU is the legal vanguard in the United States of a movement whose roots trace back to atheism and communism. The Founding Fathers warned that our liberties were dependent upon a citizenry who believed in God. Communists from Marx and Lenin on have always realized that undermining religion is a precondition to establishing their political goals, which include state control of the means of production, abolition of private property, and redistribution of income. In other words, the destruction of the capitalist state demands a war on the Judeo-Christian God. Undermining liberty cannot happen unless faith is first undermined. The point is, the founding principles of the ACLU determined as necessary that the organization existed to wage a War on God. The ACLU's hatred of God was no modern accident. Instead, the ACLU's hatred of God is a necessary consequence of the reason the organization was created.

The protection and rights of the individual—conceived as an eternal soul given life by a Supreme Being, endowed with unalienable rights, and governed by a code of natural right built into human consciousness by our Creator—are the fundamental construct that drove our Founding Fathers to write the Declaration of Independence, the Constitution, and the Bill of Rights. The ACLU understands correctly that attacking God is the only way the American people would ever permit these sacred documents to be so deeply rewritten as to subvert their original meaning. If the American people can be driven from believing in God, the consequence is that our rights are no longer unalienable, but instead our rights, such as they may be, are bestowed by a state that can as easily take away the rights as grant them in the first place.

Among a purely secular people who have no meaning for natural law, all laws are equivalent, such that even when the state dictates arbitrarily, there is no power or ultimate arbiter higher than the state itself. A people who abandon God necessarily abandons their liberty. All that remains is a secular state whose end in purpose may well be the end of any liberty or freedom, such as is expressed by the First Amendment, that predicates itself on the inherent right built into the human heart and soul to have individual recourse to a power greater than the state. A secular state that can bestow human rights can equally remove those same human rights, at the will of the state, to the extreme detriment of those believers in God who yet might remain within the state.

As I completed this book, I felt a sense of urgency. Since the organization was created in 1920, so many constitutional battles have been lost to the ACLU that time has grown short to stop the onslaught. Constitutional warriors for God must understand the ACLU has employed such sophisticated techniques—not only of legal argumentation, but also of organizational development, fund-raising, and even psychology and public relations—that reversing the tide in God's favor has no easy assurance of success.

This book does not aspire to be a comprehensive compendium of Supreme Court cases dealing with religion. Instead, I want to unmask the ACLU's hypocritical façade of defending civil liberties that the organization strives to sell to a secular public unable to appreciate how deeply liberty will be lost if God is abandoned. I will expose the secret history of the ACLU in order to encourage supporters of our faith to enter the war on God's side. We must win the war against our faith if we are to preserve for future generations the heritage of liberty our Founding Fathers so generously left for us. Our Founding Fathers bestowed on future generations a constitutional republic "if we can keep it," as Benjamin Franklin famously warned. Now is the time to prove this generation of Americans will be equal to the task of rising up against the ACLU to preserve the freedom of religion our Founding Fathers meant for citizens of the United States to enjoy, even if it means crushing once and for all the ACLU as an effective advocate for a godless public arena.

In the final analysis, I am confident the instinct God placed at the center of human consciousness to be aware of the divine will win out; the Judeo-Christian faith will not be erased from our nation and the face of the earth. But if we do not fight this battle now, the United States of America will most certainly descend into a form of paganism not seen since the darkest days of antiquity. Because of its instant mass communication tools, its financial strength, and its savvy propaganda techniques to advance its politically correct agenda, we shall descend into dark days with a list of horrors unimagined in previous eras—including abortion on demand, unrestrained pornography of every possible variation, and sexual promiscuity that knows no bounds—unless the ACLU is stopped dead in its tracks right now. The end result of the ACLU's desired freedom from religion is a libertine license that puts human desires and pleasures, regardless how petty or bizarre, on the throne where God belongs. Instead of unalienable rights bestowed by God, the state will be used to preserve, protect, and defend outrageous lifestyles, open access to vices, and the near-random killing of unborn children. Despicably, the ACLU will pervert the First Amendment to create and then to protect its desired future political reality that attempts to erase every last vestige of God that dares seek expression outside the confines of an individual human heart and mind.

Those who will be outlawed as bigots and ultimately as criminals in the atheistic, materialistic world the ACLU desires to create are the very faith believers our Founding Fathers thought they were writing the First Amendment to protect. Today the ACLU is bent on creating future generations who will renounce and despise the God of the Jews and the Christians, as the founders of the ACLU so despised all our Founding Fathers knew as holy.

We must act now if people of faith—those who continue to believe that God's law is defined by the Constitution, not by the ACLU—are to prevail ultimately.

This struggle, unfortunately, is nothing new. None less than Satan defined the first attempt to dethrone God so as to elevate himself to God's throne.

But if we allow the Judeo-Christian culture to be replaced by an atheistic view of human destiny, we are heading away from the liberties our Founding Fathers defined for us and heading down the road to slavery. Sin will be viewed as a worn-out, Old World concept derived from the Inquisition, while the fall from the garden of Eden will be dismissed as a fable designed by synagogues and churches to keep us in servitude to the secular authorities that operate and govern human religious institutions. What will provide the philosophical foundation for the libertine future that the ACLU is in the process of creating is the Darwin-derived theory that human beings can advance to a Marxist-Leninist social utopia through the natural selection as redefined by the class struggle. Abortion will be seen as eliminating the unwanted, much as the eugenics masters preached in their march-up to the Holocaust, while the open pursuit of our most selfish, most base instincts will be regarded as nothing more than a valid experiment in the survival of the fittest. While a sexual agenda unimaginable to the generation of Americans who fought World War II will be taught even in kindergarten classes, no fetus given life by God and growing in the womb of a mother will be considered safe from extinction with the blessing of the state.

If the ACLU advances unopposed in its godless agenda, the dark that is descending on America may not be lifted for generations, if ever. And as our Founding Fathers so aptly reminded us, only a moral people can preserve the liberty required to build a bright future for America in which individual initiative and free enterprise can thrive once again.

In a Judeo-Christian nation, Good Samaritans are not only welcome; they are possible. In the world desired by the ACLU, Good Samaritans will not only be rare; they are likely to be persecuted, if not prosecuted. Shared values derived from a common Judeo-Christian tradition teach us to "do to others as you would have them do to you."[2] In a secular world where the state controls what rights we are permitted as citizens, the golden rule no longer applies equally. Over its history the ACLU has been the archetypical Bad Samaritan—a stranger to the nation's religious tradition, whose founders instilled within the organization values designed to erase all vestiges of the nation's Judeo-Christian roots and replace them with a transplanted godless vision that draws its energy not from Moses or from Jesus Christ, but from Marx and Lenin. Even more insidiously, the ACLU strategy devised by its founders was predicated on a determination to wage its War on God in a stealth fashion in which the ACLU intends to destroy our religious freedom by appearing on the scene as a defender of our religious freedom.

After decades of the ACLU attacking God in court, God has become the beaten and robbed traveler lying helpless by the side of the road. In the modern parable, the Good Samaritan of the Bible does not save the traveler. Instead, the traveler is attacked, beaten, and robbed by the Bad Samaritan of the ACLU, through the intervention of its paid pack of liberal legal advocates. The hour is late, and the question is whether we as Good Samaritans can yet save God's place at the center of our nation, restoring God as the endower of our rights, in the Judeo-Christian tradition that motivated our Founding Fathers to establish this nation over two hundred years ago.

The message of this book is that the ACLU will be successfully repelled in our courts such that God will be restored to the public square of this nation—but only when an army of warriors for God stands up against the ACLU. The United States must return to an understanding of the Constitution based on natural law, just as future generations of Americans must be taught once again that true morality must be based on the religious faith expressed in the Judeo-Christian Bible, with the understanding that the unalienable rights we enjoy are derived from our Creator, not from the secular state as advised by the ACLU.

I

The War on God

We do not consider ourselves a Christian nation.

—President Barack H. Obama[1]

A t a press conference in Turkey on April 6, 2009, President Obama declared that we Americans do not consider ourselves to be a Christian nation. President Obama chose to make this pronouncement in an Islamic state. The more complete quotation makes it clear the president wanted to distance characterizing the United States by any religious values: "Although as I mentioned, we have a very large Christian population, we do not consider ourselves a Christian nation or a Jewish nation or a Muslim nation; we consider ourselves a nation of citizens who are bound by ideals and a set of values."[2]

Studying this quotation, we can see how successful the American Civil Liberties Union has been in transforming the concept of the United States from our origins, distancing our present from the initial pilgrims who landed in the New World to escape religious persecution in the Old World. Subtly, President Obama's statement erases religion altogether from the concept of the United States as a nation. Substituted instead are secular concepts of not specified "ideals" and "values." What precisely are these ideals and values if the definition must derive from other than an understanding of God? If there is no God who instills in human beings our "unalienable rights" of life, liberty, and the pursuit of happiness, are we now fully dependent on the state to define and preserve our freedoms? Consider how far we have come from the Declaration of Independence that President Obama can make today a definitional statement of the United States without reference to our Creator. This transformation of America from a Judeo-Christian nation to a secular nation that excludes God from public mention has not happened by accident.

As noted in the Preface, under the guise of protecting First Amendment freedom of religion rights, the ACLU has conducted a decades-long War on God, with the goal of erasing every trace of the Judeo-Christian religion from the public spaces of the nation. The ACLU's War on God is central to the true purpose of the Communists who founded the organization and the radical Left that promotes the organization today.

Today, the ACLU aims to remove all symbols of Judeo-Christian worship not only from the public spaces of the nation but also from the hearts and minds of the American people. For those who think this judgment is too harsh, consider that our Founding Fathers intended to welcome all religions on an equal basis, a principle they clearly articulated in the First Amendment.

Never did our Founding Fathers contemplate the creation of an organization like the ACLU—a well-funded group of leftist legal advocates who would learn how to use the principles of religious freedom defined in the First Amendment to destroy religious freedom in the United States.

Ironically, the hypocrisy of the ACLU has never been greater than today. How can the ACLU defend Islam in the same public arena in which it would have sued if the religious practices had been Judeo-Christian in nature?

These three short vignettes should leave no doubt that Judeo-Christian religious beliefs are not safe in the United States as long as the ACLU continues to win in the war it has decided since its founding to wage against God.

In 1934, members of the Veterans of Foreign Wars (VFW) put up a Latin cross on Sunrise Rock in the Mojave Desert as a memorial to soldiers who died in World War I.

Sunrise Rock became public land in 1994 when Congress passed the California Desert Protection Act, creating the Mojave National Preserve.[3] This legislation transformed the cross from being a memorial to the veterans who died in World War I to preserve our basic freedoms into what the ACLU would quickly perceive as an objectionable religious symbol that needed to be removed from government-owned land.

To get a feel for the impact of a solitary cross, regardless how prominently displayed, on a national park the size of the Mojave National Preserve, consider that the park covers some 1.6 million acres of Southern California land—an area that comprises 25,000 square miles, making the Mojave National Preserve the third-largest unit of the National Park System in the contiguous United States. Its size exceeds the combined area of the nation's five smallest states.[4] A solitary cross in a park that size is barely the magnitude of a postage stamp placed on a football field.

Yet despite the relative insignificance in size of the few feet comprising the cross monument, for more than sixty years the cross remained a poignant expression giving meaning to the ultimate sacrifice of those honored US servicemen and servicewomen who fought, bled, and died in Europe's World War I trench-lined battlefields.

Going back to the 1930s, the original caretaker of the cross was a reclusive prospector named John Riley Bembrey, reputedly a medic in World War I and part of the original group of veterans who erected the cross. Over time, caretaking for the memorial passed to Wanda and Henry Sandoz, a couple who owned private land elsewhere on the preserve. They had been on a picnic in the desert when they met Bembrey in an encounter that changed their lives.

When the *Washington Post* caught up with Wanda and Henry in 2009, they were approaching the fiftieth anniversary of their marriage; Wanda was sixty-five years old, and Henry was seventy. "Everybody in the area knew why that cross was there," Henry told the newspaper reporter. "They want to just tear it down, tear it down, tear it down, but I put it up to stay." Wanda was equally devoted to the monument. "We realize this country wouldn't be what it was without the veterans," she told the *Washington Post*. "To me, I know it sounds corny, but that cross out there in the middle of nowhere is as important to me as the Vietnam memorial. All your memorials in Washington, D.C., they're beautiful, they're impressive, they're wonderful, but they say the same exact thing as that cross is saying."[5]

Even after Henry and Wanda in their senior years had moved some 150 miles away from the Mojave Desert to be closer to their grandchildren, the couple remained as committed as ever to their mission. The cross had been replaced and repaired many times since first being put in place in 1934; in 1998 Sandoz finally built a cross of four-inch metal pipes painted white that stood eight feet tall.

For decades, the various crosses stood tall in the Southern California sky, atop the thirty-foot-high rock, equally visible from the nearest highway ten miles away and from Cima Road, a narrow strip of blacktop within one hundred feet of Sunrise Rock. Since it was first put in place, the Mojave cross served as a gathering place for Easter services, and the immediate area was used as a campsite for those who gathered to worship there. At one point, the cross was marked by wooden signs that stated, "The Cross, Erected in Memory of the Dead of All Wars," and "Erected 1934 by Members of Veterans of Foreign Wars, Death Valley Post 2884."[6]

In 1999, Frank Buono, a retired Park Service employee who had worked at nearby Joshua Tree National Park and professed to be Catholic, complained to the ACLU that he was offended by the presence of the cross as a religious symbol on public land. He felt the cross represented a violation of the establishment clause of the First Amendment. Buono argued that even though he lived in Oregon, he was a frequent visitor to the Mojave National Preserve. He asked the ACLU of Southern California to seek on his behalf an injunction against the government that would compel the removal of the cross.

Henry and Wanda Sandoz objected strenuously. Politely but firmly, Sandoz told the *Washington Post* that he was not inclined to be helpful when the superintendent of the preserve told him and his wife that there had been a complaint about the cross and asked him to take it down.

"I told her not 'no,' but 'hell, no,'" he told the reporter.[7]

In March 2001, the ACLU of Southern California, representing Buono, filed a lawsuit in federal court to compel National Park Service officials to remove the cross. "The federal government should not offer public land—owned collectively by people of every faith and no faith—as a site for the advertisement and promotion of Jesus Christ, Buddha, Pope John Paul II, or any other particular religious figure," said Peter Eliasberg, a staff attorney of the ACLU of Southern California and a First Amendment specialist, at the time the lawsuit was filed.[8]

The ACLU press release announcing the lawsuit indicated the ACLU felt it had won the previous year in negotiations about the issue after receiving a letter from the National Park Service saying the cross would be removed. But everything changed on December 15, 2000, when the US Congress passed an appropriations bill including a rider introduced by California's Republican representative Jerry Lewis that prohibited the secretary of the interior from using any federal funds to remove the Mojave cross.[9]

"If any person was allowed to place a permanent, free-standing expression of his or her political viewpoint at this site, we would have no objection," Eliasberg said, defending the lawsuit, "but that is not the case here. No other group is allowed to erect a religious symbol. This creates a situation in which the federal government favors Christian expression over any other."[10]

The ACLU press release said the Mojave cross case presented the ACLU with a "crucial first test" of the US Department of Justice under then recently appointed attorney general John Ashcroft, a strong and openly professed Christian. The ACLU noted that he "promised during his confirmation hearings that he would uphold the Constitution."[11]

At the same time he filed the lawsuit, Eliasberg sent a letter to the Department of Justice in which he urged government officials "to act responsibly, abide by the law, and reach a quick settlement rather than attempt to defend a clearly unconstitutional practice," according to the press release. "This case will put to the test Attorney General Ashcroft's commitment to upholding the principles of our Constitution," Eliasberg wrote. "This will be a clear indicator of what we can expect from this Department of Justice in upholding the First Amendment guarantees that keep us free."[12]

The ACLU expressed no doubt that the Constitution required the Bush administration to defy not only its faith-based principles and God, but also the World War I veterans to whom the cross was dedicated, in using the power of the federal government to remove this lonely white cross from the rugged granite outcrop on which it stood in one of California's most beautiful and most desolate deserts.

"The courts have consistently held," Eliasberg argued, "that a permanent religious fixture on federal land is a violation of the U.S. Constitution. An Act of Congress doesn't change that. The cross must come down, and no amount of political maneuvering or grandstanding will prevent that."[13]

Ever conscious of the public relations impact of its arguments, the ACLU of Southern California had asked Morris Radin, an eighty-two-year-old Jewish veteran of World War II, to attend the press conference in a move obviously calculated to cushion what otherwise might be interpreted as an offense against veterans.

"My father, Abe, was just eighteen when he came to America and became a citizen," Radin told the press. "As an Orthodox Jew, he knew firsthand what happens when people are not free to practice their beliefs. He and my mother Sophie both left Russia to escape the pogroms. They never told me whether they had witnessed any of the atrocities born of that nation's inability to guarantee their freedom of religion. They drew a curtain on that period of their lives and faced a new life in a different place."[14]

What was the ACLU's point? That the Holocaust could be repeated in the United States if the Bush administration in its first months in office was not compelled to use the full force and authority of the federal government to remove the Mojave cross?

On July 24, 2002, the US District Court for the Central District of California found that Buono, as a frequent visitor to the Mojave National

Preserve, had standing to sue and, after concluding the presence of the cross on federal land conveyed an impression of governmental endorsement of religion, granted Buono injunctive relief to remove the cross. "This is a huge victory not only for the ACLU but also for the First Amendment," Eliasberg celebrated on hearing the district court's ruling.[15]

In the wake of the district court ruling in 2002, a plywood box was constructed and mounted on the cross to cover the view of the horizontal bar. Instead of a cross on top of Sunrise Rock, the memorial was transformed into a rectangular box held aloft by a round, white-painted metal pole.

In 2003, once again Representative Lewis came to the rescue by inserting language into the massive fiscal year 2004 defense appropriations bill that proposed to swap out the cross and one acre of the land on which it stood in exchange for a one-acre parcel of land owned by the Sandoz family within the confines of the Mojave National Preserve. This was aimed at transferring the Mojave cross from federal ownership to sympathetic private ownership under the auspices of the Veterans of Foreign Wars.[16]

On April 5, 2005, the US District Court for the Central District of California held that the land exchange arranged by Congress in 2003 was a "sham" to avoid the Constitution, an invalid attempt to keep the cross on display, not a legitimate attempt to comply with the court's earlier issued injunction. This decision was upheld by the US Court of Appeals for the Ninth Circuit, one of the most liberal courts in America, in the decision of a three-judge panel that invalidated the land transfer on September 6, 2007, arguing that "carving out a tiny parcel of property in the midst of this vast Preserve—like a donut hole with the cross atop it—will do nothing to minimize the impermissible governmental endorsement."[17]

The Bush administration appealed, calling the ruling of the Ninth Circuit Court of Appeals a "seriously misguided decision" that would require the government "to tear down a cross that has stood without incident for 70 years as a memorial to fallen service members."[18] When it reached the Supreme Court, the case tested not only the resolve of the Bush administration but also the conservative credentials of Bush-appointed chief justice

John G. Roberts in a court that also included Justice Samuel A. Alito Jr., whom Bush appointed to replace Sandra Day O'Connor as she retired.

On April 28, 2010, in writing the majority opinion for the Supreme Court, Justice Anthony Kennedy remanded the case, *Salazar v. Buono*, 559 U.S. _____ (2010), back to the lower courts for further consideration consistent with the Supreme Court's holdings. Justice Kennedy concluded that

> a Latin cross is not merely a reaffirmation of Christian beliefs. It is a symbol often used to honor and respect those whose heroic acts, noble contributions, and patient striving help secure an honored place in the history of this Nation and its people. Here, one Latin cross in the desert evokes far more than religion. It evokes thousands of small crosses in foreign fields marking the graves of Americans who fell in battles, battles whose tragedies are compounded if the fallen are forgotten.[19]

But the liberal members of the Supreme Court were not convinced. Dissenting, Justice John Paul Stevens wrote, "The cross is not a universal symbol of sacrifice. It is the symbol of one particular sacrifice, and that sacrifice carries deeply significant meaning for those who adhere to the Christian faith."[20]

In the delicate balance that is the Supreme Court, for the moment the conservative appointments of the Bush administration held the day when they declared the Constitution does not necessarily require the removal of religious symbols from public land.[21]

Technically, the Supreme Court dodged the issue. The majority of justices decided it was better to accept the land transfer, not as the sham seen by the Ninth Circuit Court, but as a legitimate removal of the cross from federal land to private property now owned by the VFW. Still, narrowly viewed, the complex Supreme Court decision in *Salazar v. Buono* only remanded to the district court for reconsideration the land-transfer scheme the appeals court had previously rejected; the carefully crafted consensus avoided forcing the Supreme Court to take an ultimate stand on the constitutionality of the cross itself.

That a majority of the court—Justices John Roberts and Samuel Alito, along with Anthony Kennedy, Antonin Scalia, and Clarence Thomas—ruled the cross should remain in place appeared to many to represent a shift in the court toward allowing religious symbols to remain on government property. Truthfully, the decision was splintered, with concurring, dissenting, concurring-in-part, and dissenting-in-part decisions being filed by the various justices. The court took the easy way out, deciding to remand the case back to the lower courts to see if the land-transfer solution could be worked out. In other words, if the cross technically could be defined as not resting on federal land, the constitutional challenge would simply go away.

"The land-transfer statute embodies Congress's legislative judgment that this dispute is best resolved through a framework and policy of accommodation for a symbol that, while challenged under the Establishment Clause, has complex meaning beyond the expression of religious views," Justice Kennedy wrote. "That judgment should not have been dismissed as an evasion, for the statute brought about a change of law and a congressional statement of policy applicable to the case."[22]

In the final analysis, the Supreme Court ruling settled nothing.

During the night of May 9–10, 2010, unknown vandals tore off the plywood cover, physically removed the cross from its base on Sunrise Rock, and stole it. Wanda Sandoz told the Associated Press that vandals had damaged the cross in the past, but that such incidents had become rarer since her husband bolted the cross to the desert rock more than a decade earlier.

"I was really upset and I was crying," Wanda said, after learning the cross was gone, "but then I said, 'Well, we'll show them. We'll put up a bigger one and a better one.'"

But Henry Sandoz objected, "No we won't. We will put one up exactly like the veterans put up."[23]

The VFW offered—to no avail—a twenty-five-thousand-dollar reward for information leading to the conviction of those behind the cross's removal.[24] Within days, a replica cross was mounted on Sunrise Rock.

Yet on May 21, 2010, the Justice Department ordered the replica taken down. Linda Slater, a spokesperson for the National Park Service, explained that the park service employees removed the replica because the Ninth Circuit Court had not yet reversed its injunction. "We're still under a court injunction," Slater said. "We have to take it down."[25]

Besides, the National Park Service was not sure the Supreme Court's ruling applied to mandate the display of a replica cross, now that the original was gone.

After the theft, all that was left on Sunrise Rock was two protruding bolts from the old cross, jagged from being sawed when the original cross was removed, encased in a concrete pad upon which the new cross was placed.

"It just gets crazier and crazier," Wanda Sandoz told reporters.

The implications of the Mojave cross case remain enormous for the future of God in America.

"If you tear down a seven-foot cross in the middle of the Mojave Desert, 1.6 million acres, what will you have to do to the crosses in Arlington National Ceremony and all the other memorials in highly trafficked, prominent locations?" wondered Kelly Shackelford of the Liberty Legal Institute, one group that has worked on providing legal representation to keep the memorial in the desert. "The implications are large and we just don't know if the court is going there," he told WND in a printed interview. "But what about the Tomb of the Unknown, [where an inscriptions reads] 'Known but to God.' Or the Supreme Court [which has multiple images of the Ten Commandments]. They'll have to call out the bulldozers and sandblasters."[26]

As of this writing, no cross stands atop Sunrise Rock, and the future of the cross in the desert remains in doubt, despite a Supreme Court decision that was aimed at leaving the cross in place.

❧

In 2001, Judge Ray Moore, chief justice of the Alabama Supreme Court, who is also a West Point graduate and a Vietnam veteran, received national publicity for placing a massive granite monument displaying the Ten Commandments in the central rotunda of the state judicial building. Predictably, the ACLU filed suit; the Eleventh Circuit Court of

Appeals upheld the US District Court ruling that the monument had to be removed. The case ended in 2003, when the Alabama Court of the Judiciary unanimously removed Moore from his job as chief justice. The monument was removed, and Ray Moore became a national celebrity. In 2011 Moore, now known as "The Ten Commandments Judge," even considered running for president.[27]

In 2005, the US Supreme Court ruled on the Ray Moore controversy in the case *McCreary County, Kentucky, et al. v. American Civil Liberties Union of Kentucky, et al.*, 545 U.S. 844 (2005). This case involved two Kentucky counties that had decided to post large, readily visible copies of the Ten Commandments in their courthouses. The ACLU suit was predicated on the premise that the display of the Ten Commandments in any county courthouse in the nation violated the establishment clause of the First Amendment.

Before the case reached the Supreme Court, the counties had attempted to cope with adverse rulings from the district court by modifying their exhibits to include, along with the display of the Ten Commandments, different historically important documents, including the lyrics of "The Star-Spangled Banner" and the text of the Declaration of Independence. The Kentucky counties had attempted to argue that the display was a civic display, not a religious display, in that the Ten Commandments provide the moral background of the Declaration of Independence and the foundation of the US legal tradition. Despite these modifications, the ACLU was not deterred from objecting that the inclusion of the Ten Commandments gave the document display a religious purpose.

In its brief to the Supreme Court, the ACLU argued that the Ten Commandments are inherently religious; they derive from the Torah as well as Exodus 20 and Deuteronomy 5 of the Christian Bible's Old Testament. "Jewish tradition teaches that God gave the Ten Commandments to Moses on Mt. Sinai (about 3200 years ago)," the ACLU brief stated. "For this reason, many Christians and Jews deem the Ten Commandments sacred. Jews deem the Commandments 'a statement of faith'; both Jews and Christians deem them a statement of rules." Conceding that the Decalogue, as well as other ancient but unspecified documents, informed our notions of right and wrong, the ACLU drew the line that the Ten Commandments "played virtually no role in the drafting or adoption of our nation's founding documents." In the final analysis, the ACLU insisted, "because the Ten Commandments express religious beliefs that are central only to Jews and Christians, displaying the Decalogue necessarily disfavors those with other religious beliefs or none at all."[28]

The Supreme Court concurred: displaying the Ten Commandments in a courtroom violated the establishment clause of the First Amendment. Justice David Souter, writing for the majority of the court in *McCreary County, Kentucky, et al. v. American Civil Liberties Union of Kentucky, et al.*, 545 U.S. 844 (2005), sided with the ACLU. Following a long line of cases, he noted that viewing the original text of the Ten Commandments in its entirety "is an unmistakably religious statement dealing with religious obligations and with morality subject to religious sanction." Souter's conclusion followed: merely displaying the Ten Commandments in a public courtroom violated the establishment clause. "When the government initiates an effort to place this statement [the Ten Commandments] alone in public view, a religious object is unmistakable," Souter wrote. The justice rejected the argument that the religious impact of the Ten Commandments was minimized if the Ten Commandments were displayed with other historical documents. "If the observer had not thrown up his hands, he would probably suspect that the Counties were simply reaching for any way to keep a religious document on the walls of the courthouses constitutionally required to embody religious neutrality," Souter concluded.[29] Souter's view was simple: if the Ten Commandments are inherently religious, the Ten Commandments have no place in a US courtroom.

Looking at the case in retrospect, we can see that the ACLU achieved its purpose of shutting the door on any attempt to put the Ten Commandments in a courtroom, regardless how ingeniously packaged or innocuously displayed.

"The Ten Commandments play an important part in the spiritual lives of many Americans and it is precisely for this reason that the government should not be in the business of endorsing or promoting religious beliefs," said David A. Friedman, general counsel of the ACLU of Kentucky, after he had argued before the Supreme Court. "People should not be made to feel like second-class citizens in their own community because they may not share the prevailing religious view—especially in a courtroom."[30]

The ACLU filed the case against the Kentucky counties on behalf of David Howe, a sixty-nine-year-old retired radio broadcaster and the son of a retired minister. "I believe that attempts by government agencies, at any level, to endorse religious beliefs are an affront to those who do not necessarily share those particular beliefs," Howe told the press at the conclusion of the oral arguments before the Supreme Court. "I have no quarrel with the Ten Commandments, but they don't belong in my courthouse."[31]

Justice Souter's decision had sound basis in Supreme Court precedent. In reaching this conclusion, the Supreme Court followed a long line of previous decisions that supported the Supreme Court ruling the Ten Commandments, a fundamental statement of Judeo-Christian rules of conduct, had no place in a US courtroom.

Have we really reached the point where God has no place in our nation's courtrooms? How is it possible that the Judeo-Christian tradition, begun with God giving the Ten Commandments to Moses on Mount Sinai as a fundamental statement of God's law, ends with the US Supreme Court banning the Ten Commandments from all public courtrooms in the United States?

Even more curious, how is it possible that the ruling was made in the name of preserving religious freedoms? Is it really true that to enjoy our religious freedom, we have to ban public expressions of that freedom if such public expressions involve paying respect to the Ten Commandments that our Founding Fathers held as fundamental to our moral beliefs and that generations of Americans have been taught to obey, from our nation's founding until today?

According to the ACLU, this is an inevitable conclusion of the First Amendment, at least for Christians and Jews. "The relationship between individuals and their God, which is at the core of the Ten Commandments, is and should remain a private matter," said ACLU legal director Steven R. Shapiro of the McCreary case. "It is not the government's business."[32]

In the summer of 2002, the University of North Carolina at Chapel Hill let incoming freshmen know their summer reading program included *Approaching the Qur'an: The Early Revelations*, a book by Haverford College professor of comparative religions Michael Sells.[33]

In the book, Sells presented his translation of some of the Koran's earliest *suras* (chapters), along with a commentary he wrote to make the Koran more accessible to the non-Islamic reader. On July 22, 2002, the Family Policy Network, a Christian public affairs group headed by Pat Robertson and based in Virginia, filed suit in the US District Court for the Middle District of North Carolina, seeking a preliminary injunction to keep the university from conducting its summer program.[34] The Family Policy Network pointed out requiring entering freshmen to read the Bible would certainly prompt groups like the ACLU to sue to block the program. Believing that Islam should be treated no differently from Christianity in public schools, the Family Policy Network felt that requiring any reading of the Koran violated the establishment clause of the First Amendment, even if school policy allowed students to opt out of reading the book by choosing to write an essay instead.

The University of North Carolina initiated the summer reading program for freshmen in 1999, choosing one book for each incoming class. Previous titles included *There Are No Children Here* by Alex Kotlowitz, *Confederates in the Attic* by Tony Horwitz, and *The Spirit Catches You and You Fall Down* by Anne Fadiman. This selection of books changed in the wake of the 9/11 attacks against the World Trade Center and the Pentagon, when the university wanted to modify the summer reading program to address the national tragedy. The University of North Carolina argued that the decision to include Professor Sells's book in the summer reading was made not to promote Islam as a religion but to provide students with a cultural and historic context in which to understand Islam today. Critics argued that sensitizing the students to understand Islam sympathetically was a thinly veiled attempt by the university to deliver a politically correct message defusing the idea that the terrorists attacking the United States on 9/11 were religiously motivated "Islamic terrorists."

Carl W. Ernst, the university's resident expert in Islam, attempted to justify the university's statement. "The imposition of European curriculums on colonized countries familiarized generations with European literature," he explained to the *New York Times*, in a letter to the editor printed on September 3, 2002.[35] "The Koran assignment at the University of North Carolina, where I am a professor of religious studies, is a belated attempt to catch up with the one-way flow of globalizing culture." So, to defend the university's decision, the argument sought to transform the book from being perceived as a religious treatise promoting Islam to being perceived as a cultural statement promoting the idea that Islam should properly be seen as a religion of peace, despite the Islamic faith of the 9/11 terrorists.

The ACLU decided not to sue the university on First Amendment grounds. "The University of North Carolina is requiring all incoming freshman to read *Approaching the Quran* not to promote Islam but to broaden adult students' understanding of Islam in this time of crisis," John Brodie, president of the ACLU of North Carolina, wrote to the *Wall Street Journal* in a letter published on August 23, 2002.[36] "A lawsuit was filed to stop the program, but the ACLU is not participating because we believe it is permissible and desirable for a public university to teach objectively about the role of religion in the U.S. and other countries."

Brodie further argued that the ACLU would not object if the university made the Bible, the Torah, or the Bhagavad Gita a part of the secular curriculum. "It is unconstitutional for a public school to indoctrinate students in religion, and the ACLU has opposed and will oppose prayers and religious instruction by government for the purpose of religious indoctrination," he concluded. "College-level inquiry into the Koran and Islamic beliefs for the purpose of enriched understanding is just not the same thing."[37]

In defending the inclusion of his book in the university summer reading curriculum, Sells took a decidedly political view of the controversy. "Spokesmen for the Family Policy Network and Pat Robertson wave isolated verses of the Qur'an to prove their point that it commands Muslims to slay unbelievers," Sells wrote in a letter to the editor published in the *Washington Post* on August 8, 2002.[38] "For them, Islam is clearly our enemy." Arguing that the Koran is difficult for most Americans to approach, Sells justified the inclusion of his book as an alternative to the traditional translations available in bookstores—translations Sells characterized as "not what most Muslims consider to be the word of God or what they experience in their worship." Sells, however, believed his book offered a comprehensible as well as sympathetic entry into the core "literary features" and ideas of Islam. "Reading it can only strengthen any subsequent discussion of Islam and terrorism."[39]

The Family Policy Network lawsuits filed in 2002 failed. The federal courts decided it did not violate the establishment clause of the First Amendment for Professor Sells's book to be required reading for incoming freshmen at the University of North Carolina. The university later clarified the assignment to say that any students or their families opposed to reading parts of the Koran because to do so was offensive to their own faith could choose not to read the book; those students were asked to complete a one-page writing assignment on why they chose not to.

To complete the curriculum, freshmen were asked to write an essay on Sells's book, guided by questions prepared by the university. Two parts of the book were designated for consideration: first, the cultural and historical context in which the Koran came to exist, and second, the central themes and literary quality of the *suras* translated in the book. Finally, all freshmen were asked to attend a two-hour group discussion at various locations on campus, during which the topics again were focused on a positive understanding of Islam and its traditions. The written essays, though not graded, were collected. Attendance at the group discussions was not required, yet various discussion facilitators made a record of those present.

A separate legal challenge launched in 2004 by various students and their parents also failed. Chief Justice N. Carlton Tilley Jr. wrote the memorandum opinion of the US District Court, in which he ruled:

> Part of the purpose of this program was to introduce students to the type of higher-level thinking that is required in a university setting. Students

who were not members of the Islamic faith, probably the great majority of the students, were neither asked nor forced to give up their own beliefs or to compromise their own beliefs in order to discuss the patterns, language, history, and cultural significance of the Qur'an.[40]

Although the University of North Carolina (UNC) can insist that requiring incoming freshmen to read the Koran served only the purpose of secular education, few readers here will miss the political impact of the case. In the aftermath of 9/11, the university arguably wanted to make sure all incoming freshmen knew from the start that the university was not prepared to tolerate any behavior that might lead to hate crimes against Muslims in the UNC community.

What was packaged as a university summer reading program for incoming freshmen could equally be seen as propaganda, aimed at making sure all students allowed to participate in the university were first administered political reeducation disguised as sensitivity training, in which they were indoctrinated before they ever began taking regular university classes that Islam is to be perceived as "a religion of peace," not as the motivating ideology that prompted the 9/11 terrorists to perpetrate their murderous crimes.

How did the United States get to the point at which putting a memorial cross in a national park in the desert or placing the Ten Commandments in a courtroom is unconstitutional, but a public university's summer reading program that includes reading a portion of the Koran is just fine?

Interestingly, while the university required incoming freshmen to read *suras* from the Koran, there was no complementary reading assignment including Psalms from the Old Testament or the Sermon on the Mount from the New Testament. Are not Judaism and Christianity also religions of peace?

The ACLU leaves no doubt that the Constitution demands church and state be separate, but that the ACLU equally believes mosque and state must be similarly separated is by no means certain.

2

Roots in Communism

Even the American Civil Liberties Union, set up specifically
to defend the liberties of Communists and all other political
groups, began to wilt in the cold war atmosphere.

—Howard Zinn[1]

The ACLU, even today, goes to great lengths to deny that the cofounder of the organization, Roger Nash Baldwin, had Communist ties.

The "Frequently Asked Questions" section of the ACLU website poses the following: "Does the ACLU have Communist roots? Was co-founder Roger Baldwin a Communist?"

Predictably, the ACLU answers, "No, Roger Baldwin was not a Communist. Like many of his contemporaries, he observed and wrote about the social and political issues in the early years of the Soviet Union, but later he wrote, 'The Nazi-Soviet Pact of 1939, a traumatic shock to me, ended any ambivalence I had about the Soviet Union, and all cooperation with Communists in united fronts.'"[2] Baldwin, like many early Communist sympathizers in the 1920s and 1930s, learned by the 1950s that it was preferable to be seen as progressive, more in the tradition of Theodore Roosevelt, interested in social justice, not outright revolution.

The ideological shifting required worldwide when Hitler and Stalin decided to shake hands is illustrative for the point relevant here: namely, the motivation to create the ACLU came from the political Left, led in the 1920s and 1930s by youthful radicals who drew their inspiration for social justice from communism, not the freedoms defined by Jefferson and Madison. The allegiance of those radicals was to a then emerging Soviet Union that was throwing out God along with capitalism. World War I was the root not only of the Bolshevik revolution but also of the antiwar, anti-capitalist, anti-God anarchist movement in the United States, from which the ACLU sprang forth on the American scene.

Mostly, the Nazi-Soviet Pact of 1939 was a shock to Communists and committed Socialists in the United States. To American Socialists and Communists in the run-up to World War II, it was unimaginable that their beloved Stalin had made a pact with the hated Adolf Hitler. But to scholars specializing in the study of National Socialism in Germany during the rise of Hitler, it was no surprise that Hitler and Stalin could shake hands and become allies. The truth is that both ideologies—Nazism as well as Soviet communism—were totalitarian ideologies that derived their origins from the political Left. "The notion that communism and Nazism are polar opposites stems from the deeper truth that they are in fact kindred spirits," wrote political commentator Jonah Goldberg in his book *Liberal Fascism*. "Communists champion class, Nazis race, fascists the nation. All such ideologies—we can call them totalitarian for now—attract the same *types* of people."[3] Truthfully, Hitler was destined to attack Stalin, not because their two ideologies were so fundamentally different, but because they were both branches on the same tree—two totalitarian ideologies competing to claim government control over human beings and the means of production while proclaiming freedom.

Frank Marshall Davis, the Socialist-Communist African American poet and journalist who decades later played a major formative role in the young life of Barack Obama, railed at the thought Stalin would shake hands with Hitler. "I had felt betrayed when Stalin signed that nonaggression pact with Hitler," he wrote in his autobiography, *Livin' the Blues*. "So the Russians were as hypocritical as the rest of the white world! I, and other souls I knew, felt we had been deserted by our own potential champion. But after all, since the Russians were white, what else could you really expect?"[4]

For those sympathetic to Communists in the 1930s, like Roger Nash Baldwin and Frank Marshall Davis, what was so crushing about the 1939 Nazi-Soviet nonaggression pact was that their beloved Stalin had dared to make a pragmatic compromise with the hated Hitler rather than remain true to Communist principles that dictated only the internationalist movement of "workers of the world united" could bring forth the utopia that committed Marxist-Leninists saw as the future of humanity.

"The announcement of the Nazi-Soviet pact in the summer of 1939 had triggered a controversy among the American intelligentsia that brought matters to a head," wrote Baldwin's biographer, historian Robert Cottrell.[5] Before 1939, Baldwin viewed civil liberties in the context of class warfare, making it clear that even if he himself was unwilling to profess communism openly, Baldwin was comfortable with professed Communists who enthusiastically supported and promoted Soviet Russia as a model for the United States to follow. After the 1939 pact, Baldwin moved closer to the anti-Communists within the ACLU, to the consternation of dedicated Communists who had helped propel the ACLU to a position of national prominence. "When I was elected to the [ACLU] Board about eleven years ago, the fact that I was a Communist was known to Roger Baldwin, Norman Thomas, and other members of the Board," Anna Rochester, a radical historian and leftist economist, complained to the *New York Times*. "In fact, I was given to understand that one reason they wanted me on the Board was that I would represent the Communist viewpoint. I resigned of my own free will, long before they [the ACLU] became a red-baiting organization."[6]

Today, the ACLU recognizes how detrimental acknowledging the communist roots of the orginization would be. "Throughout the organization's history and particularly during the McCarthy era, the ACLU, its members, staff and founders have been accused of being Communists," the organization's FAQs continue. "The ACLU has no political affiliations and makes no test of individuals' ideological leanings a condition of membership or employment." Affirming that the members and staff of the national ACLU and its affiliates can be members of any political party or no political party, the FAQs go on to assert: "What the ACLU asks of its staff and officials is that they consistently defend civil liberties and the Constitution."[7]

Political scientist Aaron Wildavsky, writing the introduction to sociologist William A. Donohue's book *The Politics of the American Civil Liberties Union*, openly expressed his disillusionment with the ACLU. "The ACLU was never what I thought it was, an organization standing up for those people whose civil liberties were threatened by the passions of the time," Wildavsky wrote. "The ACLU has always been what Donohue says it is: an organization committed to a shifting agenda of substantive policy change as dictated by the political perspectives of its most active members."[8]

Even controversial journalist H. L. Mencken ultimately turned on the ACLU. In 1936, conservative Harold Lord Varney wrote critically about the ACLU, publishing an essay titled "The Civil Liberties Union— Liberalism à la Moscow," in *American Mercury*, a magazine founded by Mencken. Invited by Paul Palmer, then the editor of *American Mercury*, to write an article Palmer thought would defend the ACLU, Mencken submitted instead an article highly critical of the ACLU. Mencken dared to bare the truth about the ACLU: it was not a nonpartisan organization.[9] Willing to draw the ACLU's ire, Mencken charged that some of the ACLU's "most important and activist officers [were] actually strong partisans of the Left," and that they had sufficient influence "to cast 'a reasonable doubt' over the ACLU's disinterestedness."[10] Mencken proceeded to lambast various ACLU officers, including Baldwin, for their support of Soviet Russia and their ties to Communist-front organizations in the United States.

Today, the ACLU understands the necessity to reposition its defense of civil liberties from the language of class warfare that was comfortable to the organization's founders, to the more politically acceptable language of defending the Constitution. To modern readers, the shift is almost so deft as to be imperceptible. But to those appreciating the fervor with which communism hit prominent leftist intellectuals during the Russian Revolution, it remains shocking that the ACLU today works to cast as nothing more than a

McCarthy-era slur the suggestion the organization began by welcoming radical Socialists and Communists not only to the ranks but also to the group's leadership.

The historical record remains clear that the ACLU owes its organizing fervor to the American radicals from the Left who opposed the entry of the United States into World War I—then a largely unorganized rabble of bomb-throwing anarchists including "Red Emma" Goldman, early union organizers including railroad union organizer and presidential candidate Eugene V. Debs, radical Socialists who joined with outright Communists, along with various types of religious conscientious objectors and a mixture of malcontents. Refusing in 1917 to report for his physical exam at the local draft board, as required by the Selective Service Act, Baldwin was prosecuted, convicted, and sentenced to a year in prison. By that time, Baldwin, a Boston-born Brahmin and Harvard-educated social worker by profession, was heading the National Civil Liberties Bureau (an early name for the ACLU) as its executive director. He was well along the path to being a committed Socialist whose political sympathies rested with the Russian Revolution, the conflict that caused Russia to withdraw from World War I.

Like Baldwin, Eugene V. Debs went to prison, not for avoiding the draft but for giving an antiwar speech in Canton, Ohio, on June 16, 1918, for which he was prosecuted for sedition under the Espionage Act of 1917. "When I think of a cold, glittering steel bayonet being plunged in the white, quivering flesh of a human being, I recoil with horror," Debs famously said at his trial. "I have often wondered if I could take the life of my fellow man, even to save my own."[11] Nationally renowned for his Socialist embrace of the union movement, Debs was a clear role model for World War I–era antiwar protesters like Baldwin who followed his example.

According to an online reference dedicated to her life and her writings, anarchist Emma Goldman's career "served as an inspiration for Roger Baldwin, a future founder of the American Civil Liberties Union."[12] Goldman was arrested so many times that she began to carry a book with her so she wouldn't have to sit in jail with nothing to read. Finally, in 1918, she was deported to Russia for her Communist activities. Yet Goldman left after only twenty-three months. Disillusioned with the repression and lack of free speech she saw in Russia under Lenin, Goldman declared Russia a failure, much as Baldwin and other disillusioned leftists would declare the Soviet Union a failure after the 1939 nonaggression pact between Hitler and Stalin. "The Russian revolution as a radical social and economic change meant to overthrow capitalism and establish communism must be declared a failure," Goldman wrote in Stockholm, and her statement was published as an editorial in the *Chicago Herald-Examiner* on March 22, 1922. "The Marxian policies of the Bolsheviki, the tactics first extolled as indispensable to the life of the revolution only to be discarded as harmful after they had wrought misery, distrust and antagonism, were the factors that slowly undermined the faith of the people in the revolution."[13]

It is apparent that the American Left's disillusionment with communism after the Russian Revolution failed to establish the perfect society did not send the leftist intelligentsia in the United States into the embrace of the American Constitution and the principles of free enterprise capitalism. Reflecting on the coming of World War II, Frank Marshall Davis wrote, "We still had the festering memory of World War I, when we were called upon to battle the Kaiser and 'make the world safe for democracy'—only to come home and find we had merely made America safe for continued racism. We had been promised the moon of equality for our all-out support and, after the armistice, had been showered with the same old mud of discrimination."[14] For Davis, the underlying racism of the United States was a consequence of the class conflict that exploited racial minorities. In the final analysis, what the American Left rejected were the Soviet Union and Stalinism, but not the fundamental principles at the core of Marxism. "Social justice" became a code phrase in which class warfare could be argued through the "unequal justice" arguments of the civil rights movement that emerged in the 1950s. In a similar fashion, War on Poverty in the 1960s recast as entitlement programs the Communist goal of eliminating private property in favor of redistributing income under government or collectivist management. By the end of the 1960s, J. Edgar Hoover could brag there were more government agents in the Communist Party of the USA than there were Communists. Thirty years later, by the 1990s, the Clinton-era Socialist leftists recast themselves as pragmatists. Today, the term of choice is *progressive*, as those on the left dislike being called "liberals," almost as much as they disdain being called "Socialists."

So it was with Roger Nash Baldwin. Though ultimately disillusioned with Stalin and the Soviet Union, Baldwin never renounced the leftist social, political, and economic views that had attracted him to communism immediately after the start of the Russian Revolution. As Baldwin's biographer Robert Cottrell noted, by 1935, fifteen years after the founding of the ACLU, although Baldwin deplored the terrorism and authoritarianism of Soviet Russia, he could still write, "I can tolerate it only as preferable to far less hopeful concentrations of power in capitalist countries."[15] In that same year, Baldwin sent a brief note to be included in the thirtieth reunion class book of the Harvard class of 1905, saying, "I am for socialism, disarmament, and ultimately for abolishing the State itself as an instrument of property, the abolition of the propertied class and sole control by those who produce wealth. Communism is the goal."[16] What Baldwin feared most was that leftists crying "crocodile tears" for the abuses of Stalin in the Soviet Union concealed a readiness to abandon "the world's first experiment in building socialism," abandon and allow a return to czarist despotism and capitalist exploitation in Russia.[17]

In 1920, the year following his release from prison, Baldwin reorganized the National Civil Liberties Bureau into the American Civil Liberties Union, asking (among others) radical union organizer William Z. Foster to be on his original national committee. Foster came up through the part of the pre–World War I union movement that had been openly Socialist; his history included being a member of the openly Socialist Industrial Workers of the World, widely known as the Wobblies or, more simply, the IWW.

Foster officially became a Communist in 1921 when he attended a conference of the Profintern, the Red International of Labor Unions, in

Moscow. "It was my good fortune to spend four months of 1921 in Soviet Russia," Foster said in a speech delivered in Chicago on July 16, 1924. "While I was there I studied the situation diligently with all the resources at my command. I tried to see things as they were, not as I would like them to be. And finally, as a result of my investigations, I declared upon my return to the United States that, in my judgment, the Russian revolution was a success." That Foster had every intention of bringing what he considered the success of the Russian Revolution to the United States was clear: "In Russia the sun of the new social order has dawned," he declared to his Chicago audience.[18]

On his return from the Soviet Union, Foster became a formal member of the Communist Party of America in 1921. By the mid-1920s, he rose to serve as the party's national chairman, holding the title of general secretary in the then-renamed Communist Party of the United States of America (CPUSA). Foster also served as the national chairman of the Workers Party of America (WPA), the official labor union of the CPUSA.

In the list of national committee members that appears on the left margin of ACLU letter stationery from the 1920s, Foster is named as a national committee member from Chicago. Similarly, New York labor organizer B. Charney Vladeck, a prominent member of the Socialist Party of America, was on the national committee of the ACLU.

In 1925, an illustrative dispute broke out between Foster, representing the WPA, and Baldwin, representing the ACLU. The controversy involved various members of the WPA in New York City who engaged in disruptive heckling tactics designed to disrupt and break up public meetings at which prominent Russian Socialists were scheduled to give speeches attacking communism in Russia. In a series of letters exchanged between Baldwin, representing the ACLU, and the executive committee of the WPA, the WPA maintained it had revolutionary justification for preventing from speaking what were seen as reactionary Socialist critics of communism in Russia. Baldwin and the ACLU took the position that First Amendment free speech rights justified the WPA heckling, but not to the point that the Socialist critics were not permitted to speak.

In a letter dated March 19, 1925, Baldwin and various members of the ACLU executive committee explained the following to the WPA:

> You well may know that the position of the Civil Liberties Union demands the right of free speech for all groups and persons, regardless of what they have to say. The fact that William Z. Foster, your National Chairman, is on our National Committee, as well as B. Charney Vladeck, is clear evidence that your Party officially stands for the same civil rights for its opponents as it demands for itself. Yet the Party by its actions in the meetings of Dr. Abramovich and at the Town Hall meeting fails to concede the rights in fact which it recognizes in principle.[19]

The WPA responded in a letter dated April 2, 1925, addressed to Baldwin as director of the ACLU:

> We must draw your attention to the fact that the Workers (Communist) Party of America is not yet the ruling party in the United States. On the contrary, it is the most outrageously persecuted and oppressed section of the American Labor movement. Consequently, to demand as you do, that we respect the civil rights of our opponents, or that we concede them such rights, is ridiculous. The only question of concern to us in the matter of civil rights is that the working class of the United States do [sic] not permit itself to be intimidated by the capitalist dictatorship that prevails in this country and carry on its struggle for the destruction of the capitalist system and the establishment of workers.[20]

The many letters written between the WPA and the ACLU in this controversy display a difference of tactics that ultimately caused Baldwin to distance himself from the Communists. As a matter of tactics, Baldwin felt the American people would tolerate the leftist extreme in the United States only if the rights of the leftist extreme were packaged within a language of tolerance.

Among the letters found today in the Library of Congress in Washington, DC, is a letter that Baldwin wrote to the WPA dated March

14, 1925, in which he went so far as to explain the ACLU was "just as much concerned, for instance, for the rights of Catholics to condemn birth control, as we are for the right of Margaret Sanger to advocate it."[21] Truthfully, Baldwin's life and history display no evidence he held a genuine enthusiasm for defending the rights of Catholics to condemn birth control. The point is that Baldwin understood the usefulness of presenting himself as willing to defend the rights of Catholics. The causes that Baldwin and the ACLU chose to champion were anything but value neutral.

When it came down to the question of birth control, Baldwin and the ACLU were squarely on the side of Margaret Sanger, a radical eugenicist who believed the human race could be improved by genetic management and the weeding out of inferior human stock.[22] Sanger's writings go so far as to suggest she supported abortion as a means to reduce America's black population.[23] Yet Baldwin was sufficiently wily to couch his true support for abortion as a eugenicist tool with a tip of the hat not just to Christians but even to Catholics in his willingness to remark he would support even Catholics in their notion that abortion is against the law of God, however mistaken that notion might appear to Baldwin himself.

In the next sentence of the letter Baldwin wrote to the WPA, dated March 14, 1925, after expressing his equal willingness to support Catholics on abortion and Margaret Sanger on eugenics, Baldwin equated the right of the Ku Klux Klan (KKK) to hold meetings on private property unmolested to the right of the Knights of Columbus to assemble freely under the banner of their Catholic beliefs. Again, there is little historical support for the argument that Baldwin ever supported the Knights of Columbus—another Catholic organization intrinsically viewed as suspect by the Boston-Brahmin Protestants from whom Baldwin was bred. But that Baldwin should consider as equivalent the right of the Knights of Columbus to hold their meetings to the rights of a terrorist organization like the KKK to hold their meetings suggests his disdain for both.

The cleverness of Baldwin's break with Foster was not that the two disagreed on their fundamental political beliefs, but that Baldwin realized Foster's ideological purity would advance the principles of the radical Left less effectively than Baldwin's feigned indifference to the political objectives of the various groups he and his organization chose to champion. That Baldwin disagreed with Foster on methods is clear. That Baldwin disagreed with Foster's Communist political ends and objectives is unlikely at best.

Foster and the Communists in the WPA were true believers of a radical Left ideology they believed could be imposed on others with a fascist firmness, to the point of abrogating the free speech rights of political opponents. While Baldwin hated capitalists and capitalism equally as did Foster, he saw the wisdom of positioning the ACLU and its members not as true-believing ideologues, but as liberals who were tolerant of diversity in political views, to the point of mouthing a willingness to support not only Christians, but also Catholics—something Foster would never lower himself to do.

That Baldwin felt the ultimate social justice goals of the Communists and radical Socialists of his day were correct was never brought into question in the extensive correspondence between the ACLU and the WPA that is held today in the collection of the Library of Congress. The question before Baldwin was different from the question before Foster. Where Foster saw the ACLU as an engine for bringing on the revolution, Baldwin saw the ACLU as working even more insidiously.

As early as 1925, Baldwin was beginning to realize that with a constitutional republic such as the United States that adhered to the tolerant values of the Founding Fathers, the ACLU could advance radical leftist goals in court only as long as the centrist American public felt all the ACLU was asking for was fairness, not an open Communist revolution. As early as 1925, Baldwin set out the intellectual foundation on which the ACLU could weather an anti-Communist backlash. By 1940, Baldwin feared what developed as McCarthyism in the 1950s postwar period would inevitably come sooner or later in the United States. Contrary to Foster's wishes, the ACLU under Baldwin's direction was not to be a Communist organization. Instead, Baldwin positioned the ACLU to openly recruit liberals and progressives, transforming in the 1930s the ACLU into an organization the Democratic Party could strongly champion, even if Republicans continued to hold suspicions about the true politics of Baldwin and his leftist lawyers.

That the ACLU was determined to pursue First Amendment free speech rights as a question of fairness was clear in the 1925 exchange of letters with the WPA. Baldwin sought to defend his position and that of the ACLU by challenging Foster over whether the Communist Party USA would demand the same free speech rights for capitalists who supported private property and private enterprise as it demanded for itself.

The obvious answer was no.

In his letter of March 14, 1925, addressed to Earl Browder, the acting secretary of the WPA, Baldwin summarized the controversy as follows:

> The Workers Party and the Civil Liberties Union would of course disagree as to the philosophy of free speech. You regard it as a means to an end. We regard it as an end in itself. Nevertheless, William Z. Foster sits upon our National Committee just as does Charney Vladeck, whom the Workers Party so bitterly opposes, and just as do scores of other persons whose economic philosophies would clash.[24]

While Baldwin wanted the ACLU to appear tolerant, he still solidly came down on the side of fighting for the working class, not the capitalist establishment. In a letter dated April 4, 1925, to the WPA, Baldwin made this clear:

> We take no position on any struggle, whatever, except to see that the participants all get a chance to be heard openly, freely and fairly. Theoretically, we are just as much concerned about civil rights for capitalists as we are for workers . . . for the worst reactionary as for the extremist radical. Practically of course, the nature of the struggle about us and the personnel of the organization brings to us chiefly working-class cases.[25]

As Robert Cottrell points out, Baldwin's dismay over the WPA's attitude toward civil liberties "in no way lessened Baldwin's belief that U.S. capitalism needed to be transformed, nor did it diminish his identification with the Left."[26] The ACLU, Baldwin reasoned, would strive to help an oppressed class rise by using civil liberties as a means "to keep the powers of government off the backs of a rising class."[27]

By the end of 1930, Foster finally resigned from the ACLU board in protest, claiming that the ACLU had betrayed the workers' cause.[28] Still, Foster and Baldwin continued their close association and friendship. Political science professor Paul Kengor, author of *Dupes: How America's Adversaries Have Manipulated Progressives for a Century*,[29] notes that newly found declassified letters and other documents in the Soviet Comintern archives reveal a letter dated May 23, 1931, signed by Baldwin and written on ACLU stationery, addressed to Foster, asking him to help ACLU chairman Harry Ward with his then upcoming trip to Stalin's Russia. In the letter, Baldwin suggests Ward was making the trip to Russia to find "evidence from Soviet Russia" that would undermine the capitalist profit motive. John Rossomando of the *Daily Caller* points out that "Baldwin wrote the letter at a time when Stalin was deporting 1.8 million Ukrainian peasants to Siberia under his policy of the forced collectivization of agriculture," a policy that resulted in the "deaths of up to 10 million Ukrainians in the two years that followed."[30]

Kengor describes Baldwin as "the prototype dupe," a small *c* communist who was prudent enough not to have joined the Communist Party.[31] According to Kengor, Baldwin was "an atheist initially enamored with Soviet Communism, as was evident in his 1928 book *Liberty Under the Soviets*, which was based on his two-month Potemkin-village tour of the USSR in 1927."[32]

Kengor explains, "If you look at a lot of things about the ACLU's early history, you will see a lot of things that are pro-communist. What I'm trying to say about this group is that from the outset [it] was on the farthest extremes of the left. It was atheistic. Certain members were pro-communist, . . . as defined by the writings and the beliefs of its founders, key officials and board members."[33] In particular, Kengor has in mind Corliss Lamont, an American philosopher and philanthropist who served as ACLU director from 1932 to 1954. An outspoken advocate for Stalinist Russia, even after the Hitler-Stalin pact, Lamont first achieved notoriety with the 1935 publication of *The Illusion of Immortality*, the book version of his Columbia PhD dissertation that Kengor characterizes as "an immediate atheist classic," which remains in print today.[34] A star pupil of John Dewey, Lamont published in his life a series of books and pamphlets devoted to promoting the Soviet Union and trashing God.

In 1932, Foster published *Toward Soviet America*,[35] a book that Francis E. Walter, the Democrat who chaired the House Committee on Un-American Activities, called in his introduction to the 1961 reprinting "easily the best-known book dealing with Communism by any American Communist."[36] Pointing out that Foster was "an open, admitted Communist" when he wrote the book, Walter made it clear that Foster, "the highest official of American Communism," wrote every word with the approval of Moscow. Walter explained the plan Foster proposed for communism to overtake the United States was a "soft" policy. "Instead of battering down our ramparts from without, victory now was to be achieved from within," he wrote. "Trojan Horse tactics would be employed."

"From capitalism to Communism, through the intermediary stage of Socialism; that is the way American society, like society in general, is headed," Foster wrote in the final chapter of his book—boldly titled "The United Soviet States of America."[37] His view was that the Communist Party would establish a dictatorship in America:

> Under the dictatorship all the capitalist parties—Republican, Democratic, Progressive, Socialist, etc.—will be liquidated, the Communist party functioning alone as the Party of the toiling masses. Likewise, will be dissolved all other organizations that are political props of the bourgeois rule, including chambers of commerce, employers' associations, rotary clubs, American Legion, Y.M.C.A., and such fraternal orders as the Masons, Odd Fellows, Elks, Knights of Columbus, etc.[38]

Foster saw all housing being made available at no charge to workers:

> The great hotels, apartments, city palaces, country homes, country clubs, etc., of the rich will be taken over and utilized by the workers for dwellings, rest homes, children's clubs, sanatoria, etc. The best of

the skyscrapers, emptied of their thousand and one brands of parasites, will be used to house the new government institutions, the trade unions, cooperatives, Communist party [sic], etc. The fleets of automobiles and steam yachts of the rich will be placed at the disposition of the workers' organizations. A great drive will be made to demolish the present collection of miserable shacks and tenements and build homes fit for workers to live in.[39]

Fairly typical for radical Socialists and Communists of his era, Foster believed that the elimination of capitalism would welcome in a new era of sexual expression as the moral restrictions needed to keep oppressed workers in a class-subjugated state were eliminated in the new dawn of the classless society. Foster wanted to liberate American women, whom he saw as confronting "medieval sex taboos, assiduously cultivated by the church, State and bourgeois moralists."[40] American women freed economically would also be free in sex, emulating their sisters in Russia: "The free American woman, like her Russian sister, will eventually scorn the whole fabric of bourgeois sex hypocrisy and prudery."[41] Instead of being enslaved in the kitchen, American women would benefit from great factory kitchens that would prepare "hot, well-balanced means for home consumption by the millions," while children were reared in "the most elaborate system of kindergartens and playgrounds in the world—in the cities and villages, in the neighborhoods and around the factories."[42]

For modern readers, it is difficult to perceive that in the 1930s, as the Great Depression progressed, Communists openly professed their vision of the future as an appealing alternative to the unemployment, economic misery, crime, and despair realized by millions of Americans at the time. Foster's Communist utopia reduced to a personal vision of bliss in which factories thrived, workers lived in the abodes of the wealthy and drove their vehicles, while women were spared nothing sexually, and children were watched without conflict in collectivist kindergartens and grade schools—all at public expense.

That not everyone would embrace openly such a social agenda was unimaginable to Foster; he wrote with the conviction that the benefits of his utopia were self-evident. Foster's utopia was materialistic—a world where human desires were always fulfilled, where carnal desire could be satisfied without guilt or boundary, with no discussion of any limits as to who, when, where, what, or how lust could be fulfilled. Everyone would live in harmony once the evil of capital and greed was banished from Foster's Soviet USA. But God was nowhere to be found in Foster's pages. What replaced the divine as an instrument of human motivation and morality was the scientific certainty that communism would succeed, as proved by a worshipful view of what Soviet Russia had achieved since the revolution.

Today, the ACLU takes pains to erase from the organization's official history all these inconvenient historical associations with communism. Equally forgotten is the Fish Committee, a special committee constituted by the US House of Representatives in 1931, which reported:

> The American Civil Liberties Union is closely affiliated with the communist movement in the United States, and fully 90 percent of its efforts are on behalf of communists who have come into conflict with the law. It claims to stand for free speech, free press and free assembly, but it is quite apparent that the main function of the ACLU is an attempt to protect the communists in their advocacy of force and violence to overthrow the government, replacing the American flag by a red flag and erecting a Soviet Government in place of the republican form of government guaranteed to each state by the Federal Constitution.[43]

The Fish Committee report singled out Baldwin: "Roger N. Baldwin, its [the ACLU's] guiding spirit, makes no attempt to hide his friendship for the communists and their principles."[44]

Attorney J. Matt Barber, vice president of Liberty Counsel, a legal advocacy group committed to promoting religious freedom, commented on this Special House Committee, concluding that the main function of the ACLU is "entirely counter-constitutional."[45]

Barber continued, "A shared objective between both Communism generally, and the ACLU specifically is the suppression of religious liberty; principally, the free exercise of Christianity. Karl Marx, high priest of the ACLU's beloved cult of Communism, once said: 'The first requisite for the happiness of the people is the abolition of religion.'"[46]

In 1925, the leadership of the ACLU decided the Butler Act, a Tennessee law that prohibited the teaching of evolution in public schools, represented an opportunity to advance its goals. In the routine job of scanning newspaper articles, Lucille Milner, the ACLU's executive secretary, came across a three-inch headline, "Tennessee Bans the Teaching of Evolution," which she brought to the attention of Roger Baldwin. He "saw its import in a flash" and ordered Milner to bring the Tennessee law to the attention of the ACLU board when it met the following Monday.[47]

The ACLU board agreed a case brought under the Butler Act would test the teaching of religion in the public schools, raising issues that might advance the case all the way to the Supreme Court. On May 4, 1925, the Chattanooga *Daily Times* ran a story reporting the ACLU would pay for the defense lawyers of any teacher willing to be arrested and tried for violating the Butler Act.[48] Within a few days, the ACLU received a telegram reporting that John Thomas Scopes, a high school science teacher, would be arrested for violating the Butler Act.

The case came to national prominence when William Jennings Bryan, the three-time presidential nominee of the Democratic Party and a Christian fundamentalist widely recognized for his openly professed faith, agreed to represent the Tennessee attorney general. Clarence Darrow, the well-known Chicago-based criminal defense lawyer and ACLU member who was also an agnostic, volunteered to help represent Scopes. In 1924, Darrow had achieved national notoriety for presenting a psychological defense of Nathan Leopold and Richard Loeb, the sons of two wealthy Chicago families who had kidnapped and killed a teenage boy simply for thrills. Bryan was still renowned for his fiery "Cross of Gold" speech at the

Democratic Party's 1896 National Convention, in which he championed the average worker against the avarice of the wealthy, who advocated for maintaining the gold standard. Darrow was the modern high-priced city-slicker lawyer, willing to champion cutting-edge scientific theories as legal defenses in court trials. Bryan was a well-loved populist Democratic Party politician, known for giving political speeches that rivaled the best sermons fundamentalist preachers could deliver from the pulpit.

With the subject matter of the trial and the selection of lawyers in place, Roger Baldwin and the ACLU leaders got exactly what they wanted: a case the public was sure to see as "the Good Book against Darwin, bigotry against science, or as popularly put, God against the monkeys," as Baldwin so aptly encapsulated the coming courtroom drama.[49]

Soon Baltimore journalist and satirist H. L. Mencken, who traveled to Tennessee to cover the trial, memorialized Baldwin's insight by tagging the event the "Monkey Trial."[50] Mencken quickly characterized the trial as a contest between eighteenth-century Enlightenment, as represented by science and the teaching of evolution, versus primitive pre-Enlightenment thinking, as represented by the Bible and the Genesis account that God created the world. "The so-called religious organizations which now lead the war against the teaching of evolution are nothing more, at bottom, than conspiracies of the inferior man against his betters," Mencken reported, casting the Scopes trial into the battle between God and science that attracted Baldwin and the leaders of the ACLU. "What all this amounts to is that the human race is divided into two sharply differentiated and mutu-ally antagonistic classes, almost two genera—a small minority that plays with ideas and is capable of taking them in, and a vast majority that finds them painful, and is thus arrayed against them, and against all who have traffic with them."[51]

With the Scopes case, the ACLU developed the following theme: science was for the educated, the enlightened class, while religion was relegated to the masses, the great unwashed, including those too stupid to be educated. Karl Marx had put this concept more simply eighty-two years earlier, argu-ing that religion was the opiate of the people. Clearly, the inevitable Marxist conclusion was that communism defined the path for the advancement of the species—an evolutionary-sounding theme that would have appealed to the worst of the Himmler-inspired geneticists among the Nazi persecutors of the Jews.

The satirist Mencken descended upon the opportunity presented by the Scopes trial to present these ideological principles to the masses through newspaper articles dripping in sarcasm. He aimed his opprobrium on Bryan and those foolish enough to read the Bible as if it were the word of God. Bizarrely, Mencken lined up the educated classes with the monkeys, claiming the enlightened could easily see how far we had come from the apes. The Bible, by default, was lined up with the unenlightened people who were yet naïve enough to believe Scripture to be the Word of God. All this was right up the ACLU's alley. What could be better in advancing the War on God than portraying religion as belonging to the stupid? Who reading Mencken would not want to include himself among the superintelligent, the elite, who stood in unison against the prejudices of the Dark Ages?

Scopes, the teacher who had come to the ACLU's attention, was unknown to the public before the trial. The twenty-four-year-old general science instructor and part-time football coach had been filling in, substitute teaching the biology course while the usual teacher, the principal of the school, was ill. To break the law, all Scopes had to do was take a state-approved biology text to use for his personal review in preparing his classroom instruction to include Darwin's theory of evolution. "I explained that I had got the book out of storage and used it for review purposes while filling in for the principal during his illness," Scopes later recalled. "He [the principal] was the regular biology teacher." In taking the substitute teaching opportunity, Scopes had not planned to make himself the principal actor in the emerging test case. Frank E. Robinson, the owner of the Dayton drugstore, was responsible for recruiting Scopes to accept the ACLU offer. Scopes, single and easygoing, was considered the ideal defendant for the test case. What really did he have to lose? At most, he would be charged with a misdemeanor.[52]

Scopes had not engaged in a transgression of epic proportions. Nor was the trial defined to fight out in court epic legal principles. The trial judge

John T. Raulston ruled narrowly that the only issue in question involved the authority of the state legislature to develop the public school curriculum. This narrowing of the question effectively threw out all the expert testimony the ACLU had intended to introduce at trial. The ACLU's initial strategy was to argue that evolution was a valid scientific theory that described the creation of the world and the emergence of human beings. The ACLU wanted to contrast this with the Bible's religious account of how God created everything, including human beings. The ACLU's goal was to prove evolution was science while demonstrating that the Bible was prejudice.

The problem was that Raulston, as trial judge, felt no experts were needed to shed light on the meaning of the statute itself. In his view, the statute was perfectly clear: "the crime of teaching against the story of biblical creation was specifically defined [by the law] as teaching that 'man descended from a lower order of animals.'"[53] So even if Darrow could succeed in proving religion had no scientific basis, that conclusion was irrelevant. In Raulston's narrow definition of the question in dispute, if the jury decided the state legislature had the authority to decide the public schools could be forced to teach religion, Scopes was guilty, even if religion was nonsense. All Raulston wanted the jury to decide was whether the state legislature had the authority under law to demand the public schools could be forced to teach God, the Bible, and creationism over science, Darwin, and the theory of evolution.

Despite this narrowing of the question before the court, Judge Raulston allowed Darrow to put Bryan on the stand, even after Darrow asserted that Bryan was an expert on the Bible. Raulston was probably taken aback by what amounted to one of Darrow's more famous courtroom maneuvers: swearing in *as a defense witness* the lawyer representing the state in the prosecution of the case.

Once Bryan was on the stand as a sworn witness, Darrow pressed him to admit everything in the Bible should be interpreted literally. When Bryan responded that what the Bible said "should be accepted as it is given there," Darrow demanded Bryan had to respond with precise answers to a series of questions difficult, if not impossible, to answer with precision. How old was the earth, measured in days, weeks, months, years—maybe even hours? Was Eve the first woman, and how exactly was she constructed out of Adam's rib?

"Did you ever discover where Cain got his wife?" asked Darrow.

"No, sir. I leave the agnostics to hunt for her," Bryan shot back in response.[54]

On the witness stand, Bryan was obviously frustrated by Darrow's overt attempt to humiliate him for believing that the Bible provided a precise, historically accurate account of creation, not an illustrative or allegorical account. But even under the pressure of Darrow's persistent questioning, Bryan maintained his composure and responded with dignity and humor.

In his Pulitzer Prize–winning account of the Scopes trial, historian Edward J. Larson, author of *Summer for the Gods: The Scopes Trial and America's Continuing Debate over Science and Religion*, recounted that the crowd in the courtroom cheered Bryan on with applause, even though Darrow scored most of the jabs.

"The only purpose Mr. Darrow has is to slur the Bible, but I will answer his questions," Bryan stated on the witness stand. "I object to your statement," Darrow retorted, as both men stood and shook their fists at each other. Larson noted that Judge Raulston then abruptly adjourned the court for the day, having heard enough of the theatrics. The next day, Raulston barred further examination of Bryan and ordered his testimony struck from the record. "I feel that the testimony of Mr. Bryan can shed no light upon any issue that will be pending before the higher court," he ruled from the bench. "The issue now is whether or not Mr. Scopes taught that man descended from a lower order of animals."[55]

What is largely forgotten in the account of the Scopes case taught to schoolchildren today is that Darrow failed to win the trial. Scopes was found guilty, and Bryan was vindicated in his prosecution of the case. The jury decided that the Tennessee state legislature did have the authority to determine evolution should not be taught in the public schools. Scopes was found guilty and fined one hundred dollars.

But once the judge gaveled the trial to an end, the politically correct version of the trial began to be written. Journalists like Mencken rushed to file stories, telling the world how Darrow had triumphed. Perhaps not surprisingly, even decades ago the *New York Times* reporters went to rural Dayton, Tennessee, bringing with them their city-bred antipathy toward fundamental Christians, representing a newspaper that itself was already "religiously committed to evolution" as a proven scientific truth.[56] Predictably, the *Times* portrayed Bryan's testimony as "an absurdly pathetic performance," insisting the famous politician and religious fundamentalist had been the "butt of a crowd's rude laughter."[57]

In truth, Darrow failed to score a knockout punch against Bryan, with most observers remembering that Bryan sat calmly and answered Darrow's questions confidently, stating what he knew and admitting frankly what he did not know and would not speculate upon. Darrow paced back and forth across the platform in an emotional and agitated manner, as if to dramatize the importance of his questions and punctuate the ridiculousness of Bryan's answers with an air of exasperation.[58]

Through his courtroom theatrics, Darrow succeeded in his goal of identifying religious fundamentalism with the suppression of free speech, so as to argue religion required restraining the advancement of scientific knowledge. Darrow, H. L. Mencken, the *New York Times*—all shared the same accusation: that Bible-believing Christians like William Jennings Bryan stood in the way of enlightenment. If only God could be moved out of the way, human beings would continue to evolve to superhumans, as Nietzsche, the Communists, and Darwin had predicted—a theme the Nazis could equally comprehend.

A quarter of a century after the Scopes trial, the highly successful 1955 Broadway play *Inherit the Wind*, written by Jerome Lawrence and Robert Edwin Lee, carried forward this theme. This stage play was brought to the big screen in 1960, with a Hollywood adaptation of the Lawrence and Lee play directed by Stanley Kramer, in which a still youthful-looking Spencer Tracy played Henry Drummond, a character based on Clarence Darrow, and the obviously aging Fredric March played Matthew Harrison Brady, a character based on William Jennings Bryan.

The movie climaxes with Spencer Tracy grilling an obviously befuddled

Fredric March into a near nervous breakdown on the stand. It did not matter to the unsuspecting millions watching the movie that Lawrence and Lee crafted for their Darrow-like character questions that were never actually asked of Bryan at the trial. What mattered was that audiences around the nation saw a spectacle in which an increasingly confused Fredric March stumbled to come up with answers to questions the audience thought Darrow had asked at the trial. With the help of the Lawrence and Lee script and an adaptation of the play by screenwriters Nedrick Young and Harold Jacob Smith, Spencer Tracy was sharp, brilliant, and engaging, while Fredric March looked like he was trying to answer today's questions with yesterday's answers.

In the stage play and the movie, the climactic courtroom scene ends with Fredric March mindlessly reciting from memory the names of the books of the Bible in order, physically broken by what has just transpired during Spencer Tracy's sharply crafted cross-examination. With the judge leaving the stand and the courtroom emptying, Fredric March falls into the arms of his wife, calling out, "Mother. They're laughing at me, Mother!" She comforts him, assuring him the courtroom spectators were not laughing at him. "I can't stand it when they laugh at me!" Fredric March repeats pathetically, in an obvious physical deterioration that in the play ultimately has him keel over from a heart attack and die.[59] His wife takes him in her arms and says, "It's all right, baby. It's all right. Baby . . . Baby."

The point Lawrence and Lee wanted to make was clear: under precise questioning from the legal sharpshooter, the religious zealot crumbles and is so reduced psychologically that his last refuge is the loving arms of his aging wife as the courtroom observers ridicule him with laughter and the judge walks away.

The problem with this version of events is that nothing of the sort actually happened in the Dayton, Tennessee, courtroom, and it's easy for viewers to forget that the play and movie are fictionalized. On the stand, Bryan did not break down.

In the public imagination even today, the Scopes monkey trial is remembered for the politically correct version the playwrights Lawrence and Lee invented out of whole cloth. Clarence Darrow did not win in that 1925 courtroom in Dayton, Tennessee, except perhaps in the minds of the agnostic Clarence Darrow and the articles the reporters from New York filed with their newspapers. How easy it was to forget that the ACLU had concocted the entire affair, advertising in the newspaper to find a defendant like Scopes who was willing to be the guinea pig and challenge the statute. After the Scopes trial, the Butler Act was never again enforced, and in the view of the mainstream press at the time, Bryan and God were the losers.

"It was plain to everyone, when Bryan came to Dayton, that his great days were behind him—that he was now definitely an old man, and headed at last for silence," H. L. Mencken summed up.

> There was a vague, unpleasant manginess about his appearance; he somehow seemed dirty, though a close glance showed him carefully shaved, and clad in immaculate linen. All the hair was gone from the dome of his head, and it had begun to fall out, too, behind his ears, like that of the late Samuel Gompers. The old resonance had departed from his voice: what was once a bugle blast had become reedy and quavering. Who knows that, like Demosthenes, he had a lisp? In his prime, under the magic of his eloquence, no one noticed it. But when he spoke at Dayton it was always audible.[60]

Mencken demonized Bryan and, in the process, demonized fundamental Christianity itself. "Bryan was a vulgar and common man, a cad undiluted," the journalist concluded.

> He was ignorant, bigoted, self-seeking, blatant and dishonest. His career brought him into contact with the first men of his time; he preferred the company of rustic ignoramuses. It was hard to believe, watching him at Dayton, that he had traveled, that he had been received in civilized societies, that he had been a high officer of state. He seemed only a poor clod like those around him, deluded by a childish theology, full of an almost

pathological hatred of all learning, all human dignity, all beauty, all fine and noble things.[61]

Ironically, Lawrence and Lee always said their play *Inherit the Wind* was written not to be a historically accurate representation of the Scopes trial. Instead, they crafted it as a polemic against an ACLU bogeyman of the era in which the play was written; they intended *Inherit the Wind* to serve as a broadside attack against McCarthyism, not specifically to be an argument for teaching evolutionary theory in the public schools. In a similar fashion, *The Crucible*, an Arthur Miller play about the 1692 Salem witch-hunt trials, was aimed at attacking McCarthyism.

In an interview given on the seventy-fifth anniversary of the Scopes trial, professor of history Edward J. Larson admitted as much.[62] "I had the good fortune to meet and work with both Jerome Lawrence and Bob Lee, the writers of the play, in preparing my book [about the Scopes trial]," Larson said in the interview.

> And as they [Lawrence and Lee] were always candid from the very beginning, they weren't writing about the Scopes trial; they were writing a play about McCarthyism. It was written during the period of the blacklisting of authors and playwrights; indeed, actually, some blacklisted playwrights helped in writing it. And they were just projecting back, much as was done with *The Crucible* by Arthur Miller, projecting back to another event, and then making a play about, trying to expose, really, how awful McCarthyism was. And so it's a wonderful play, but it tells you about the '50s, not the '20s.[63]

Oddly, with the production of *Inherit the Wind*, the ACLU managed to come full circle with the origins of the ACLU itself. Opposing religion in order to advance science, the Scopes trial ended up advancing the argument the ACLU used to defend Communists in the 1950s. If evolution was the victor in the politically correct version of the Scopes trial, the ACLU was ready to develop the subplot, namely, that communism itself—another supposedly scientifically based economic theory—was unjustly oppressed by mindless religious zealots who had no more justification than the deeply disturbed and demented Christians that Lawrence and Lee presented in their play.

To put the theme in the motif of Arthur Miller and *The Crucible,* Senator Joe McCarthy's investigation into Communists in government and the arts—including the writing of plays and movies—was equivalent to burning witches to death in Salem, Massachusetts, in 1692. Just as the American Left was unwilling to comprehend that William Jennings Bryan and his fundamental belief in God had any value in a modern scientific world, the American Left was unwilling to admit the extensive number of card-carrying Communists who actually were in government and the arts in the 1950s and, perhaps, even today.[64] Had Roger Baldwin taken the ideologically rigid position that Foster urged in 1925, the ACLU would have been forced to proclaim openly its ideological support of communism in order to defend Communists in the 1950s. By positioning itself as value neutral in its choice of which causes to champion, the ACLU avoided having to admit the organization had Communist roots and Communist sympathetics in order to come forward supporting the particular Communists being attacked by McCarthy in the Cold War backlash that Baldwin had long anticipated.

In retrospect, Baldwin's strategic calculations proved right. With the Scopes trial, the ACLU transformed a relatively unimportant misdemeanor into one of the most well-known courtroom dramas of the twentieth century. What the ACLU got with the Scopes trial was a chance to put religion itself on trial. What the ACLU achieved by not professing to be an openly Communist organization was the ability to defend openly professed Communists in the 1950s without having to admit the ACLU was, in effect, defending itself. By championing Scopes and the theory of evolution, the ACLU further advanced a main objective of the Communist assault on America. As long as Americans held to Judeo-Christian beliefs, the odds that America would become a radically Socialist or outright Communist state were virtually nil. Attacking God in the name of science proved a much more effective tactic given that the goal was to eliminate

Judeo-Christian belief in God in a nation that never would tolerate a direct attack on religious faith, a principle our Founding Fathers believed they had enshrined in the heart of the First Amendment.

What was emerging under Baldwin's direction was an ACLU that could achieve great success advancing political goals on the extreme left that traced back to the group's radical roots in the revolutionary politics of the 1920s and 1930s, as long as those in the organization hid the group's leftist political goals from an unsuspecting public. Step-by-step through a series of seminal cases beginning with the Scopes trial in 1925, the ACLU devised the strategy of always claiming to defend American freedoms, while surreptiously advancing its true purpose to advance communism in the United States. The ACLU even today likes to proclaim its roots derived from a determination to protect the free speech rights of antiwar protestors during World War I, deflecting attention from the degree to which the ACLU embraced the radical leftist politics exposed by many of the most prominent World War I protestors, including Eugene V. Debs.

The Scopes trial—which occurred just five years after the ACLU's founding—marked an important tactical turning point for the organization. The ACLU was no longer willing to restrict its activity to reactive legal defense cases the ACLU undertook to represent defendants who came forward because they believed their civil liberties needed protecting. Instead, the Scopes trial taught the ACLU the advantage of becoming proactive. With the Scopes trial, the ACLU realized the organization could push its ideological agenda against God and creationism by picking and choosing cases in which a point could be made with the American public. After the Scopes trial, activist legal advocates within the ACLU were encouraged to find and develop demonstration cases to utilize the courts in order to change public policy in accordance with ACLU objectives. Even though the ACLU lost the Scopes case, the organization expected that eventually it could find judicial activists at the appellate level who would see things its way.

Moreover, the Scopes case proved to the ACLU that casting religion as the suppressor of scientific-free expression in an enlightened secular society was a winning strategy.

Piety had not prevented millions around the globe from being mas-sacred in World War I, the most horrific conflict experienced in human history to that date. In the secular America developing after World War I, God was under cultural attack. If God was not the solution to solving human problems, maybe removing God from the human equation alto-gether could be sold as the solution. Marxism had long sought to place human beings on the throne of God. For the ACLU, evolution provided an ideal scientific theory to champion precisely because Darwin had attempted to explain the emergence of human beings without reference to God.

The Communists in the ACLU could embrace evolution whether or not the theory could ever be conclusively proven, much as they embraced communism whether or not any Communist country would ever succeed in producing the economic abundance theorists had postulated. The point was that both evolution and communism were presented to a gullible public as scientifically established facts, even though both were at best postula-tions. What made evolution and communism by nature complementary was that neither had any use for God.

It would take the Supreme Court another forty-plus years to rule that state laws prohibiting the teaching of evolution in the public schools were unconstitutional (in *Epperson v. Arkansas*, 393 U.S. 97 [1968]). Two decades later, in *Edwards v. Aguillard*, 482 U.S. 578 (1987), the Supreme Court struck down as unconstitutional a Louisiana law that demanded public schools teach creation science whenever evolution was taught, ruling the "preeminent purpose of the Louisiana Legislature was clearly to advance the religious viewpoint that a supernatural being created humankind."[65] Such results would have been unthinkable before the Scopes trial had begun. Persisting in the strategy to create test cases to champion in the courts, the ACLU has continued since 1925 its pitched battle to use the nation's courts to drive the God of our Founding Fathers and their Judeo-Christian reli-gion completely from the public arena once and for all, a reality that today is almost fully accomplished.

Even during his lifetime, Edward Bernays was widely credited with being the father of modern public relations. But it is equally important to understand the influence the Viennese psychoanalyst Sigmund Freud, Bernays's uncle, had on the mass marketing techniques developed by Bernays and introduced to the American public via Madison Avenue. From Freud, Bernays learned that people could be manipulated to modify their behavior or to internalize key social and political ideas by appealing to their subconscious desires. It's rarely appreciated that Freud had launched his own war on religion, a war Bernays ultimately advanced by developing the techniques of propaganda.

In 1927 Freud published a short but influential book called *The Future of an Illusion*, in which the illusion under discussion was religion. He followed this with the 1929 publication of another short book, *Civilization and Its Discontents*. The key idea of both polemics was that human beings created religion in order to restrain and control subconscious sexual desires that would be disruptive to society if allowed full expression. Freud believed this social control mechanism was detrimental, in that evolutionary theory required human force and power to be fully expressed if natural selection and the survival of the fittest were to be allowed to operate. The goal, according to Freud, was to advance the species with the science of psychology, every bit as much as Darwin sought to advance the species with the science of evolution. For Freud and for Darwin, religion stood as an impediment, an illusion created by human beings that inevitably produced discontent in the midst of civilization, thereby restraining human progress.

In his own short book—titled *Propaganda* before that term had derived sinister implications—published in 1928, Bernays put forth a theme compatible with his uncle's psychoanalytic concepts. He argued that an invisible government, the "true ruling power of our country," manipulates democratic societies, such that a relatively small elite "pull the wires which control the public mind." He defined *propaganda* as "a consistent, enduring effort to create or shape events to influence the relations of the public to an enterprise, idea or group."[66] Although he avoided attacking religion directly, Bernays advocated a conscious manipulation of public opinion by appealing to people through subtle, psychologically constructed images and messages.

The message was not lost on the ACLU. Attacking religion head-on would be far less effective than attacking religion as a prejudice—a prejudice that blocked the expression of other religions as well as a prejudice that blocked human advancement through restraining science. Science, viewed from this perspective, becomes a competing religion—a competing set of beliefs that puts human beings at the center of their own salvation, not in some future kingdom in the afterlife, but in the here and now. In other words, a civilization anxious for material advancements could be repositioned to see God as a barrier to a religion that transcended belief in God. That superior religion was science itself, predicated on human knowledge that promised advancements in a wide range of fields, including the health sciences, possibly even life extension, and certainly in the evolution of future human beings as an advanced species unto themselves.

In retrospect, the ACLU seized upon the Scopes trial as if its objective from the beginning was not to champion evolution per se, but to see God banned from all public spaces in America, with science put in the place of God. In its War on God, championing evolution became a means to an end, not an end in itself. Somehow, the American public had to be convinced that the only way to preserve religious freedom was to ban every vestige of government support for religious expression in the public arena. That God could ever be banned completely from the public sphere was an idea our Founding Fathers never would have contemplated, given the pains they took to write the language of the First Amendment so as to protect religious expression in America. For our Founding Fathers, religious freedom was so important the amendment designed to preserve religious freedom was positioned first in specifying the Bill of Rights. For the lawyers of the ACLU, eliminating God from America would be difficult but, after the Scopes trial, not impossible. With the Scopes trial, the ACLU lawyers managed to elevate science to the status of a religion. Now all that was needed was to elevate atheism to the status of a religion.

3

A WALL OF SEPARATION

I cannot see how an "official religion" is established by letting those who want to say a prayer say it.

—JUSTICE POTTER STEWART, *ENGEL V. VITALE*, 370 U.S. 421 (1962)

According to a 2010 study conducted by the First Amendment Center, 53 percent of Americans believe the US Constitution establishes a Christian nation, but 66 percent of them require a clear separation of church and state.[1] What exactly does "a clear separation of church and state" mean, and how does that understanding affect what we mean when we say the Founding Fathers created the United States as a Christian nation?

We can appreciate how important it was to our Founding Fathers to establish freedom of religion once we understand the initial words of the First Amendment: "Congress shall make no law respecting an establishment of religion, or prohibiting the free exercise thereof." The Founding Fathers gave no further elaboration of this simple two-clause statement, the first ten words of which have, over time, become known as the establishment clause and the last six words as the free exercise clause.

When we review the history, we learn that the Founding Fathers did not write even these sixteen words easily or quickly, nor is the amendment's meaning easy to interpret because the number of words was few.

In the debate during the Constitutional Convention of 1787, the Federalists, led by James Madison—those supporting the Constitution and the establishment of a stronger federal government to replace the deficiencies of national leadership under the Articles of Confederation ratified in 1781—did not feel it necessary to specify a Bill of Rights that included the right to freedom of religion. Madison's argument was that Congress did not have the power to establish a national religion because it was not specifically given the authority to do so under the Constitution being debated to replace the failed Articles of Confederation. James Wilson, a lawyer from Philadelphia, echoed Madison's call to limit the power of the federal government to enumerated powers. Wilson also worried that if the Constitutional Convention adopted a Bill of Rights, the rights specified there might be considered exclusive of other rights not mentioned.[2] The Constitution emerged from the Constitutional Convention without any specification of free speech rights.

The anti-Federalists—those opposed to the Constitution because they continued to fear a strong central government—won the day, as their demand for a specified Bill of Rights soon captured the popular imagination. Madison's home state of Virginia ratified the Constitution only after recommending the addition of a religion amendment, worded as follows:

> That religion, or the duty we owe our Creator, and the manner of discharging it, can be directed only by reason and conviction, not by force or violence; and therefore all men have an equal, natural and unalienable right to the free exercise of religion, according to the dictates of conscience, and that no particular religious sect or society ought to be favored or established, by law, in preference to others.[3]

Interestingly, this formulation of religious freedom prefigured what ultimately emerged as the language in the First Amendment, with the first half of the paragraph devoted to describing the free exercise of religion as an unalienable right, echoing the Declaration of Independence's insistence that all human rights flow from God, and the second half devoted to outlawing a government-established state religion. The two halves of religious freedom— free expression and no established state religion—appear unified under the concept that religion cannot be imposed by force and violence, but instead must be allowed to flow openly and in public from personal conviction.

During the debate over the Bill of Rights by the first Congress, Madison simplified Virginia's language, while retaining the key ideas of the Virginia formulation: "The Civil Rights of none shall be abridged on account of religious belief or worship, nor shall any national religion be established, nor shall the full and equal rights of Conscience be in any manner, or on any pretext infringed."[4]

After being debated by the House of Representatives, the language of the First Amendment was revised to read: "Congress shall make no law establishing religion, or prohibiting the free exercise thereof, nor shall the rights of conscience be infringed."[5] Although the House version was closer to the final language, the Senate voted the amendment to state: "Congress shall make no law establishing articles of faith or a mode of worship, or prohibiting the free exercise of religion."[6] As the language proceeded toward final form, the rights of conscience were eliminated as an increasing emphasis made sure that Congress passed no law establishing a state religion.

Legal commentators who consider Madison the chief architect of the First Amendment language have concluded that the language as influenced by Madison was "merely aimed to prevent the *federal* government from establishing a *specific* state-sponsored church."[7] Supporting this view, the first clause of the First Amendment as finally written addressed the establishment issue first, whereas previous drafts had not done so, with rights of free expression placed second.

Yet it is not altogether clear that the only requirement for free expression of religion was that government refrain from establishing a state religion. Granted, a possible interpretation of the First Amendment language is that a necessary condition of religious freedom is that government refrain from establishing a state religion, but that alone is not a sufficient condition to establish religious freedom. It may also be required that the federal government refrain from imposing on religious expression any constraints that would disallow citizens from openly expressing their belief in God and practicing their religion as they see fit, without government restraint.

So the question is whether the First Amendment puts any positive obligation on government to provide the necessary and sufficient conditions required for free expression of religion or whether government's responsibility under the First Amendment is limited only to preventing a state religion from being established—a requirement that could easily be interpreted as demanding government avoid any and all involvement in promoting or deterring religious beliefs and practices. In other words, is the free expression clause of the First Amendment a competing principle to the establishment clause—such that once government intervenes to protect free expression of religion, the danger is present that government is moving to establish religion? Or is the free expression clause a complementary principle to the establishment clause—imposing upon government the obligation to intervene as a referee to permit free expression of all religious beliefs, such that establishing one religion as a state religion becomes impossible?

The point is that government may have a positive responsibility to allow robust expressions of religious beliefs, especially if the language of the earlier drafts of the First Amendment is to be taken seriously. If this is so, then the First Amendment compels government not to eradicate religion from the public arena but to promote religion within the public arena. If the expression of religious beliefs is an inherent God-designed part of human nature, as the Declaration of Independence proclaimed, then a government acting to remove religion from the public sphere would have seemed to our Founding Fathers to be acting in a manner antithetical to our founding principles.

Although the First Amendment was passed by Congress as part of the Bill of Rights in 1789 and ratified by the states in 1791, the Supreme Court did not directly address the establishment clause until 1947, when the court decided *Everson v. Board of Education*, 330 U.S. 1 (1947).[8] The case involved a New Jersey statute that allowed the parents to be reimbursed for the fares paid to public carriers for transporting their children to both public schools and Catholic parochial schools. Justice Hugo Black, a Democratic senator from Alabama who had joined the KKK in his youth and had been known for his anti-Catholic views, wrote the majority opinion of the court. In doing so, Black articulated for the first time the legal standard of imposing a wall of separation between church and state.

In its amicus brief (that is, "friend of the court": someone not a party to a case who volunteers to offer information to assist a court in deciding a matter before it) to the Supreme Court in the *Everson* case, the ACLU noted "the use of public moneys to transport children attending parochial school is in aid and support of such schools and of religious institutions and tenets, and that the statute and resolution authorizing such expenditures violate the fundamental American principle of separation of church and state and the constitutional prohibition respecting an establishment of religion." In advancing the establishment clause argument against the New Jersey policy of reimbursing Catholic parents the cost of using public buses to transport their children to parochial schools, the ACLU amicus brief specifically used the phrase "separation of church and state." The ACLU argued the case "presents a situation which, however innocent or plausible it may be made to appear, constitutes a definite crack in the wall of separation of church and state. Such cracks have a tendency to widen beyond repair unless promptly sealed up."[9]

In writing the majority opinion in the Supreme Court's 5–4 decision, Justice Hugo Black penned what was to become one of the most important formulations in religious freedom jurisprudence. "The First Amendment has erected a wall between church and state," Justice Black wrote, echoing the words of Thomas Jefferson. (Jefferson, writing to the Danbury [Connecticut] Baptist Association in 1802, used the phrase "wall of separation between Church & State.")[10] "That wall must be kept high and impregnable." Black expounded on that view as follows:

> The "establishment of religion" clause of the First Amendment means at least this: neither a state nor the Federal Government can set up a church. Neither can pass laws which aid one religion, aid all religions, or prefer one

religion over another. Neither can force nor influence a person to go to or to remain away from church against his will or force him to profess a belief or disbelief in any religion. No person can be punished for entertaining or professing religious beliefs or disbeliefs, for church attendance or non-attendance. No tax in any amount, large or small, can be levied to support any religious activities or institutions, whatever they may be called, or whatever form they may adopt to teach or practice religion. Neither a state nor the Federal Government can, openly or secretly, participate in the affairs of any religious organizations or groups, and vice versa.[11]

Although the principle articulated by Black suggested the Supreme Court would declare the New Jersey law unconstitutional, the court actually decided just the opposite. The majority of the court drew the distinction that New Jersey did not contribute money directly to the school, but "to help parents get their children, regardless of their religion, safely and expeditiously to and from accredited schools." As a legal commentator noted, "In response to the contention that the state was establishing religion by upholding New Jersey's law, the court stated that the First Amendment required the state to be *neutral* in its relationship with both religious and nonreligious groups; it did not allow the state to be hostile toward religion."[12] Justice Black drew a comparison with police officers who protect from traffic accidents students who attend parochial schools on an equal basis to the police protection extended to students attending public schools. "Similarly, parents might be reluctant to permit their children to attend schools which the state had cut off from such general government services as ordinary police and fire protection, connections for sewage disposal, public highways and sidewalks," he wrote.[13] Clearly, he argued, the First Amendment did not require the state to cut church schools off from general government services to the point that church schools would find it difficult to operate.

Somehow, articulating a principle that there should be a wall between church and state seemed to be softened because the Supreme Court in the *Everson* decision did not rule the government subsidy of public transportation to parochial schools unconstitutional. But the important part of the

Everson case was not that the Supreme Court allowed the state of New Jersey to use tax money to subsidize public transportation for parochial-school children. The important part of the *Everson* case stems from a comment that Justice Felix Frankfurter made in concurring with the opinion of the court. Frankfurter commented that James Madison's words characterizing Thomas Jefferson's Bill for Establishing Religious Freedom and his own letter written to the Virginia Assembly displayed to Frankfurter a "technical precision" that allowed Frankfurter to conclude Jefferson and Madison were both proponents of a clear separation of church and state in the interest of making sure government does not establish a national state-sponsored religion. "The [First] Amendment's purpose was not to strike merely at the official establishment of a single sect, creed, or religion, outlawing only a formal relation such as had prevailed in England and some of the colonies," Frankfurter wrote in his concurring opinion to *Everson*. "Necessarily, it was to uproot all such relationships. But the object was broader than separating church and state in this narrow sense. It was to create a complete and permanent separation of the spheres of religious activity and civil authority by comprehensively forbidding every form of public aid or support for religion."[14]

Even though the ACLU was on the losing side, it got what it wanted in the language of the majority decision. "More importantly, the Supreme Court accepted the ACLU's assertion of a 'separation of church and state,' and the *Everson* case, with its stark 'wall' imagery, became the foundation for the ACLU's subsequent Establishment Clause cases," wrote Claremont Institute political scientists Thomas Krannawitter and Daniel Palm in their 2005 study of the ACLU and religion in American politics. "But perhaps the best measure of the ACLU's success came with the media, which gradually but steadily through the 1950s and 1960s began to refer to the 'Constitution's separation of church and state,' leaving many Americans with the mistaken impression that the words are part of our fundamental law."[15]

In the years since *Everson*, federal courts "have referenced Jefferson's celebrated phrase almost too many times to count," stated legal scholar Daniel Dreisbach in his book *Thomas Jefferson and the Wall of Separation Between Church and State*.[16] "Remarkably, the Jeffersonian metaphor has eclipsed and supplanted constitutional text in the minds of many jurists, scholars, and the American public." Today, it is almost hard to remember that the language regarding the creation of a wall of separation between church and state derives not from the language of the First Amendment but from an otherwise relatively obscure letter Thomas Jefferson wrote in 1802.

It does not matter that Jefferson never used the wall metaphor again in any of his subsequent writings on religious freedom. Nor does it matter that Jefferson was not a key architect of the First Amendment, as was Madison, or that Jefferson wrote the letter to the Danbury Baptists eleven years *after* the Bill of Rights was ratified. The truth is that Jefferson was in France when the first Congress debated the Bill of Rights. Nowhere in the debate over the First Amendment in the first Congress is there any mention of "separation between church and state."[17]

But everything changed when Justice Black managed to incorporate Jefferson's image of a wall of separation into Madison's thinking, to produce what amounted to a virtual rewrite of the First Amendment. Is this what Madison meant when he argued against the United States having a national religion, much as Great Britain had elevated the Church of England following King Henry XIII's 1534 rift with the Roman Catholic Church? Is this what Jefferson meant when he insisted freedom of religion was an unalienable right derived from God? It was almost as if Justice Black decided the First Amendment was equivalent to the biblical admonition to render unto Caesar what was Caesar's and unto God what was God's, under the assumption that a discernible distinction could be drawn without conflict between what was Caesar's and what was God's.[18] The whole point of the First Amendment's attempt to protect freedom of religion is that over time Caesar tends to intrude upon God.

As if to advance the impression that the wall metaphor was nothing more than Madison's words incorporating Jefferson's meaning, the Supreme Court appended to the *Everson* decision the complete text of Madison's "Memorial and Remonstrance Against Religious Assessments," delivered in 1785 to the General Assembly of the Commonwealth of Virginia.[19] What else was the reader to think than that Madison and Jefferson were of like mind in concurring that a wall of separation between church and state was required in order to preserve religious freedom, even though the First Amendment said no such thing? Cleverly, Black wrapped his "wall of separation between church and state" metaphor within the history of Virginia, a colony and state revered for the fight to establish religious freedom for its citizens. The end result was to imply the establishment clause demanded an impregnable wall be placed between government and religion, so as to protect religion. Strangely, Justice Black's reasoning edged into the type of paradoxical thinking expressed in the apocryphal statement made popular during the Vietnam War: namely, "we had to destroy the village to save the village." How far would the wall metaphor advanced by Justice Black in *Everson* go? Conceivably, the metaphor could be extended so as far as to assert that government might have to destroy religion in order to save religion—all done in the name of clarifying and implementing the establishment clause to the detriment of the free expression clause.

In writing his opinion, Black relied on the Virginia Statute for Religious Freedom, a document that "Jefferson wrote and Madison sponsored in opposition to Virginia's tax" supporting an established religion.[20] Yet that Jefferson's and Madison's views on religious freedom were identical is by no means certain. Madison, a Federalist, was most concerned that there be no nationally established state religion; Jefferson, an anti-Federalist, was most concerned that no government action be permitted that should in any way constrain the freedom of religious expression, a right Jefferson believed God placed in the hearts and minds of human beings by their very nature.

No less than Chief Justice William Rehnquist, dissenting in the 1985 Supreme Court decision *Wallace v. Jaffree*, 472 U.S. 38 (1985), rebelled against Justice Black's use of Jefferson's letter to the Danbury Baptists to establish a judicial theory that would ultimately end up banning religion from the public sphere in America. Rehnquist's sharply worded protest conveys his frustration: "The Court's opinion in *Everson*—while correct in bracketing Madison and Jefferson together in their exertions in their home State leading to the enactment of the Virginia Statute of Religious Liberty—is totally incorrect in suggesting that Madison carried these views onto the floor of the United States House of Representatives when he proposed the language which would ultimately become the Bill of Rights."[21]

Rehnquist insisted the concern of our Founding Fathers in the debate over the First Amendment during the first Congress was to prevent government from establishing a state religion, not to "require that Government be absolutely neutral as between religion and irreligion." In this dissent to *Wallace v. Jaffree*, Rehnquist objected that the Supreme Court had used Justice Black's citation of Jefferson's letter to restrict religion. "The evil to be aimed at, so far as those who spoke were concerned, appears to have been the establishment of a national church, and perhaps the preference of one religious sect over another; but it was definitely not concerned about whether Government might aid all religions evenhandedly," Rehnquist wrote.[22] In conclusion, Rehnquist expressed in the strongest possible terms his simple recommendation that the wall of separation metaphor introduced by Justice Black in *Everson* "should be frankly and explicitly abandoned."[23]

The *Everson* test invites us to assume language of the First Amendment prohibiting Congress from passing any law that would establish a state religion is equivalent to the meaning implied in the wall metaphor. Professor Dreisbach thinks not, arguing that it differs in significant respects from the meaning of the First Amendment language. "The First Amendment's laconic text imposes explicit restrictions on Congress only," Dreisbach noted. "A wall, by contrast is a bilateral barrier, a structure of unambiguous demarcation that inhibits the movement of traffic from one side to the other. The separation principle, interpreted strictly, proscribes all admixtures of religion and politics, denies all governmental endorsement of and aid for institutional religion, and promotes a religion that is strictly voluntary and essentially private, personal, and nonpolitical." The final result of applying the wall metaphor strictly, in Dreisbach's view, ends up inhibiting religious intrusions on public life and politics. Sadly, Dreisbach concludes, "Jefferson's architectural metaphor, in the course of time, has achieved virtual canonical status and become more familiar to the American people than the actual text of the First Amendment."[24]

We do not need to parse Jefferson's many writings on religion to realize he considered belief in God and politics to be intertwined. The principal architect of the Declaration of Independence, Jefferson began by asserting that human rights were unalienable, in other words, derived not from some compact among human beings that could be taken away easily by human beings changing their minds, but that human rights are unalienable because they are bestowed by God and, as such, are not subject to being granted or taken away by the consent of human beings. The entire view of the Declaration of Independence derives from a concept of natural right, conceptualized as those characteristics of human beings and laws of human behavior that are inherently placed within the nature of human beings by their Creator. This was an extremely important idea. Government, in Jefferson's view, does not exist to perpetuate government. Government exists "to secure these Rights." Only then can governments be considered to have derived "their just Powers from the Consent of the Governed."

The whole point of the Declaration of Independence is that government has a responsibility to God to be formed and to function so as to preserve the unalienable rights that God placed within the fabric of every human being. Remove God from the Declaration of Independence and human rights have no stated meaning. Jefferson clearly did not intend to accomplish this by articulating a metaphor of a wall separating church and state. God necessarily enters politics for Jefferson because political structures are required to protect the unalienable rights that God bestowed upon human beings by our very nature, including religious freedom.

We need also remember that Jefferson, an anti-Federalist, wrote the letter to the Danbury Baptists precisely because the congregation was concerned that simply by writing the First Amendment, the first Congress had begun the process of transforming religious freedom from an unalienable right to express belief in God into a right granted and conditioned by the state.[25] That Jefferson regarded his letter to the Danbury Baptists as consistent with his view of natural right is clear from the last sentence to his second paragraph, the sentence immediately following his articulation of the wall metaphor: "Adhering to this expression of the supreme will of the nation in behalf of the rights of conscience, I shall see with sincere satisfaction the progress of those sentiments which tend to restore to man all his natural rights, convinced he has no natural right in opposition to his social duties."[26]

Clearly, Jefferson did not intend to articulate a principle that would invite government to intrude upon freedom of religious expression. If a wall were needed to separate church and state, Jefferson's point was that the wall should function to keep government out of religious affairs, not to empower government to remove religion from the public arena, lest we run the risk of creating a state-established religion. In other words, Justice Black in the *Everson* decision used the wall metaphor to establish the exact opposite of what Jefferson intended. Jefferson's wall, intended to keep government's hands off religious practices, had been turned by Black's interpretation to invite government intervention any time a religious practice slipped out of the privacy of the home into some form of expression open to the community in the public arena. While Jefferson wrote the letter to mitigate the fears of the Danbury Baptists that the First Amendment invited government regulation, Black ended up interpreting the Danbury letter by doing just that: namely, inviting government to put all Americans of faith on notice that government would be prohibited from taking any steps to promote the free expression of religion even if that put an end to open expression of Judeo-Christian beliefs in the public sphere.

Jefferson's point was that the human rights specified in the Declaration of Independence derived from a view of political philosophy known as *natural right* or *natural law* theory in which human beings have an inherent right built by God into the structure of human nature to express their religious beliefs openly, without government interference. The concept of rights and freedoms under natural right and natural law theory differs fundamentally from the scientific views of human nature that are expressed in what were proposed as modern scientific and political theories, including the scientific theory of evolution and the political philosophies behind socialism and communism. It is impossible to conceptualize natural right and natural law theory as political philosophy without a clear notion of God. In sharp contrast, modern scientific and political theories, including both socialism and communism, typically proceed with the presumption that science advances through a logic that does not depend on the presumption of a Supreme Being. Without God in the equation, questions of morality are seen "value judgments" arbitrarily made by human beings, such that the values of one person or group may not be the values of others and that the values of today may not be the value of tomorrow, while nobody's values have any claim to being superior to anybody else's values.

Under modern scientific and political theory, the state—not God—confers rights and freedoms upon citizens. This disconnect is one reason modern scientific and political thinkers argue that intelligent design explanations of creation are just another form of creationism, letting God in through the back door. Darwin, like Marx, saw human beings as advancing in history, reaching new heights of perfection through advances in human reason and knowledge as defined within the scientific method alone. Darwin viewed the progress of humans from apes as an ongoing part of the continuing process of natural selection in which more adaptive future humans would exceed the capabilities of humans seen today. Marx, following Hegel, also saw progress in history, such that the social dialectic would force into creation a classless society in which benign bureaucrats would administer social justice such that human societies would prosper and economic inequalities would disappear. So, when the ACLU insists that God should not intrude on the public arena, the ACLU sides with the scientific materialism that binds together Darwin and Marx, such that God is seen not as the completion of human nature, but as an unfortunate human invention that detracts from the progress of human nature toward completion.

In the Judeo-Christian tradition, human nature is the same today as it was two thousand years ago—equally flawed now as it was then—and as it will be almost certainly two thousand years from now. Rather than start with perfectible human beings, the Bible starts with fallen human beings who are expelled from the garden of Eden in the persons of Adam and Eve, the first two human beings. Following the fall from grace, all subsequent human beings born are necessarily flawed by Adam and Eve's original sin, such that we humans are destined by nature to be sinners, imperfect beings perfected only by the grace of God and, for Christians, the redemption made possible by Christ's death on the cross. Reading Justice Black in the Everson decision, these contemplations of original sin and the necessity of Jesus Christ for salvation are absent. The secular world devoid of Judeo-Christian religious practices that inevitably results from Justice Black's construction of Jefferson's wall is a world in which Darwin, Marx, and their modern, secular successors can and do live comfortably—all without a necessary or daily consciousness of God.

The natural right view known to Jefferson and his contemporaries could not have been more different from Justice Black's modern, virtually god-less view of the public sphere. What Jefferson expressed in his letter to the Danbury Baptists was the view that a strong government depended upon a people free to openly express their religious beliefs, whatever their religious beliefs might be. The whole point of the wall metaphor, as Jefferson penned it, was to constrain government, not to articulate a principle upon which government might constrain religion. Truly, Jefferson would have considered twisted the reasoning that his wall of separation metaphor was being used by the Supreme Court to empower the state to place the wall squarely between believers and their God. "If the purpose of Jefferson's letter to the Danbury Baptists was to establish a wall preventing government from advancing religion, he would have been violating his own rule in the very document in which he pronounced it," concluded Krannawitter and Palm. "One must conclude, therefore, that either Jefferson was so confused that he contradicted himself, or the interpretation of Jefferson's words offered by the Supreme Court and the ACLU is grossly mistaken."[27] But ever since *Everson*, as Dreisbach has pointed out, the wall metaphor "has become the central icon of a strict separationist dogma that champions a secular polity in which religious influences are systematically stripped from public life."[28]

Moreover, by saddling the First Amendment with the due process provisions of the Fourteenth Amendment, Justice Black in crafting the majority opinion in *Everson* managed to separate "religion and civil government at all levels—federal, state, and local."[29] The First Amendment limited only the federal Congress from passing laws representing an establishment of religion.

But after *Everson*, Justice Black managed to use the Fourteenth Amendment to transform the First Amendment into the tool an activist federal government could use to deliver mandates concerning religion that no state or locality in the nation could afford to ignore. Perhaps Justice Black could feel secure in having interpreted the establishment clause to remove any concern that by protecting religious freedom, the federal government was establishing a state religion. But ironically, what Justice Black succeeded in doing was authorizing the federal government to establish a state religion comfortable to modern-day atheists, all in the name of the First Amendment.

Under the First Amendment language as originally written, the states were unrestrained to pass whatever laws the states desired regarding religion, without concern for whether or not they were consistent with laws regarding religion at the federal level. Applying the Fourteenth Amendment after *Everson*, no state could pass any law the Supreme Court viewed as objectionable, not just because the state law might lead to the establishment of a state religion or to the support of a particular religion over another religion at the state level, but because the state law might just violate what the Supreme Court saw as the need to maintain an impregnable wall of separation between government and religion at all levels of government. After *Everson*, the meaning of the First Amendment was reduced to requiring all levels of government to keep religion out of American public life, even if that meant removing completely all references to the God worshipped by Christians and Jews from the public view in America—a result that would have astounded our Founding Fathers, given the language they thought they were crafting into the First Amendment to protect open expression of religious beliefs in America.

The driving force we have to thank for this perverse result is the ACLU—an organization that has remained dedicated since the Scopes trial to the public policy of removing God from sight.

⌁

The Supreme Court decision in *Everson* was a failure, even for the ACLU.

Instead of establishing a bright-line test, *Everson* resulted in mass confusion in the federal courts. As one scholar noted, the phrases "rife with confusion," "in hopeless disarray," and "suffer[ing] from a sort of jurisprudential schizophrenia" were just a few of the disparaging ways that federal courts described the Supreme Court's establishment clause jurisprudence following *Everson*.[30] Federal courts couldn't decide which government practices regarding religion were sufficiently neutral as to be constitutional and which government practices favored religion so much that they were unconstitutional. This result should have been expected. Wise judges and judicial scholars have warned for centuries that metaphors adapted to be principles of law are intrinsically difficult to decipher and apply in subsequent fact situations. Justice Black employed Jefferson's wall metaphor as if the image were simple conceptually and immediately comprehensible to all without further explication or debate. Unfortunately, subsequent court cases proved how unenlightening the wall metaphor served to be, applied as a rule of law.

In the forty years following *Everson*, "the question of the 'wall of separation' between church and state became one of the most hotly contested political issues in America," wrote Samuel Walker in his sympathetic history of the ACLU. "On the one side stood the forces of organized religion that sought to maintain their traditional prerogative of using the state's machinery—particularly the schools—to advance religious doctrines. On the other side stood the ACLU and other separationist groups, insisting that in a pluralist society, government had to be neutral in religious matters."[31] During this time, the ACLU achieved major civil rights victories with landmark cases in the social arena, including the 1954 decision *Brown v. Board of Education* that established separate schools could not provide equal education, overturning decades in which racial segregation had been an accepted practice in the United States. Following *Brown v. Board of Education*, a broad consensus developed in civil rights litigation, with nearly unanimous agreement that racial prejudice of all types was to be eliminated from American society. Consensus, however, was lacking in freedom of religion cases.

In examining more than two decades of cases following *Everson*, scholars have found it difficult to discern a bright-line test that would allow

American citizens and communities to know whether a certain religious practice would be found constitutional or not. In 1948, the Supreme Court ruled in *McCollum v. Board of Education*, 333 U.S. 203 (1948) that religious education provided by churches on public school grounds in Illinois during the school day was unconstitutional. Then in 1952, in *Zorach v. Clauson*, 343 U.S. 306 (1952), the Supreme Court found that allowing New York students to leave public school grounds for religious education was constitutional. Dissenting in *Zorach*, Justice Black wrote, "I see no significant difference between the invalid Illinois system and that of New York here sustained." If Justice Black, the author of the court's majority opinion in *Everson*, could not distinguish these cases, how could a state, county, city, or municipal school official be expected to make the distinction reliably?

Moreover, a deeply divided court has decided most of the school prayer cases following *Everson*. "That division raises questions concerning the robustness of the principles governing school prayer and whether changes in the Court's composition could alter the jurisprudential logic applied to situations involving some form of prayer in schools," commented three legal scholars in an article in the *Journal of Law and Education*.[32]

In an attempt to clarify the wall of separation test, the Burger court developed a new test in *Lemon v. Kurtzman*, 403 U.S. 602 (1971). The case struck down various arrangements in Rhode Island and Pennsylvania that provided state funding of teachers at Catholic parochial schools, with the court deciding the laws in question involved an "excessive entanglement" between government and religion, in the words of Chief Justice Warren Burger, who wrote the court's decision.[33]

In so doing, Chief Justice Burger established a new test that subsequently became known simply as the *Lemon* test. The *Lemon* test was distinguished by having three prongs of analysis. First, the statute in question had to be shown to have a secular legislative purpose to be considered constitutional. Second, the primary effect of the statute had to be to neither advance nor inhibit religion. Third, the statute must not foster an excessive entanglement with religion. If the state law in question failed any of these three tests, it was unconstitutional. The first prong, requiring the statute to have a legitimate government purpose that was not a sham, became the most important. The second prong tended to be satisfied as long as the government did not prefer one religion to others. The third prong was the most vague, requiring that in administering the law, the government did not become "excessively entangled" with religion, as articulated by Chief Justice Burger.[34]

"With the *Lemon* decision, the ACLU had succeeded in establishing a constitutional doctrine that had the effect of making religion's presence in the public square inherently tenuous," concluded Krannawitter and Palm.[35] Returning to the case *Wallace v. Jaffree*, 472 U.S. 38 (1985), the Burger court ruled unconstitutional a 1981 Alabama statute authorizing a minute of silence in all public schools "for meditation or voluntary prayer." The majority of the Supreme Court decided that the intent of the Alabama legislature was to find a way to return voluntary prayer to the schools. In his dissent, Justice William Rehnquist commented not only on Justice Black's wall of separation test as a principle of constitutional law but also on the *Lemon* test in particular. "The secular purpose prong has proved mercurial in application because it has never been fully defined, and we have never fully stated how the test is to operate," Rehnquist wrote. "If the purpose prong is intended to void those aids to sectarian institutions accompanied by a stated legislative purpose to aid religion, the prong will condemn nothing so long as the legislature utters a secular purpose and says nothing about aiding religion."[36]

Rehnquist's concern was that any state statute that provided any aid whatsoever to religion would be seen as lacking a sufficiently secular purpose to be construed as constitutional. He dismissed the *Lemon* test as having "no more grounding in the history of the First Amendment than does the wall theory upon which it rests."[37] He then proceeded to make a mockery of both cases, noting the federal courts had ruled that a state may lend to parochial-school children geography textbooks containing maps of the United States, but the state may not lend maps of the United States for use in geography class; a state may lend textbooks on American colonial history but may not lend a film on George Washington or a film projector to show it in history class; a state may pay for bus transportation to religious schools but may not pay for bus transportation from the parochial school to the public zoo or natural history museum for a field trip. Rehnquist objected strenuously, arguing that the establishment clause should not forbid governments from providing benefits to private individuals, even though many of the private individuals may elect to use those benefits in ways that aid religious instruction or worship. Rehnquist suggested abandoning the *Lemon* test in favor of a simpler view of the establishment clause that would allow government to be involved in regulating religion only when a case involved some particular government action that discriminated against a particular religious sect and would be limited to prohibiting government action only when the government took specific steps that could be construed as designating a particular church or sect as a state or national religion.

Political scientists Krannawitter and Palm noted the victory for the ACLU came in Justice Sandra Day O'Connor's concurring opinion in *Wallace v. Jaffree*, in which she held that the establishment clause should be read as forbidding any "endorsement of religion."[38] In her concurring opinion, O'Connor admitted that despite its initial promise, "the *Lemon* test has proved problematic." Yet she was not willing to abandon the test. She felt it could be applied to examine "whether government's purpose is to endorse religion and whether the statute actually conveys a message of endorsement." And she believed the establishment clause precludes "government from conveying or attempting to convey a message that religion or a particular religious belief is favored or preferred." She conceded that a moment of silence is not inherently religious. She even conceded that a moment of silence law "that is clearly drafted and implemented so as to permit prayer, meditation, and reflection within the prescribed period, without endorsing one alternative over the others, should pass the test."[39]

Nonetheless, O'Connor found the Alabama law unconstitutional because its text and legislative history left the conclusion unavoidable that the purpose of the statute was to endorse prayer in public schools. Krannawitter and Palm concluded that the *Lemon* doctrine, as applied by O'Connor, contrary to the Founders' thinking about the proper place of religion in the republic, "laid the groundwork for further removal of expressions of faith in years ahead."[40]

With the tests developed in the *Everson* and *Lemon* cases, the Supreme Court began the process of elevating the importance of the establishment clause over the free exercise clause in evaluating the First Amendment's definition of religious freedom. After *Lemon*, legal commentators commonly began to accept the proposition not only that the establishment clause was determinative in Supreme Court jurisprudence regarding freedom of religion but also that the establishment clause and the free exercise clause were actually competing theories. "On one hand the Free Speech Clause, intended to protect private religious expression, forbids content-based restrictions on private expression in the public forum," wrote a legal commentator in the *Brooklyn Law Review*. "Yet, on the other hand, the Establishment Clause requires that the government not favor one religion over another. As a result, an inherent conflict exists between these two doctrines because when the government allows religious speech in a public forum it appears to be sponsoring religion."[41]

Here we have come full circle from the view of the Founding Fathers that government's role in religion should be limited. We should not discount that the First Amendment begins "Congress shall make no law" either establishing a state religion or prohibiting the free exercise of religion. Rather than articulate an affirmative responsibility for government to protect religion, the Founding Fathers felt it was enough to keep government out. If nothing else, the language of the First Amendment makes it clear the goal was to restrain government when it came to religion. There is no suggestion the Founders felt the establishment clause and the free exercise clause were in any way competing. Otherwise, why would the Founders include the two clauses together? The point was to keep government out of both realms. Both clauses were needed because it was not sufficient to restrain government from establishing a state religion; government also had to be restrained from any attempt to interfere with religious practices and beliefs. The negative language of the First Amendment does not prohibit Congress from passing a law that promotes religion, provided the judgment does not promote one religion over others.

With the decisions in *Everson* and *Lemon*, the First Amendment had been turned on its head. The Supreme Court had granted itself license to use the Fourteenth Amendment to regulate state and local laws regarding freedom of religion, something the First Amendment never could have contemplated. Ignoring a possible distinction between a government law to establish a state religion and a government law that might simply benefit religion, the Supreme Court also granted itself license to strike down any law at all levels of government that impacted religious practices or beliefs in any way at all. So, after *Everson* and *Lemon*, it was not good enough that the Supreme Court struck down all laws that it felt tended to establish a state religion; the Supreme Court wanted the authority to strike down any law that discussed or impacted religion in any way at all.

The president of the Catholic League, William A. Donohue, advances the argument that the ACLU pursues specific public policy objectives when it decides which particular civil liberties to champion. He has commented that freedom *of* religion has not been given the same priority as freedom *from* religion in the ACLU's determination of which religious freedom cases to pursue.[42] "The ACLU has interpreted the First Amendment to mean that there ought to be more than a wall between church and state—there ought to be an iron curtain," Donahue concludes.[43] After *Everson* and *Lemon*, the ACLU appeared bent on a political path to establish public policy in the United States to prevent passage of laws on the federal, state, or local level that could be construed to benefit or promote a Judeo-Christian religious practice or a belief in the Judeo-Christian diety expressed in the public sector. From there, it was a small step to the conclusion that any reference to God in the public sector should simply be disallowed.

In his second book on the ACLU, a 1994 volume called *Twilight of Liberty: The Legacy of the ACLU*, Donohue recounted the case of the ACLU and Nat Hentoff, a professed atheist known for his leftist views and his published music criticism. Hentoff joined the ACLU board wanting to see "In God We Trust" taken off all US coins. Hentoff figured, "When I was elected to the national board of the American Civil Liberties Union some years ago, I thought I would be the most anti-clerical kid on the block." He soon found out he was wrong. After three years on the board, Hentoff left, realizing "there are members of that board—and of the far-flung affiliates of the ACLU—who see the separation of church and state as so absolute that not a single religious word must be allowed to pass a schoolhouse door."[44]

"For eight decades, the ACLU has been America's leading religious censor, waging a largely uncontested (until recently) war against America's core values—all not only without protest but with the support of much of the media—cloaking its war in the name of liberty," wrote Alan Sears and Craig Osten, two officers of the Alliance Defending Freedom, a legal advocacy group created specifically to counter the ACLU, in the introduction to *The ACLU vs. America: Exposing the Agenda to Redefine Moral Values.* "We now live in a country where our traditional Christian and Jewish faith and religion—civilizing forces in any society—are openly mocked and increasingly pushed to the margins."[45] In their 2005 book, Sears and Osten depicted the ACLU as operating with an annual budget of $45 million and an endowment of $41 million, used to finance an army of sixty full-time attorneys, three hundred chapters, more than one thousand volunteer attorneys, as well as sympathetic members of the judiciary, the faculties of law schools, and the media. Separately, the ACLU Foundation had net assets exceeding $176 million as of May 31, 2004, bolstered by an $8 million gift—the largest individual single donation the ACLU had ever received to that date—from ACLU member Peter Lewis, the chairman of Progressive Insurance and one of the largest contributors to leftist causes and politicians in the nation. Previously, when the Ford Foundation provided the ACLU a $7 million grant in 1999, Lewis matched the grant with another $7 million, to bring the total to $14 million. The ACLU Foundation's IRS tax return for 2010 showed $74.8 million in total revenue and support,[46] of which $64.7 million, approximately 86 percent, came from grants, including foundation grants; the previous year, total revenue and support amounted to $89.4 million, of which $78.2 million, approximately 87 percent, came from grants, including foundation grants.[47] "The ACLU's goal is a secularized 'tolerant' America where religious speech is not only silenced but punished," Sears and Osten concluded, "where unwanted human life is quickly and easily discarded, hopefully at taxpayer expense; where the God-ordained institution of marriage and the family is on its way to becoming a distant memory, and where their 'tolerance' is the silence of many others."[48]

That the ACLU has been wildly successful in accomplishing its objectives regarding religious freedom can be appreciated by realizing that since *Everson*, the metaphor of creating a wall separating church and state has become the central image defining religious freedom in much of the public's imagination, even though the wall metaphor is mentioned nowhere in the language of the First Amendment. Moreover, since *Wallace v. Jaffree*, media references to "the Constitution's ban on preference for religion" have become commonplace— another "significant advance for the ACLU's underlying propaganda efforts."[49] Today no town or municipality would dare erect a Ten Commandments tablet in a courtroom; students in public schools are legitimately concerned they will be reprimanded or suspended if they dare to wear a necklace bearing a cross or a Star of David; and sports coaches in public schools are appropriately worried that simply saying a prayer in the locker room with the team before, during, or after a game could cost them their jobs.

In 2004, the ACLU threatened to sue the city of Redlands, California, if it did not remove from the city seal a small cross that represented the city's religious heritage as a city of churches. Unable to afford the cost of litigation and the possibility that losing in court might force Redlands to pay the ACLU's attorneys' fees in addition to its own attorneys, the Redlands City Council agreed to change the seal. Since there were insufficient funds to replace the seal, the city council decided to use blue tape to cover the seal on city vehicles, while other city employees used electric drills to "obliterate" the cross from their badges.[50] Following the success with Redlands, the ACLU next decided to press Los Angeles County to remove from its seal a small cross symbolizing the Spanish missions that played a key role in the county's history. Rather than face litigation, Los Angeles County agreed to redesign the seal at a cost of approximately $1 million. The change involved replacing the seal on ninety thousand uniforms and six thousand buildings.[51] "Some Americans view these events as victories over governments endorsing a particular religion in violation of the First Amendment's Establishment Clause and attempting to force religion upon their citizens," a case note in the *Vanderbilt Law Review* observes. "Others believe that these events are examples of communities being coerced into abandoning all acknowledgment of their religious values and heritage."[52]

⎯

Not only does the ACLU's interpretation of Jefferson's letter to the Danbury Baptist Association twist Jefferson's meaning; there is no historical support for the contention that our Founding Fathers separated church and state in their public lives.

On April 30, 1789, when George Washington took the oath to be the first president of the United States at Federal Hall in New York City, he held his hand on a Bible opened to Genesis 49–50, and he ended the oath by adding the words "So help me God"—words that have been added to the presidential oath by every president taking office since then. After taking the oath, Washington led a group to the nearby Saint Paul's Chapel to pray. That pew where Washington worshipped as president is marked off for public display today. Before that, Washington had been a member of the first two Continental Congresses. The first act of the first Congress was to pray—a devotion in which Washington knelt and prayed together with the other members of the first Congress. John Adams wrote to his wife, Abigail, documenting the prayer and everything else that happened on September 6 and 7, 1774, the first two meetings of the newly formed Congress. "This prayer not only began America, but it began the continuing congressional tradition of prayer and the work of our chaplains among our government officials," wrote pastor Peter A. Lillback in his definitive book on Washington's faith, *George Washington's Sacred Fire.*[53] The title derives from Washington's first inaugural address, in which he proclaimed, "The preservation of the sacred fire of liberty and the destiny of the republican model of government are justly considered, perhaps, as *deeply*, as *finally*, staked on the experiment entrusted to the hands of the American people."[54] In his 1796 farewell address to the nation as he left the presidency, Washington maintained, "Of all the dispositions and habits which lead to political prosperity, religion and morality are indispensable supports."[55]

On May 6, 1982, President Ronald Reagan commented on Arnold Friberg's famous 1975 painting of Washington kneeling in prayer in the snow of Valley Forge during the brutal winter of 1777–78 (now on display at Mount Vernon). "The most sublime picture in American history is of George Washington on his knees in the snow at Valley Forge," Reagan said in a tribute that evokes the Friberg painting. "That image personifies a people who know that it is not enough to depend on our own courage and goodness; we must also seek help from God, our Father and Preserver."[56] A substantial oral history exists as proof of Washington having knelt in prayer in the snow at Valley Forge, including five individuals who gave an account of the incident.[57] Friberg painted the work for the nation's 1976 bicentennial celebration. Today, thanks largely to the efforts of the ACLU, that painting has been removed from courtrooms and public school classrooms around the nation.

On December 23, 1783, Washington resigned his commission as general of the Continental Army with the words: "I consider it an indispensable duty to close this last solemn act of my Official life, by commanding the Interests of our dearest Country to the protection of Almighty God, and those Who have the superintendence of them, to his holy keeping."[58] Modern secular scholars determined to maintain even Washington appreciated the separation of church and state have doubted the prayer in the snow at Valley Forge ever happened, arguing, for instance, that Washington was a man of private devotions who "would never have prayed so ostentatiously outdoors, where soldiers could have stumbled upon him."[59]

Margaret Bayard Smith, whose letters and notebooks were collected and published in *Forty Years of Washington Society*, was well positioned to know firsthand how Thomas Jefferson practiced his religion while serving as the nation's second vice president (to President John Adams), from 1797 to 1801, and as the nation's third president from 1801 to 1809. Smith's father, Colonel John Bubenheld Bayard, was a Revolutionary War officer who served with George Washington, was Speaker of the Pennsylvania Assembly, and was a delegate for Pennsylvania to the Continental Congress for 1785–1786.[60] Her husband, Samuel Harrison Smith, was a journalist and founder of the newspaper *National Intelligencer* and a close friend of Thomas Jefferson; eventually he became president of the Washington branch of the Bank of the United States. Samuel Harrison Smith's father was Jonathan Bayard Smith, who fought in the Revolutionary War, signed the Articles of Confederation, and served in the Continental Congress in 1777 and 1778. In this tightly knit group, Samuel Harrison Smith and his wife, Margaret Bayard Smith, were second cousins, both with a lineage that placed them at the formation of the United States.[61]

Smith tells the story that Jefferson, throughout his presidential administration, regularly attended religious services that were then held in the House of Representatives. The seat Jefferson chose the first religious service he attended there and the adjoining seat were reserved for Jefferson and his private secretary "ever afterwards by the courtesy of the congregation" that assembled in the Capitol for Sunday prayer meetings. The Marine band, wearing their scarlet uniforms, provided musical accompaniment to hymn singing. "Not only the chaplains, but the most distinguished clergymen who visited the city, preached in the Capitol," Smith recalled. "Preachers of every sect and denomination of christians [*sic*] were there admitted—Catholics, Unitarians, Quakers with every intervening diversity of sect. Even women were allowed to display their pulpit eloquence, in this national Hall."[62]

Jefferson's Federalist Party foes, led largely by John Adams, vilified him as an infidel and atheist, with rhetoric so vitriolic that when news of Jefferson's election swept across the country, housewives in New England were rumored to have buried their Bibles in their gardens rather than risk the confiscation of the holy books by Jefferson's new administration in Washington. Throughout his life, Jefferson never fully outlived the reputation that while serving as an ambassador in France from 1785 to 1789, he had supported prominent intellectuals behind the French Revolution that had begun in 1789, and that after returning to the United States, he had not renounced that revolution's widespread desecration of religious symbols in France.

As a backstory to Jefferson's now famous letter, the Danbury Baptists were outsiders to the Congregational Church that when Jefferson wrote the letter was officially the state-established religion in Connecticut. "The Baptists, who supported Jefferson, were outsiders—a beleaguered religious and political minority in a region where a Congregationalist-Federalist axis dominated political life," noted legal scholar Daniel Dreisbach in a Heritage Foundation report that preceded his seminal book on the subject. Dreisbach argues, "Although today Jefferson's Danbury letter is thought of as a principled statement on the prudential and constitutional relationship between church and state," the letter was in fact "a political statement." Jefferson penned the letter on New Year's Day, 1802, intending to send a rebuke to John Adams and the Federalists—"a political statement written to reassure pious Baptist constituents that Jefferson was indeed a friend of religion," crafted "to strike back at the Federalist-Congregationalist establishment in Connecticut for shamelessly vilifying him as an infidel and atheist in the recent campaign."[63]

Ironically, since *Everson* the Supreme Court has given disproportionate attention to this letter while neglecting a much more thoughtful statement on religious freedom. The Supreme Court appended to the Everson case, the Virginia Statute of Religious Freedom, written by Jefferson and passed by the Virginia General Assembly on January 16, 1786. It is frequently referred to as a precursor to the First Amendment's formulation of religious freedom. Jefferson drafted the statute at a time when Virginia had established the Anglican Church as a state religion. Jefferson proclaimed that "no man shall be compelled to frequent or support any religious worship, place, or ministry whatsoever, nor shall be enforced, restrained, molested, or burthened in his body or goods, nor shall otherwise suffer on account of his religious opinions or belief; but that all men shall be free to profess, and by argument to maintain, their opinions in matters of religion, and that the same shall in no wise diminish, enlarge, or affect their capacities."[64] Again, Jefferson specified that freedom of religion was among the "natural rights of mankind," placing his defense of free religion squarely within the context of the doctrine of natural right. The Virginia statute was not passed until 1786 and only then thanks to the intervention of James Madison, the principal architect of the First Amendment's language. The Virginia Statute for

Religious Freedom is one of three accomplishments inscribed on Jefferson's tombstone—the other two being that he was the author of the Declaration of Independence and the father of the University of Virginia. Not surprisingly, his letter to the Danbury Baptists goes unmentioned in this short final testament list of accomplishments.

Of the first four presidents, only Jefferson did not proclaim a day of national thanksgiving. In October 1789, Washington left no doubt he felt government could support religion, proclaiming the day of national thanksgiving "as acknowledgement that God deals with nations as well as men; that nations may pray, supplicate and give thanks, be pardoned, enjoy protection and favor, or endure deserved condemnation; a recognition that God may interpose, that He is the Author of all good."[65] One of the first acts of the first House of Representatives was to elect a chaplain. A joint House-Senate committee was established to discuss coordination of the selection of chaplains and the issue of denominations. In 1789, Congress implemented the recommendations of this joint committee by passing legislation that specified congressional chaplains would be paid an annual salary of five hundred dollars from federal funds.[66]

In his comprehensive study of the history of religious freedom in the United States, political scientist Robert L. Cord charged that "the excessively broad interpretation of the First Amendment requiring a virtual absolute separation of Church and State . . . is both historically unsupportable and erroneous." Cord proposed a narrow interpretation of the First Amendment's establishment clause that was reduced to the following three points: (1) the national legislature, Congress, was denied the power to establish a national religion; (2) Congress was also forbidden to give any religion or religious sect a legally preferred status; and (3) the issue of the establishment or disestablishment of state churches in the states constituting the federal government was to be decided by the governments of the individual states.[67]

As we have seen, the states were not prohibited under the First Amendment from establishing religion until the Supreme Court applied the First Amendment to the states by invoking the due process clause of the Fourteenth Amendment in *Everson*. Cord's conclusion was clear:

In sum, as to the various interpretations that the U.S. Supreme Court—and the lower courts that have followed its decisions—has given to the Establishment Clause since the precedent of *Everson* in 1947, I must conclude that the Court has never logically, carefully, or fully considered all the available historical evidence and consequently has, for the most part, erred in its definition and application of the American constitutional doctrine of separation of Church and State.[68]

The point cannot be stressed enough: the idea that the Supreme Court could use the First Amendment to erase God from the United States of America would have been abhorrent to our Founding Fathers. Yet with the encouragement and coaching of the ACLU, that is exactly what the Supreme Court is in the process of doing.

4

ENTER THE ATHEISTS

Religion poisons everything. As well as a menace to civilization, it has become a threat to human survival.

—CHRISTOPHER HITCHENS, *GOD IS NOT GREAT*[1]

A h! Ah! Don't turn that dial now," a female voice admonished on KTBC Radio in Austin, Texas, on June 3, 1968. "You are going to hear, for the first time in American history, on a major radio station, the very first broadcast of a regularly scheduled weekly radio program of an Atheist."

So began the broadcasting career of Madalyn Murray O'Hair.

"I am not just any Atheist either," she continued. "No matter who you are, or what your age, sex, race or creed, I have affected your life in recent years because everyone in America either goes to school or has gone to school in his life, and I am Madalyn Murray O'Hair—you recognize that name—the American Atheist who removed Bible reading and prayer recitation from the public schools of our country."

Basically, she was telling the truth.

"My teen-age son, Bill Murray, and I did this by fighting a legal case in the courts of our land, clear up to the United States Supreme Court and the United States Supreme Court agreed with us and ruled on June 17, 1963, that Bible reading and prayer recitation should indeed not be in the public schools, for this *did* violate the American principle of separation of church and state, protected by our constitution."[2]

The case was *Murray v. Curlett.* At the Supreme Court, Murray's case was combined with a similar case from Pennsylvania, and it was decided as *School District of Abington Township, Pennsylvania v. Schempp,* 374 U.S. 203 (1963), commonly known as *Abington Township School District v. Schempp.* When the Supreme Court rendered its 8–1 majority decision on June 17, 1963, prayer in public schools was found to violate the establishment clause of the First Amendment. Madalyn Murray O'Hair was well along her way to being "the most hated woman in America"—a tagline first pinned on her in 1964 by *Life* magazine. In October 1965, *Playboy* published an interview with her, under the headline "A Candid Conversation with the Most Hated Woman in America." None less than the famed World War II reporter Richard Tregaskis, author of the 1943 classic *Guadalcanal Diary,* conducted the interview.[3] Brashly, O'Hair told Tregaskis that she was an atheist because "religion is a crutch, and only the crippled need crutches."

In the interview, Murray (who had not yet married O'Hair) praised attorney Clarence Darrow and condemned the Bible. "I read that Clarence Darrow didn't believe in the Bible either," she told Tregaskis. "So I read everything he had ever written, all of his trials, everything—to search out the philosophy of his disbelief." Regarding Christianity, she was less kind. "Christianity has held mankind back in politics, in economics, in industry, in science, in philosophy, in culture," she said. "Anyone who has even a surface knowledge of the Middle Ages, when the Church held unchallenged sway, can recognize this."[4]

And she had absolutely no use for the Bible. "Well, I picked up the Bible and read it from cover to cover one weekend—just as if it were a novel— very rapidly, and I've never gotten over the shock of it," she went on. "The miracles, the inconsistencies, the improbabilities, the impossibilities, the wretched history, the sordid sex, the sadism in it—the whole thing shocked me profoundly. I remember I looked in the kitchen at my mother and father and I thought: Can they really *believe* in all that?"[5]

In 1980, William J. Murray, Madalyn's son and coplaintiff in bringing the school prayer case against the Baltimore public schools, underwent a Christian conversion. Today, he serves as the chairman of the Religious Freedom Coalition, a nonprofit group headquartered in Washington, D.C., dedicated to protecting Christians in the Middle East, including assisting Palestinian Christian families and supporting Christian schools in the West Bank.[6] In 1982, he published the book *My Life Without God*, providing an illuminating view into his life with his famous self-professed atheist mother and his own journey from darkness into light.[7]

"Mine was not the typical American family, where a dad and a mom and the kids cuddled up on the couch with hot chocolate and popcorn to watch *Father Knows Best*," Bill Murray wrote. "At my house we argued about the value of the American way, whether or not the workers should revolt, and why the Pope, Christians, Jews—anybody who believed in God—was a moron." Next, Murray described an incident in which his enraged mother flung dishes at his grandfather's head, with the dishes smashing against the wall, all while she screamed, "I'll kill you[!]"[8] The cause of the argument? Madalyn had taken offense at her father's comments about the unborn child she was carrying without marrying the father; Bill was also born out of wedlock some eight years earlier. "Not that Grandfather was a moralist, but he wanted his daughter to be pure even if he wasn't," Bill commented about the incident. "This night he had been unable to resist a comment on her blossoming illegitimate motherhood."[9]

Serving on General Eisenhower's staff as a member of the Women's Auxiliary Army Corps in Italy, Madalyn met a young Eighth Army Corps officer named William J. Murray Jr., the son of a large and supposedly wealthy Roman Catholic family from Long Island, New York. Even though she was married at the time to a marine fighting in the Pacific, Madalyn became intimate with Murray, and her first child, Bill, was conceived—in September 1945, the month Japan formally surrendered. "I'm sure she hoped he would honor his commitment to her and to the unborn child by obtaining a divorce," Bill wrote of his mother and father. "Not only did he not seek a divorce, he refused to admit he was the father of the child."[10] Madalyn later won a paternity case against the hapless Murray, from whom she received child support payments of fifteen dollars per week until Bill was eighteen years old. "In particular, Mother came to hate the Roman Catholic church and the Pope for preventing her marriage to a man of considerable wealth," Bill concluded years later. "My father had told her point blank that it was his devotion to the church that would not permit him to divorce his wife."[11] Bill was born on May 25, 1946, and his mother named him William Joseph Murray III.

By the late 1950s, Madalyn had become an openly professed Communist, having found the Socialist Workers Party and the Socialist Labor Party not sufficiently revolutionary for her. She became determined to move herself to the Soviet Union along with her two illegitimate sons, Bill and his brother, Garth. Sometime during 1959, Madalyn made her first application for Soviet citizenship through the Soviet embassy in Washington. Failing to get a positive response, she decided to take matters in her own hands. On August 24, 1960, she and her two sons departed from New York City on the *Queen Elizabeth*, headed for Paris, where somehow Madalyn thought her appeal to immigrate with her children might find a more receptive audience. She was wrong. The Soviet embassy in Paris suggested Madalyn might do better to take her two children back home, where she could work for the revolution in her native land. Rejected and nearly broke, Madalyn, Bill, and Garth returned to Baltimore.

The next month Madalyn took Bill to Woodbourne Junior High School in Baltimore to enroll him for classes. That morning was probably the moment the decision to begin the school prayer case was born. "We walked down the long hall in silence, following the signs pointing to the school office," Bill remembered. The doors to the classrooms were open. "As we passed one class we saw the students standing with their hands over their hearts, reciting the pledge of allegiance to the flag." This was more than his mother could bear. "My mother's face reddened. 'Do they do this every day or is this something special?' she demanded." Then they passed another classroom where the students were standing beside their desks with their heads bowed, reciting the Lord's Prayer. "During the drive home, Mother questioned me more about the prayers and the Bible reading," Bill explained. "When I told her I had been participating in these for years at school, she cursed me roundly, accusing me of being stupid and brainless like all men."[12]

Finally, Madalyn resolved that if she could not go to the Soviet Union, where she perceived there was real freedom, then she would just have to change America. "I'll make sure you never say another prayer in that school!" she told her son, after assigning him to keep a notebook to record all the verses cited from the Bible, the number of times the children recited the Lord's Prayer, and when they stood to pledge allegiance to the flag, a pledge that by 1960 included the added phrase "under God."[13]

The ACLU initially indicated only moderate interest in taking Madalyn Murray's case, largely because the ACLU had already committed to a nearly identical case, *Abington Township School District v. Schempp*, that had begun in Pennsylvania two years earlier. Besides, Bill remembered, his mother was not keen to sign up with the ACLU, especially since the ACLU required that all fund-raising done for the case be done through the ACLU. "My mother was communist, but she wasn't stupid," Bill recalled decades later.[14] A local attorney named Leonard Kerpelman took the case, agreeing to handle the case for expenses only, waiving his fee. Bill recalled that his mother and Kerpelman were an odd couple—he was an Orthodox Jew—but she adored him because he let her do most of the work. "She was a bit of a lawyer herself," Bill noted. "She had obtained a law degree from South Texas College of Law but had never been able to pass the bar exams in Texas or Maryland."[15] As the case achieved local notoriety, Bill faced taunts at school: "Where's your mommie, commie?" and "Hey commie! Go back to Russia!"[16]

Associate Justice Tom C. Clark delivered the Supreme Court's 8–1 majority decision in *School District of Abington Township, Pennsylvania v. Schempp*, 374 U.S. 203 (1963), the case that had consolidated *Murray v. Curlett*, the case brought by Madalyn and Bill Murray against the Baltimore public schools. The court decided that the First Amendment's establishment clause, as applied to the states through the Fourteenth Amendment, made unconstitutional state laws authorizing public schools in Pennsylvania and Maryland to require passages from the Bible to be read or the Lord's Prayer to be recited at the beginning of each school day—even if individual students could be excused from attending or participating in such exercises at the written request of their parents. Put simply, Madalyn Murray was correct in asserting that the Supreme Court case brought by her and her son was the reason that school-sponsored Bible reading is today outlawed in public schools.

Justice Clark based his decision on a conclusion that the First Amendment requires the government must maintain strict neutrality, "neither aiding nor opposing religion." Clark's view was that the First Amendment freedom of religion was absolute only when the religion was expressed or practiced within the heart, the home, and the church—not in the public schools. "The place of religion in our society is an exalted one, achieved through a long tradition of reliance on the home, the church and the inviolable citadel of the individual heart and mind," he wrote. "We have come to recognize through bitter experience that it is not within the power of government to invade that citadel, whether its purpose or effect be to aid or oppose, to advance or retard. In the relationship between man and religion, the State is firmly committed to a position of neutrality."[17]

Only Justice Potter Stewart dissented. Stewart insisted that the establishment clause and the free exercise clause of the First Amendment fully complement each other, and he rejected what he called "a doctrinaire reading" of the establishment clause, which, he explained, would lead to irreconcilable conflict with the free exercise clause. As an example, he gave the following: "Spending federal funds to employ chaplains for the armed forces might be said to violate the Establishment Clause. Yet a lonely soldier stationed at some faraway outpost could surely complain that a government which did not provide him the opportunity for pastoral guidance was affirmatively prohibiting the free exercise of his religion."[18]

Stewart argued that the Supreme Court ended up not maintaining a policy of neutrality with regard to religion but establishing a religion of secularism by banning prayer in the schools. "For a compulsory state educational system so structures a child's life that, if religious exercises are held to be an impermissible activity in schools, religion is placed at an artificial and state-created disadvantage," he argued.[19]

Bill Murray reported that on hearing the decision, "Mother was elated; I was relieved. The ordeal was over, or so we thought."[20] What followed was "another barrage of attention—from the media, fellow dissidents, and opponents. The story was on the front page of newspapers across the country and became a lead story on many radio and TV newscasts."[21] Former president Harry S. Truman recalled that when he was in fifth grade, the teacher opened each day with a prayer. "It never hurt anybody," Truman said. "It made good citizens out of them." Governor George Wallace of Alabama, a Democrat, vowed to stand in the schoolroom himself, if necessary, to read the Bible.[22]

But despite the obvious disapproval coming even from the former president of the United States, Madalyn held true to her principles.

Edward Schempp, the father who created the case against the public schools in Abington Township, Pennsylvania, was a Unitarian Universalist. He did not hate the Bible or the Lord's Prayer. His objection was that the specific religious doctrines conveyed by a literal reading of the Bible were contrary to the religious beliefs he wished his children to hold. Madalyn Murray was an unabashed atheist who objected to religion itself, as she made clear in a letter published in *Life* magazine, April 12, 1963, before the court's decision was announced, where she resumed her attack on the Bible: "We find the Bible to be nauseating, historically inaccurate, replete with the ravings of madmen. We find God to be sadistic, brutal, and a representation of hatred, vengeance. We find the Lord's Prayer to be that muttered by worms groveling for meager existence in a traumatic, paranoid world."[23]

Her disdain for God and religion was equally obvious. The letter to *Life* magazine continued: "The business of the public schools, where attendance is compulsory, is to prepare children to face the problems on earth, not to prepare for heaven—which is a delusional dream of the unsophisticated minds of the ill-educated clergy."[24]

Justice Stewart, in his dissenting opinion in the Abington Township School District case, expressed his conviction that state legislatures and local school boards could design procedures to allow the children to pray in the public schools in a manner consistent with the requirements of the First Amendment. "What our Constitution indispensably protects is the freedom of each of us, be he Jew or Agnostic, Christian or Atheist, Buddhist or Freethinker, to believe or disbelieve, to worship or not to worship, to pray or keep silent, according to his own conscience, uncoerced and unrestrained by government," Stewart wrote.

> It is conceivable that these school boards, or even all school boards, might eventually find it impossible to administer a system of religious exercises during school hours in such a way as to meet this constitutional standard—in such a way as completely to free from any kind of official coercion those who do not affirmatively want to participate. But I think we must not assume that school boards so lack the qualities of inventiveness and good will as to make impossible the achievement of that goal.[25]

Stewart's argument undoubtedly left Madalyn Murray unimpressed. Her point was clear: nothing would satisfy her until God was removed completely from America. For her, the public schools were simply convenient places to start, especially since she could build a case around her son attending a Baltimore public school where they dared begin the day with Bible reading and prayer. Why was Madalyn Murray so determined? The answer was simple. As an atheist, she did not believe in God. But more than that, she had come to the point that she felt belief in God was detrimental, especially to children so unfortunate as to be exposed to religion by state force. Even though Madalyn rejected the legal assistance of the

ACLU because she wanted to collect all donations for herself, ideologically, Madalyn Murray O'Hair and the ACLU were on the same page.

～

Professor Bryan F. Le Beau, in his book *The Atheist: Madalyn Murray O'Hair*, published a photograph of Madalyn in Austin, Texas, holding a book she wanted the world to know she was reading.[26] That book, *The Big Lie: An Unmasking of Our Untruthful Religious and Political Past,* was authored by American Communist Howard J. Dodge and published in 1971. Dodge portrayed Americans as ancient Romans, maintaining that the United States, like ancient Rome, was corrupted by materialistic capitalism. In contrast, Dodge portrayed the historic Jesus Christ as if he were the first Socialist, prefiguring communism. "True, communism is contrary to the thrust of the pagan Roman capitalistic system, with its goals and values that we still continue today," he wrote, "but communism is not contrary to the socialistic teachings of Jesus and the Ten Commandments." For Dodge, Soviet Russia represented the ideal state. "Since 1917, the Russians have transformed their country from one with wholesale starving and illiterate masses under capitalism, into a thriving nation under communism. And Russia is today making as great, or even greater, economic strides than America is."[27]

Reading Dodge's *The Big Lie* is like reading William Z. Foster's *Toward Soviet America,* updated by the leftist criticism of America made by Socialists and Communists during the late 1960s. As examples of American corruption, Dodge played upon the assassinations of President John Fitzgerald Kennedy, Senator Robert Kennedy, and civil rights leader Martin Luther King. He paraded the race riots and black urban poverty as signs of America's exploitation of race. He vilified the Vietnam War as a war of capitalist imperialism. Through all his attacks, he repeated the theme that "mankind, Christianity, America and the world are not as we have been told."[28] He embraced Darwinism in order to argue human beings are continuing to evolve as history unfolds. He portrayed Karl Marx as "a deep-seated humanist, in the mode of ones like Socrates, Jesus, Jefferson, Darwin and Lincoln." He argued Marx "only wished to establish a new blueprint of a 'Kingdom of men on earth,' as Jesus had."[29] Dodge praised Marx as having laid the principles for a utopia on earth: "As with Jesus, Marx's idea for a [K]ingdom of men was not that a few privileged people should control the vital resources of the land, but that all the people should share it equally."[30] Here Dodge was saying openly what Roger Baldwin toiled to bury as the intellectual history of the ACLU.

Predictably, Dodge and the ACLU ended up in the same place: attacking God. In *The Big Lie*, Dodge explains the "religion of communism" was destined to replace the belief in a Judeo-Christian God that characterized American religious beliefs. "True, communism is not a praying religion— but with Jesus being just a man, and Yahweh a fake, there can be no holy ghost or other imagined guidance from the heavens anyway," he wrote. "Thus, no breech [*sic*] of the 10 Commandments, or of Jesus, or of any honest god is made by not praying. In fact, to pray to Jesus or Yahweh as the Judaic-Christian-Islam religion teaches, is in effect, *kneeling down to a graven image, is heathen and unenlightened*."[31] There the circle is completed. The theme from the Scopes trial is brought forward. Belief in God is antithetical to belief in the advancement of science. Why bother teaching children to pray in the schools when religion is nothing more than a lie created to imprison the unenlightened?

Nor did Dodge ignore the theme of sex. Having liberated themselves from the capitalist-imperialist ideas of ancient Rome and having embraced the true religion of communism, the Russian people were liberated and able to enjoy the open sexuality that a corrupt America can only envy, or so said Dodge. Among his many illustrations, Dodge included pictures of young, scantily clad Russians enjoying the beach and each other's obvious sexual appeal. "Fourth generation Communist Russians are . . . uninhibited, hip and better off than any in their history," Dodge wrote as a caption, highlighting the point we are supposed to draw from viewing the four photographs on that page depicting happy Russian youths in their bathing suits on the beach.[32]

In contrast, he attacked the idea of celibacy among the clergy in the

Catholic Church as having been issued by homosexual popes and "copied from the vestal virgins" of ancient Rome, women he portrayed as lesbians.[33] He ridiculed, in one sentence, Mary, the mother of Christ, together with Joseph Smith, the founder of the Mormon faith. "The idea that Mary was taken into heaven in her entire flesh and bones body is about as silly as Joseph's tale of the City of Zion being taken to heaven in its entirety for Enoch," he argued.[34] His point is clear: when communism is the religion of the people, sex is wholesome, unrestrained, and pure; but when people worship God, sex is reduced to sin, such that even Mary, the mother of Jesus, is portrayed as having been nothing more than a prostitute.

That Madalyn Murray would be reading Howard J. Dodge should come as no surprise. Dodge, for all his praise of Jesus as an early Socialist, was an atheist, who agreed with Murray that Soviet Russia was the utopia.

Historian Bryan Le Beau recounts an incident in which Murray was asked what would happen if a majority of the people in the United States decided to have organized prayer in the public schools. Murray did not agree that the people of the United States had that right. "Rather than belittle the person, she [Madalyn Murray] pointed out that such majority rule had permitted child labor, refused to give suffrage to women, and maintained slavery," Le Beau noted.[35] Again, the point was unmistakable. An atheist like Murray felt completely comfortable insisting God and religion had to be banned from America. In other words, her belief in atheism did not permit her to be tolerant of those who believed in God, not when she perceived that false religion had done nothing to prevent historical tragedies, including slavery. Conveniently, Murray forgot that in antebellum America, abolition had first been proclaimed from the pulpit or that believers in God had organized and operated the Underground Railroad responsible for freeing slaves from captivity.

At the start of the 1965 academic year, Susan Epperson, a young woman who had obtained a master's degree in zoology at the University of Illinois, prepared to teach tenth-grade biology at Central High School in Little Rock, Arkansas. She was planning to use a textbook that presented the theory of evolution, even though Arkansas law prohibited the teaching of any theory that suggested human beings had evolved from a lower order of animals. The Arkansas statute was a counterpart to the Tennessee law passed in the fundamentalist religious sentiment of the 1920s. In taking up the case of *Epperson v. Arkansas*, 393 U.S. 97 (1968), the US Supreme Court noted that the Tennessee Supreme Court in 1927 had upheld the constitutionality of the law that led to the Scopes trial. In an interview with the ACLU given in 2010, Epperson maintained the Arkansas Education Association chose her to be the plaintiff in the case because she was a Christian. "I think they [the Arkansas Education Association] were . . . looking for a Christian believer," Epperson said. "Because some people equate believing in evolution with being an atheist, the AEA wanted to demonstrate that one can believe in God and also believe all the scientific evidence for evolution."[36]

Writing the majority opinion of the Supreme Court, Associate Justice Abe Fortas struck down the Arkansas law not because it was vague but because it violated the establishment clause of the First Amendment. "The overriding fact is that Arkansas' law selects from the body of knowledge a particular segment which it proscribes for the sole reason that it is deemed to conflict with a particular religious doctrine," Fortas wrote, "that is, with a particular interpretation of the Book of Genesis by a particular religious group." Fortas insisted that the law violated the principle that government must be neutral in religious theory, doctrine, and practice. "It [state and national government] may not be hostile to any religion or to the advocacy of no-religion, and it may not aid, foster, or promote one religion or religious theory against another or even against the militant opposite," Fortas continued. "The First Amendment mandates governmental neutrality between religion and religion, and between religion and nonreligion."[37]

Reading *Epperson*, one could reasonably conclude that the Supreme Court would require all levels of government to maintain an equally neutral posture that would permit the teaching of creation science alongside the teaching of evolution. Yet this is not the case. In 1987, some nineteen years after *Epperson* was decided, the Supreme Court ruled unconstitutional a Louisiana statute that required the teaching of creation science whenever evolution was included in the school curriculum. Why? Because the Supreme Court continued to insist that creation science or the theory of intelligent design is religion masked in science, while the court uncritically accepts that the theory of evolution is established science. That underlying bias seems to explain the outcome in *Edwards v. Aguillard*, 482 U.S. 578 (1987). Here, the ACLU represented Aguillard pro bono; that is, without charge.

The case involved a Louisiana statute that did not require teaching either creation science or the theory of evolution but required the teaching of creation science in the public schools whenever evolution was taught. Writing the majority opinion of the Supreme Court, Justice William J. Brennan declared the Louisiana statute unconstitutional because it violated the establishment clause of the First Amendment. "Families entrust public schools with the education of their children, but condition their trust on the understanding that the classroom will not purposely be used to advance religious views that may conflict with the private beliefs of the student and his or her family," Brennan wrote. "Students in such institutions are impressionable, and their attendance is involuntary." He argued the state exerts "great authority and coercive power" through mandatory attendance requirements and because of the students' "emulation of teachers as role models," as well as the young students' susceptibility to peer pressure.[38]

Applying the first prong of the *Lemon* test, Brennan concluded the Louisiana statute had a religious purpose behind it. He noted that the legislative sponsor of the bill, state senator Bill Keith, had aimed to narrow the science curriculum to avoid the subject entirely. During the legislative hearings, Keith said, "My preference would be that neither [creationism nor evolution] be taught."[39] Brennan also noted that no Louisiana law prohibited public school teachers from teaching creation science if they chose to do so. He rejected the premise that the goal of the law was to promote "basic fairness" by noting that the law required curriculum guides be developed for creation science, without requiring comparable guides to be prepared for evolution. The law further forbade school boards from discriminating against anyone who chose to teach creation science but failed to provide similar protection for those who chose to teach evolution or any other noncreation-science theory or those who refused to teach creation science. The law also did not require the teaching of evolution if creation science were taught.

"If the Louisiana Legislature's purpose was solely to maximize the comprehensiveness and effectiveness of science instruction, it would have encouraged the teaching of all scientific theories about the origins of humankind," Brennan concluded. "But under the Act's requirements, teachers who were once free to teach any and all facets of this subject are now unable to do so." Accordingly, the court ruled, "The preeminent purpose of the Louisiana Legislature was clearly to advance the religious viewpoint that a supernatural being created humankind." In the view of the majority, the point of the Louisiana statute was "to restructure the science curriculum to conform with a particular religious viewpoint."[40] In other words, rather than view creation science as science, the Supreme Court chose to see creation science as religion wrapped in the appearance of science. "The Louisiana Creationism Act advances a religious doctrine by requiring either the banishment of the theory of evolution from public school classrooms or the presentation of a religious viewpoint that rejects evolution in its entirety," Brennan said. "The Act violates the Establishment Clause of the First Amendment because it seeks to employ the symbolic and financial support of government to achieve a religious purpose."[41]

A dissent authored by Justice Antonin Scalia and joined by Chief Justice William Rehnquist noted that the majority of the Supreme Court demonstrated "an instinctive reaction that any governmentally imposed requirements bearing upon the teaching of evolution must be a manifestation of Christian fundamentalist repression."[42] Scalia and Rehnquist countered by arguing that convincing scientific evidence does exist for theories such as intelligent design, while credible scientists have expressed doubts about important aspects of the theory of evolution:

> The people of Louisiana, including those who are Christian fundamentalists, are quite entitled, as a secular matter, to have whatever scientific

evidence there may be against evolution presented in their schools, just as Mr. Scopes was entitled to present whatever scientific evidence there was for it. Perhaps what the Louisiana Legislature has done is unconstitutional because there is no such evidence, and the scheme they have established will amount to no more than a presentation of the Book of Genesis. But we cannot say that on the evidence before us in this summary judgment context, which includes ample uncontradicted testimony that "creation science" is a body of scientific knowledge, rather than revealed belief. *Infinitely less* can we say (or should we say) that the scientific evidence is so conclusive that no one could be gullible enough to believe that there is any real scientific evidence to the contrary, so that the legislation's stated purpose must be a lie.[43]

The point is that Scalia and Rehnquist, with their dissent in *Edwards*, dared to contend that no scientific consensus exists that the theory of evolution is proven fact. Even more daring, Scalia and Rehnquist suggested that a theory with religious implications such as creation theory or intelligent design might also have a basis to be considered legitimate within the rigors of science. If the question had involved the big bang theory of the creation of the universe, would the Supreme Court equally have decided that big bang scientists were presenting nothing more than a thinly veiled version of Genesis? The truth is that many of the most progressive scientists today, including physicists specializing in advanced particle theories, are proposing and seriously considering the validity of many aspects of physics that also have positive implications for affirming the existence of God.

Science does not necessarily exclude God, unless we understand that in order to be valid, science must by definition be secular, materialistic, and atheistic. Here Scalia and Rehnquist were challenging a central point of the ACLU. Since the Scopes trial, the ACLU had sought to structure the controversy as a choice between religion and science. In their dissent to *Edwards*, Scalia and Rehnquist dared to suggest that science might actually end up confirming the existence of God, a thought antithetical to the argumentation that premised the ACLU's War on God since the organization was founded.

In his book *Parallel Worlds: A Journey Through Creation, Higher Dimensions, and the Future of the Cosmos*, Michio Kaku, the Henry Semat Professor of Theoretical Physics at the Graduate Center of the City College of New York and a frequent science contributor on Fox News, contemplates "the ridiculously narrow band of parameters that makes intelligent life a reality, and that we happen to thrive in this band." The thought brings Kaku to contemplate God: "One can debate whether this fortuitous circumstance is one of design or accident, but no one can dispute the intricate tuning necessary to make us possible." Further, Kaku reflects that contemplating the mysteries of quantum physics forces us to comprehend the phenomenon of consciousness itself: "The infinite chain of observers, each one viewing the previous observer, ultimately leads to a cosmic observer, perhaps God himself."[44] Whether the universe exists because there is a God to observe it is a question obviously beyond the scope of this book. What is not beyond the scope of this book is the realization that a new generation of highly credible scientists is taking seriously the possibility that God might need to be present in their equations in their scientific theories.

How ironic it will be for secular atheistic scientists and their lawyer counterparts in the ACLU if it turns out that God exists. "If God exists, then He must have created science and thus, honest scientific inquiry will lead directly back to Him," warns commentator Roy Masters, the founder of the Foundation of Human Understanding.[45] "A few thousand years before physicists conceived of general relativity, the space-time theorem, quarks, supersymmetry, unified field theories, and vibrating strings, a written document described extra-dimensional reality," wrote Hugh Ross, PhD, a Christian who earned his doctorate in astronomy from the University of Toronto. "That document is the Bible."[46]

Charles Darwin worried that what is known as the Cambrian explosion presents one of the main scientific objections to his theory of evolution. The Cambrian explosion is one of the great mysteries in geologic time: namely, the appearance of many major animal and plant groups for the first time in the fossil record some 545 million years ago without any evidence of the gradual transitional steps that Charles Darwin predicted. "The big question that the Cambrian Explosion poses is where does all this new information come from?" asks Stephen Meyer, who received his PhD from the University of Cambridge in the philosophy of science. He is currently the director of the Center for Science and Culture at the Discovery Institute in Seattle, which advocates for intelligent design.[47] Meyer, the author of *Signature in the Cell: DNA and Evidence for Intelligent Design*, asks this important question: "Yet, if natural selection, as Darwin called this process, could improve the speed of a horse or an antelope, why couldn't it also produce those animals in the first place?"[48]

Yet despite increasing contemporary scientific contemplation that science might end up affirming God, the ACLU persists in its determination to portray science as knowledge and religion as prejudice.

In the case *McLean v. Arkansas Board of Education*, 529 F. Supp. 1255, 1258–1264 (E.D. Ark. 1982), the ACLU supported the state of Arkansas, arguing that a state law requiring public school teachers to teach creation science alongside the theory of evolution was unconstitutional. The ACLU won the case on appeal when US District Judge William Overton affirmed the decision of trial judge Jones that creation science is religion, not science—hence in violation of the establishment clause of the First Amendment. The decision applied only to the Eastern District of Arkansas, and the plaintiffs—various parents, ministers, including Rev. William McLean, a United Methodist minister, and representatives of various religious groups supporting the Arkansas law—decided not to appeal.[49] The case was eclipsed by *Edwards*, the Louisiana case discussed above, since it involved a state law essentially the same as the *McLean* case.

The opponents of the Arkansas law, represented by attorneys working for the ACLU, called the well-known British philosopher of science Michael Ruse to testify in their support. At the trial, Ruse testified not that creationism was wrong but that creationism did not qualify as science, by definition. To make this case, Ruse argued a scientific theory had to meet the following criteria: the theory must be "(1) guided by nature, (2) explanatory by reference to natural law, (3) testable against the empirical world, (4) tentative in its conclusions, and (5) falsifiable." He argued that under these specifications, creation science was pseudoscience masking what truly was nothing more than religious prejudice.[50]

Reviewing Ruse's testimony and Judge Jones's decision rendered in the *McLean* case, Stephen Meyer criticized the reasoning as circular, or question-begging logic. Ruse's definition demanded that anything considered "science" had to be justified entirely by empirical evidence, ruling out by definition any reference to God. "Though the ACLU won the *McLean v. Arkansas* case in 1981, leading philosophers of science, none sympathetic to creationism, later severely criticized Ruse's use of demarcation arguments in his testimony," Meyer wrote. "They pointed out that many of the definitional criteria that Ruse had used to establish creation science as pseudoscience could actually be used to establish creation science as a scientific theory. They also pointed out that the same criteria, if applied strictly, could have the effect of disqualifying Darwinian evolution from that same honorific discussion."[51]

Meyer concludes the question of what distinguishes science from pseudoscience is fundamentally uninteresting. The question truly framed is whether the theory is true or supported by the evidence. Or as Meyer has observed, "Reclassifying an argument does not refute it."[52]

It is not accidental that the ACLU wants to remove from schools not only prayer but also any theory attacking Darwin. The ACLU has found that if there are contemporary scientists willing to include God within the framework of their scientific theories, there are also contemporary atheists who are willing to maintain the traditional enlightenment attack on religion and God. Atheists such as Richard Dawkins, the Charles Simonyi Professor of the Public Understanding of Science at Oxford University, and the late author Christopher Hitchens, who once held a position as a visiting professor of liberal studies at the New School, realize how vital it is to defend Darwin to maintain the reasonableness of their beliefs—or their lack of beliefs—when it comes to God. Contemporary atheists like Dawkins and

Hitchens provide the ACLU the philosophical underpinning it needs to form legal arguments countering today's new breed of theistic scientists.

In his book *The God Delusion*, Dawkins compared the challenge of defending Darwin to the problem of explaining how a hurricane sweeping through a scrap yard would have the luck to assemble a Boeing 747. Dawkins's answer is that Darwin's principle of natural selection is the solution to the problem of improbability. Natural selection, Dawkins argued, "is a cumulative process, which breaks the problem of improbability up into small pieces." Dawkins conceded that each of the small pieces is slightly improbable but not prohibitively so. "When large numbers of these slightly improbable events are stacked up in series, the end product of the accumulation is very, very improbable indeed, improbable enough to be far beyond the reach of chance."

Yet somehow Dawkins does not see the argument as begging the question, assuming natural selection had to work simply because complex natural phenomena turn out as they do. Instead, he argues that creationists insist on "treating the genesis of statistical improbability as a single, one-off event," while he comprehends the power of accumulation.[53] But Dawkins is still begging the point. Human beings and flowers, as well as millions of complex structures we observe in the natural world, exist. Theists find it impossible to view the complexity of the natural world without seeing a teleology, or a God-determined end-in-view that produced the natural world as we experience it. Does Dawkins truly want us to believe the complex world we experience is an accident of natural selection that just happened to turn out this way?

Irreducible complexity is an argument used to counter Darwin by arguing that half an eye or half a wing is functionally useless, raising the question of how the next incremental change could have a chance of being reinforced and adopted by the organism. "A cataract patient with the lens of her eye surgically removed can't see clear images without glasses, but can see enough not to bump into a tree or fall over a cliff," he argued. "Half a wing is indeed not as good as a whole wing, but it is certainly better than no wing at all."[54] In other words, the design of the eye or the wing of a bird is seen as intelligently designed, with a functional end point determining how the eye or the wing came to exist. Intelligent design assumes a teleology—a logic of a pre-determined end point determining the outcome. The designer is presumed to be God. This is the emerging scientific idea developing to challenge the godless view of evolution. This is the answer William Jennings Bryan lacked to counter Clarence Darrow and the ACLU in the Scopes trial.

Dawkins rejects the analysis, even though he agrees natural selection had no alternative but to accumulate to the point where the eye sees or the wing flaps. What he denies is that end purpose had anything to do with God. Dawkins is forced to concede that Darwin's theory works only if complex organs result from numerous, successive, slight modifications that somehow or other end up with the correct result. But there is no reason, he insists, for assuming that "correct results" have anything to do with God, or intelligent design. Even when the evolutionist cannot explain how the perfect whole got formed from the imperfect parts, Dawkins rejoices in what he calls "temporary uncertainty"—an admission evolution cannot always know where it is going. "It is utterly illogical to demand complete documentation of every step of any narrative, whether in evolution or any other science," Dawkins finally protested.[55]

Predictably, Dawkins's explanation for why religion and God exist is that they are pseudoconcepts: contrived and embraced by human beings because theological notions have a survival value. In other words, religion to Dawkins is reducible to a coded message—a *meme* in the language of genetics—that makes us more fit to survive because we have religion and believe in God than would be the case if we abandoned religion and quit believing in God. What Dawkins proposes is a theory of religion based on chromosomes—or, more specifically, on memes, information sequences, ultimately traceable back to sequences embedded into human DNA and RNA. "In the early stages of a religion's evolution, before it becomes organized, simple memes survive by virtue of their universal appeal," Dawkins wrote.[56] Organized religions, then, are nothing more than complexes of memes—ideas about culture and behavior, including ideas about right and wrong and notions of God—that work together to promote human survival. Dawkins posits that memes will continue to evolve such that at some point natural selection will create human beings evolved enough to no longer need a meme that manufactures for us a God concept.

Dawkins crafted his conclusion about why religion and God exist to be cleverly ironic: "Religions probably are, at least in part, intelligently designed, as are schools and fashions in art."[57] That is it—religion is nothing more than a fashion, a set of current ideas, about the mystical and unknown that make human beings more fit to survive. Dawkins does not believe in God because he appears to have had no transcendent experience of God. Reading Dawkins is somewhat like trying to talk to a dog about colors. A dog does not see colors, and if we could speak with dogs, we would get nowhere trying to discuss a world of colors the dog just does not see. Similarly, Dawkins seems determined to explain away God and religion by invoking intellectual constructs that are the same as arguing that colors are reducible to nothing more than various shades of gray. Dawkins is a self-proclaimed atheist, but rather than argue that religion and notions of God are harmful to human beings, Dawkins seems merely irritated that human beings have not yet evolved to the point where we no longer need religious ideas to advance our survival.

Dawkins is completely confident that when human beings have pushed God and religion out of our consciousness, we will be better off. Here Dawkins and Freud agree that religion ultimately brings nothing but discontent to civilization. But we should not be surprised. Fundamental to the atheist purpose is to dislodge God and religion, elevating human beings and human consciousness to the place earlier civilizations and previous generations had reserved for God and religion. Ultimately, the atheist argument is not complete until God is dead, much as Nietzsche postulated, with the superhuman moving forward to take God's place.

No wonder the ACLU and the atheists with whom the organization aligns itself fight so hard to remove every trace of God and creationist theories, including intelligent design, from the schools. If our children are not taught evolution as the sole scientific truth, there is always the risk that God will slip back into the picture. As long as the Dawkinses of the modern scientific world and the H. L. Menckens in today's mainstream media agree that evolutionary theory remains sufficiently urbane and secular for their taste, God will still look to them like a throwback to the fundamentalist days of William Jennings Bryan. By shifting the argument to the utility of science, the ACLU needs atheists like Dawkins, if only to make sure the godless secular society the ACLU wants to create can remain confident there is nothing to lose by excluding God from the public arena.

The godless society sought by the ACLU is a natural consequence of the secular view of life made popular by modern atheists such as Dawkins. But to fully appreciate the modern Freud-like argument that religion is a human creation that is ultimately harmful to human progress, we need to turn to Christopher Hitchens. Hitchens agreed with Dawkins that defending Darwin demands defending atheism, but—much like Madalyn Murray O'Hair before him—he had much less use for the fineness of scientific argument advanced through intricate metaphors and images. Hitchens, like Madalyn Murray O'Hair, was much more visceral and in your face with his ridicule of believers and his insistence that we only believe in God because the human species has not yet advanced from a transitional God-believing lower state in our evolution. Still Hitchens left no doubt he considered God and religion bad ideas from the get-go. In his book-length statement of his atheistic beliefs, *God Is Not Great*, Hitchens managed to reduce his objections to religious faith to these four: "that it wholly misrepresents the origins of man and the cosmos, that because of this original error it manages to combine the maximum of servility with the maximum of solipsism, that it is both the result and the cause of dangerous sexual repression, and that it is ultimately grounded on wish-thinking."[58] So, like Dawkins, Hitchens gave God no role in creation. That might be tolerable, except that God also restricts sex. Then, in the final analysis, the idea of heaven seems childish wishing-it-were-so. That eternity could be spent in fulfillment of our human nature seemed to Hitchens nothing more than a gloss over having to endure endlessly the dictatorship of God. One wonders whether Hitchens would have found the concept of heaven more endurable had eternity been filled with a dictatorship of Hitchens.

In the second chapter of *God Is Not Great*, entitled "Religion Kills,"

Hitchens explained how religion causes human beings to war upon one another, not to love one another as the Gospels proclaim. He acknowledged that he could think of "a handful of priests and bishops and rabbis and imams who have put humanity ahead of their own sect or creed," but he concluded that was a compliment to humanism, not to religion. When Hitchens picked sides in religious conflicts, he fancied that he sided with the underdog: "If it comes to that [complimenting humanism, not religion], these crises have also caused me, and many other atheists, to protest on behalf of Catholics suffering discrimination in Ireland, of Bosnian Muslims facing extermination in the Christian Balkans, of Shia Afghans and Iraqis being put to the sword by Sunni jihadists, and vice versa, and numerous other such cases."[59] But when it came to how religious authorities view these religious conflicts, Hitchens was critical. "The general reluctance of clerical authorities to issue unambiguous condemnation, whether it is the Vatican in the case of Croatia or the Saudi or Iranian leaderships in the case of their respective confessions, is uniformly disgusting," he wrote.[60]

Regarding the theory of evolution, Hitchens rejoiced that "the courts have protected Americans (at least for the moment) from the inculcation of compulsory 'creationist' stupidity in the classroom."[61] Except that Hitchens wrote with a dry British wit and his style was slightly more modern, his prose could easily be mistaken for that of H. L. Mencken. Both shared the same urbane, sarcastic cynicism when contemplating believers in God. Public relations founder Edward Bernays would feel vindicated today to know the argument that fundamentalist God-believers are the stupid people is safely in the hands of accomplished writers such as Richard Dawkins and Christopher Hitchens. With the Supreme Court throwing any and all creationist arguments out of the public schools—including arguments from intelligent design—what conclusion are children to reach? Obviously, the Supreme Court agrees with Dawkins and Hitchens: any theory that includes God to explain the origin of human beings is not worth wasting time teaching in the classroom. As noted earlier, Clarence Darrow may have lost the legal case in the Scopes trial, but he won the case in the court of public opinion.

Hitchens dismissed intelligent design by reference to Whittaker Chambers, the informant who exposed Alger Hiss in the 1950s, after having first renounced communism himself. "Whittaker Chambers in his seismic book *Witness* recounts the first moment when he abandoned historical materialism, mentally deserted the Communist cause, and embarked on the career which would undo Stalinism in America," Hitchens noted. It was at the moment when Chambers glimpsed the ear of his baby daughter and thought the beauty of the ear must be divine in origin. Hitchens rejected the validity of the observation. "Well, I too have marveled at the sweet little ears of my female offspring," he countered, "but never without noticing that (a) they always need a bit of a clean-out, (b) that they look mass-produced even when set against the inferior ears of other people's daughters, (c) that as people get older their ears look more and more absurd from behind, and (d) that much lower animals, such as cats and bats, have much more fascinating and lovely and more potent ears." Just in case anyone missed the point, Hitchens ended the argument with ridicule: "To echo Laplace, in fact, I would say that there are many, many persuasive arguments against Stalin-worship, but that the anti-Stalin case is fully valid without Mr. Chambers's ear-flap-based assumption."[62]

Predictably, Hitchens rejected that intelligent design is a scientific theory, calling it instead "well-financed propaganda."[63] He was equally less convincing when he took off examining the paleontologist Stephen Jay Gould—a scientist Hitchens noted "imbibed a version of Marxism" in his youth and, along with Marxism, an expectation of progress in history. Hitchens was captivated by Gould's study of the Burgess shale formation, discovered in the Canadian Rockies, on the border of British Columbia. The Burgess shale contains a remarkably intact record of the Cambrian explosion. In studying the Burgess shale, Gould came to the conclusion that the evolution of human beings was by no means certain but was instead dependent upon a set of accidents that might not be replicated had the same animals and plants in evidence within the Burgess shale been alive today. Gould focused, in particular, on an early vertebrate named *Pikaia gracilens*—a two-inch creature that swam in the water much like a modern-day eel. Gould had written that if the *Pikaia gracilens* had not survived then in what he cast as a thought-experiment replay of the Cambrian period, all vertebrate creatures might have been wiped out in future history—from the shark to the robin to the orangutan to the human being. Hitchens, however, was not disturbed. He was comfortable explaining human beings as a happy accident, even if it meant abandoning the determinism Darwin and Dawkins read into evolutionary theory, in favor of the mathematics of chaos theory and the uncertainty of the Heisenberg principle.[64]

In the end, Hitchens's objections to God were petulant, if not downright childish. "If Jesus could heal a blind person he happened to meet, then why not heal blindness?" Hitchens asked. "Why all this continual prayer, why no result? Why did I have to keep saying, in public, that I was a miserable sinner? Why was the subject of sex considered so toxic?"[65]

But there is another basis upon which Hitchens and Madalyn Murray O'Hair would agree—atheism can be profitable. After her successful Supreme Court case, O'Hair found—to her great surprise—that people began sending her money. Suddenly, a woman who had never held a job found herself able to move to Austin, Texas, where she could buy the house of her dreams and establish what turned out to be a multimillion-dollar empire, all structured under her American Atheist Center. She published *American Atheist* magazine, hosted her own radio show, and created an American Atheist Library that grew to forty thousand volumes, twenty-five thousand individual pieces of archival material, and twenty thousand periodicals.[66]

Madalyn Murray O'Hair suffered a severe setback in 1980 when her son William J. Murray III defected from her cause and apologized for his role in the Supreme Court case that bears his name. Bill Murray castigated his mother as a "cult leader," and he blamed the defeat of school prayer as leaving in its wake "a nation basically devoid of any moral principles."[67] Even more difficult for Madalyn to bear, Bill rejected atheism and turned his life to God. On Mother's Day, 1980, Bill declared he had decided to dedicate his life to Christ. During the 1980s, Bill served as director of Freedom's Friends, an organization dedicated to reaching out to victims of communism worldwide. In the 1990s, Bill founded the first commercial

Bible publishing company ever established in the Soviet Union; he also conducted evangelistic tours taking Christians to the Soviet Union.[68]

In the end, Madalyn died a horrible death. Along with her son Jon Garth Murray and a granddaughter, she was kidnapped and murdered by an ex-employee, whose motives appeared to be a combination of jealousy over Madalyn's financial success and resentment at being fired. Throughout her disappearance, her older son, Bill Murray, worked desperately to spur the Austin Police Department to action. Her murder was gruesome; found buried in a shallow grave, all three bodies had been sawed apart, doused with gasoline, and burned. Madalyn's funeral was private, and only a handful of people stood at the grave site—two lawmen, two FBI agents, Bill Murray, his mother's biographer, and a preacher. No prayers were said. "Baptists don't pray for the dead," Bill told the newspapers afterward. "They either accepted Christ before they died or they didn't."[69]

It is said that some present at the grave site recalled when they were in high school on November 22, 1963, and the principal was not permitted to lead a prayer for the soul of the slain president—all because of Madalyn Murray O'Hair.[70]

But with the modern-day atheists, the ACLU had reached a point where atheism itself had reached the status of a protected First Amendment religion. If the right not to believe in God is equivalent to the right to believe in God, then in a secular society that sees no intrinsic value to believing in God, why should the rights of atheists be compromised in the public square simply because a few misguided and ill-informed Jews or Christians want to pray openly?

In recent years, the ACLU War on God has gained momentum. The success forcing the Bible reading and prayer out of the public schools has emboldened the ACLU to attack God wherever God appears in the public arena. Under the ACLU interpretation, the right of an atheist to protest because open expressions of religion are offensive has moved to center stage. The ACLU has so built the wall between church and state that God is being driven from all aspects of American life, such that even the phrase "In God We Trust" is no longer safe to be printed on US money. A Supreme Court agreeing with the ACLU is on the verge of defending the First Amendment free expression of religion only as long as that expression of faith is confined to the four walls of one's home, one's church, or one's synagogue. The moment a person walks out the door with an open proclamation of belief in God, the ACLU is ready to pounce to the defense of the atheist and the fear that the state might be in the process of establishing the United States as a Judeo-Christian nation. Underpinning the ACLU argument is the modern atheistic view that belief in God restrains the progress of the human endeavor—a view in direct opposition to the view of our Founding Fathers, who felt without an openly proclaimed belief in God there was no human endeavor that had any real prospect of success in advancing the human condition.

5

THE GODLESS
PUBLIC SQUARE

It has not been our American constitutional tradition,
or our social or legal tradition, to exclude religion from
the public square. Whatever the Establishment Clause
means, it certainly does not mean that government cannot
accommodate religion, and indeed favor religion.

—JUSTICE ANTONIN SCALIA[1]

That the ACLU could make America safe for atheists through advancing the establishment clause was taught by no one better than secular humanist and legal scholar Leo Pfeffer. In his classic 1953 book *Church, State and Freedom*, Pfeffer acknowledged that the language specifying separation of church and state does not appear in the Constitution or the first ten amendments. He maintained, however, that the establishment clause was the key to understanding the meaning and application of the First Amendment. "It was inevitable that some convenient term should come into existence to verbalize a principle so clearly and widely held by the American people," Pfeffer wrote of Jefferson's phrase. "For example, the phrase 'Bill of Rights' has become a convenient term to designate the freedoms guaranteed in the first ten amendments; yet it would be the height of captiousness to argue that the phrase does not appear in the Constitution."[2]

Similarly, Pfeffer acknowledged that the First Amendment contains two prohibitions: the first in the establishment clause prohibiting Congress from a state religion, and the second in the free exercise clause prohibiting Congress from passing laws limiting freedom of religious expression. Despite this, Pfeffer insisted the First Amendment's freedom of religion guarantee was "unitary," such that the establishment clause and the free expression clause were two sides of the same coin. For Pfeffer, then, religious freedom and church-state separation "were inextricably intertwined."[3] In other words, in Pfeffer's view, religion would be free only as long as government was kept out of the sphere of religion. While he acknowledged that some cases placed more emphasis on free expression issues, for instance, "statutes prohibiting polygamy, or requiring all children to attend secular public schools,"[4] he felt the key issue was to keep government out of religion—something that could be achieved only if the establishment clause was applied in an absolute manner. For Pfeffer, separation of church and state had to be absolute separation if expression of religious beliefs was to have a chance to be free. "A secular state, then, became the guarantor of religious freedom," one legal scholar summarized Pfeffer's views.[5]

In taking the position that separation of church and state had to be absolute, Pfeffer was, in effect, arguing that any involvement of the state in religious affairs was tantamount to the state acting so as to establish religion. "The Amendment does not say 'Congress shall make no law establishing religion,' but 'no law respecting an establishment of religion,'" he observed. "It may reasonably be argued that the latter phraseology imposes a broader prohibition than the former."[6] There is an argument that Americans are and always have been a religious people, such that those who drafted the First Amendment were the friends of religion, not its enemies; therefore, the Founding Fathers framing the First Amendment could not have intended to harm religion by depriving it of government support. To this, Pfeffer responded the argument confuses friendship for religion with friendship for government aid to religion. "Madison himself exposed the fallacy of this reasoning during the debate on the Virginia Assessment Bill," Pfeffer argued. "The issue, he said, was 'not is religion necessary—but are Religious Establishments necessary for Religion.'"[7] So, Pfeffer concluded, government support was not only unnecessary for religious expression to flourish freely; government support was actually detrimental to free expression. Pfeffer's jurisprudence is correctly described as absolutist with respect to the establishment clause, in that he felt government in all instances must remain neutral with regard to religion.[8]

In the 1980s, Pfeffer received strong criticism from Richard John Neuhaus, a prominent Christian cleric and author who first served as a Lutheran minister and then became a priest after converting to Catholicism. Neuhaus, a conservative evangelical leader and widely read author, advised President George W. Bush on a wide range of issues, including abortion, cloning, stem-cell research and the defense of marriage movement. His influential 1984 book, *The Naked Public Square: Religion and Democracy in America*, leveled an attack against Pfeffer's argument that separation between church and state must be absolute. Here, Neuhaus argued that Pfeffer had inverted the meaning of the First Amendment by asserting that the establishment clause and the free exercise clause were unitary in purpose.

According to Neuhaus, the purpose of the First Amendment is to establish free exercise of religion, such that the establishment clause is properly construed not as an end in itself but as a means to an end. A noted scholar summarized the argument: "This 'Pfefferian Inversion,' as Neuhaus called it, has resulted in the marginalization of religion in public life or, in his famous phrase, a 'naked public square.'"[9] In so doing, Pfeffer provided strong support for the next campaign the ACLU planned to conduct in its War on God. With prayer and Bible reading driven out of the public schools, the ACLU resolved to drive God completely out of the public square. Without the intellectual support and constitutional legal arguments formulated by Pfeffer, the ACLU would not have been able to carry the debate before the Supreme Court nearly as easily as it did.

As a consequence of the Pfefferian Inversion, Neuhaus believed the Supreme Court would engage in a process of demanding that the public square in the United States be completely secular, devoid of any reference to religion. The result would be that a secular Supreme Court driven by a Pfefferian interpretation of the First Amendment would push God and religion inside the churches and synagogues of America and ultimately inside the minds of the believers themselves. "As time went on, however, the court's references to religion had less and less to do with what is usually meant by religion," Neuhaus cautioned, in his attempt to warn religious believers where he saw a Pfefferian-driven Supreme Court heading. "Religion, in the court's meaning, became radically individualized and privatized. Religion became a synonym for conscience." This, Neuhaus feared, would complete the loop of Pfeffer's insistence that the establishment clause's separation of church and state must be absolute. "It [religion] is no longer a matter of communal values but of individual conviction," Neuhaus concluded, pointing out the ultimate consequence of the Pfefferian Inversion. "In short, it [religion] is no longer a public reality and therefore cannot interfere with public business."[10]

But for religion to leave the public square had severe consequences for society, Neuhaus argued. "When religion in any traditional or recognizable form is excluded from the public square, it does not mean that the public square is in fact naked," he insisted. "When recognizable religion is excluded, the vacuum will be filled by *ersatz* religion, by religion bootlegged into public space under other names."[11] He marveled at how quickly America's religion had become the religion of secularism. In 1931, the Supreme Court had asserted with conviction, "We are a Christian people, according to one another the equal right of religious freedom and acknowledging with reverence the duty of obedience to the will of God."[12] By 1984, Neuhaus observed, even if the society remained strongly religious, the state had become secular. "Such a dysjunction between society and state is a formula for governmental delegitimation," he wrote. "In a democratic society, state and society must draw from the same moral well. In addition, because transcendence abhors a vacuum, the state that styles itself as secular will almost certainly succumb to secular*ism*. Because government cannot help but make moral judgments of an ultimate nature, it must, if it has in principle excluded identifiable religion, make those judgments by 'secular' reasoning that is given the force of religion." The result is that the state begins ruling through principles of "secular humanism," the ersatz religion that of necessity fills the vacuum in the public square when traditional religion is pushed out and forced to evacuate.[13]

From there, Neuhaus feared the secular state was inevitably the prelude to totalitarianism. When religion is reduced to privatized conscience, the public square has only two actors in it—the state and the individual. Gone is religion as a mediating structure that transmits moral values and serves as a countervailing force to the ambitions of the state. "Whether in Hitler's Third Reich or in today's sundry states professing Marxist-Leninism, the chief attack is not upon individual religious belief," he warned. "Individual religious belief can be dismissed scornfully as superstition, for it finally poses little threat to the state." The chief attack, Neuhaus feared, would be on the institutions of religion, the institutions "that bear and promulgate belief in a transcendent reality by which the state can be called to judgment." In his view, only religious institutions have the power to threaten the totalitarian proposition "that everything is to be within the state, nothing is to be outside the state."[14]

Neuhaus agreed with our Founding Fathers that maintaining vibrant religious freedom in the public square is central to the purpose of establishing and holding on to the constitutional republic the Founding Fathers had crafted. In this sense, the First Amendment's defense of religious freedom was not incidental to the American enterprise, but central to the formulation of the nation under the Constitution. Reading Jefferson's wall metaphor as demanding an absolute separation between church and state made inevitable the ultimate destruction of religious freedom itself. Reading the establishment clause and the free expression clause as unitary assured that over time, organizations like the ACLU would find a welcome ear in the war the ACLU intended to wage systematically against God. The only hope was that the Supreme Court would reject the wall metaphor and embrace a view where the two clauses—the establishment clause and the free expression clause—were meant to work together. The Neuhaus formulation of the First Amendment shows the way the battle against the ACLU must be waged if religious freedom in the United States is to have any meaning protecting the religious future of Jews and Christians in America. The goal in fighting back against the ACLU must be the same goal Neuhaus sought in fighting back against Pfeffer: free and open religious expression must be reestablished in the public square, such that the presence of God in America is once again welcomed, in an America where Jews and Christians need not hide in their basements to pray to God.

In the Supreme Court case *Santa Fe Independent School District v. Doe*, 530 U.S. 290 (2000), a student elected as Santa Fe High School's student council chaplain used the public address system to deliver a prayer before each home varsity football game. Several Mormon and Catholic students or alumni and their mothers (together identified as "Doe" in the case) filed suit, challenging the prayer under the establishment clause of the First Amendment. The ACLU sided with the protesting students by filing an amicus brief in the case.

While the suit was pending, the Santa Fe Independent School District adopted a different policy involving two student elections—the first to determine whether prayer invocations should be offered at games and the second to determine who would deliver the prayer invocations. After the students held elections by secret ballot authorizing the prayers and selecting a person to deliver them, the district court entered an order modifying the policy to permit only nonsectarian, nonproselytizing prayer. The Fifth Circuit Court of Appeals held that even as modified by the district court, the football prayer policy was unconstitutional. The Supreme Court upheld the decision of the Fifth Circuit, ruling that the football prayer was unconstitutional under the establishment clause of the First Amendment.

Justice John Paul Stevens delivered the 5–3 majority opinion of the Supreme Court. Stevens distinguished between government speech endorsing religion, which the establishment clause forbids, and private speech endorsing religion, which the free speech clause and the free exercises clauses of the First Amendment protect. He distinguished that in this case involving a Texas high school, the invocations were authorized by a government policy and took place on government property at government-sponsored school-related events. Stevens was concerned that the student election system deemed appropriate only one invocation to be delivered at the football games and only one student selected to make the invocation. He was concerned that a minority of students objecting to the invocation would be coerced to listen to the invocation.

Stevens was also concerned that the Santa Fe School Independent District had done nothing to "divorce itself from the religious content in the invocations." Applying the *Lemon* test, the majority further decided the school policy had a religious purpose in that the invocation was designed "to solemnize the event." Under the test, if the purpose of the speech were deemed religious in nature and government sponsored because it was delivered with school endorsement, the only conclusion was that the speech was unconstitutional under the establishment clause. "The delivery of a message such as the invocation here—on school property, at school-sponsored events, over the school's public address system, by a speaker representing the student body, under the supervision of school faculty, and pursuant to a school policy that explicitly and implicitly encourages public prayer—is not properly characterized as 'private' speech," Stevens wrote, making the point clear.[15]

The *Santa Fe v. Doe* decision is important precisely because the majority decision leaves no doubt that the Supreme Court has moved to a Pfefferian public space that may be populated only by secular speech—the exact result Neuhaus feared. "Nothing in the Constitution as interpreted by this Court prohibits any public school student from voluntarily praying at any time before, during, or after the schoolday," Stevens continued. "But the religious liberty protected by the Constitution is abridged when the State affirmatively sponsors the particular religious practice of prayer."[16]

Justice William H. Rehnquist wrote a dissenting opinion, with Justice Antonin Scalia and Justice Clarence Thomas joining him in the dissent. "The Court distorts existing precedent to conclude that the school district's student-message program is invalid on its face under the Establishment Clause," Rehnquist began. "But even more disturbing than its holding is the tone of the Court's opinion; it bristles with hostility to all things religious in public life."[17] What was obvious was that not only did Rehnquist, Scalia, and Thomas disagree with the majority opinion in the case; the three were getting angry at the determination of the majority to use the establishment clause to crush religious expression. "Neither the holding nor the tone of the opinion is faithful to the meaning of the Establishment Clause, when it is recalled that George Washington himself, at the request of the very Congress which passed the Bill of Rights, proclaimed a day of 'public thanksgiving and prayer, to be observed by acknowledging with grateful hearts the many and signal favors of Almighty God,'" Rehnquist noted.[18]

The Rehnquist dissent suggests the possibility that a conservative coalition could form on the court to push back against the "separation of church and state" principles that have dominated the Supreme Court cases involving religious freedom since *Everson* was decided in 1947. As long as this principle remains unchallenged, Pfefferian logic will ultimately demand that all traces of God and religion be removed not only from public schools in the United States but also from the public square. A godless public square could not be more antithetical to what our Founding Fathers thought they were achieving when drafting the First Amendment. Ironically, the very language crafted to protect religious freedom has now reached the point at which Americans can only be assured freedom from religion in all places within this nation, with the possible exception of prayer confined to the church and free expression of religion confined to the four walls of a home—if not to the narrower realm of a person's mind and conscience, provided the person is sensible enough not to articulate in public the religious thoughts the person cherishes in private.

John Adams, the nation's first vice president and second president, admonished future generations that "our Constitution was made only for a moral and religious people. It is wholly inadequate to the government of any other."[19] Our Founding Fathers studied history, asking themselves why great civilizations like ancient Rome had lost their liberty and fallen. Ultimately, two very diverse thinkers—Thomas Jefferson and John Adams—concluded that without virtue, based on a solid belief in God, liberty was inevitably lost. In other words, if the Supreme Court through ACLU prompting succeeds in removing the Judeo-Christian God from American public life, a foundation pillar upon which American liberty has depended will have been removed, perhaps irretrievably. Without the open expression of religious freedom so fundamental to American liberty that it is written into the First Amendment of the Bill of Rights, American liberty will not long persist.

The ACLU has grabbed hard onto the principle that church and state must be separated precisely because the ACLU has come to appreciate the necessity of winning that argument if it is to succeed ultimately in its War on God. Understanding fully the public relations utility of advancing its cause in the name of religious freedom, the ACLU will not stop until the God of Jews and Christians is completely removed from the public square.

In this context, it is somewhat surprising to see how strongly the ACLU has advocated for Islam, with a case in point being the Islamic community center near the site of the World Trade Center in New York City, where the twin towers were destroyed when Islamic terrorists flew two hijacked airplanes into the buildings on September 11, 2001.

The project involved building a community center that would contain a Muslim prayer space—quickly designated the "Ground Zero Mosque"—at 45-51 Park Place, in a building previously occupied by a Burlington Coat Company retail outlet that was damaged in the 9/11 attack. The controversy began when the *New York Times* reported on December 8, 2009, that Imam Feisal Abdul Rauf was organizing to purchase the Park Place property he had been using for months as an overflow prayer space for about 450 Muslims. The location was a selling point for the group of Muslims who bought the building in July 2009: a presence so close to the World Trade Center, "where a piece of the wreckage fell sends the opposite statement to what happened on 9/11," Imam Feisal told the *Times*. "We want to push back against the extremists."[20]

But not everyone was equally enthusiastic. Opposition leaders argued that building a mosque so close to the former World Trade Center location would dishonor the memory of the 9/11 victims who died at the hands of Islamic terrorists. An example was drawn to the late Pope John Paul II intervening in the 1980s to prevent Carmelite nuns from establishing a convent at Auschwitz, which today is not only a memorial to the horror of the Holocaust but also a cemetery containing the physical remains of countless thousands of Jews killed there by the Nazis. "Pope John Paul II understood that building a Christian institution on a mass Jewish grave would be an unacceptable act of appropriation," wrote Morton A. Klein, the national president of the Zionist Organization of America (ZOA), and Dr. Daniel Mandel, the director of the ZOA's Center for Middle East Policy, in an op-ed piece published in the *Washington Post*. "He [Pope John Paul II] called upon the Carmelite nuns to relocate."[21]

The ACLU became particularly vocal in supporting the Ground Zero Mosque after the New York City Landmarks Preservation Commission voted against protecting the 152-year-old building standing in the way of developing "Park51," the name Imam Feisal had adopted for the community center and mosque his group planned to build. On August 3, 2010, the *New York Daily News* reported that after Mayor Bloomberg spoke to the Landmarks Preservation Commission, the commissioners voted 9–0 against giving landmark protection to the Italian palazzo-style building that would need to be demolished for the community center and mosque to be built.[22]

Almost as soon as the commission voted, the New York Civil Liberties Union and the ACLU in Washington, D.C., issued a press release praising the New York City Landmarks Preservation Commission for "standing up for the principles of religious freedom and tolerance" in approving a proposal to build a thirteen-story Islamic cultural center and mosque near the World Trade Center site in New York City. "We congratulate the Landmarks Preservation Commission for promoting our nation's core values and not letting bias get in the way of the rule of law," the New York ACLU and the national ACLU said in the joint press release. "The free exercise of religion is one of America's most fundamental freedoms. For hundreds of years, our pluralism and tolerance have sustained and strengthened our nation. On 9/11 religious extremists opposed to that very pluralism killed three thousand Americans. Those fanatics would want nothing more than for our nation to turn its back on the very ideals that made this country so great." The ACLU groups rejected opposition arguments. "For those who have sought to ban the construction of the cultural center, we must remember that our precious ideals extend to all Americans, regardless of creed or color. We see the center as a monument to pluralism, symbolic of America's commitment to religious freedom."[23]

As the controversy continued, the ACLU produced a print advertisement that showed three views of the Park Place location, with the shiny-blue glass structure in the first view showing a cross on its façade, the same structure in the second view showing a crescent and star, and the third view showing a Star of David. The advertisement poses the question, "Would there even be a controversy if this weren't a mosque?" In presenting the advertisement to the public, the NYCLU and the national ACLU issued a statement saying, "Throughout America's history, almost every religious group, including Jews, Protestants, Catholics and Muslims, has been the target of discrimination. Tolerance and fairness have generally prevailed, but only after principled voices have transcended the fear and hatred."[24] The message was clear: the ACLU was on the side of religious freedom, while those opposing the Ground Zero Mosque had no motivation other than Islamophobia—that is, hatred of Muslims—and a desire to discriminate because a mosque—not a Christian church or a Jewish synagogue—was being contemplated so close to the World Trade Center site.

The ACLU has even created a Ground Zero Mosque petition on the national website. "I stand with the ACLU and people all across America in defense of religious liberty," the petition reads. "I also affirm my support for leaders like Mayor Michael Bloomberg of New York City who boldly oppose religious discrimination rooted in cultural stereotyping and resist those who seek to trade away our most precious values for political advantage." The petition continues: "Throughout our nation's history, Jews, Protestants, Catholics and Muslims have all been victims of fear and discrimination. To see that tolerance and justice prevail, it is our duty to speak out for what we know is right."[25]

The ACLU's various statements on the issue avoid recognizing that the responsible opposition to the Ground Zero Mosque had no problem with a mosque being built in the southern tip of Manhattan, even in close proximity to the World Trade Center site. The opposition was to this particular location, within two blocks of the WTC, where debris from the wreckage of the World Trade Center on 9/11 had actually done damage to the building. The ACLU sought to position the issue as if the opposition's primary motivation was hatred of Islam and a desire to discriminate against the religion. In taking sides, the ACLU sought to characterize Islam as the underdog to which an injustice had been done. In turn, this positioned Christians and Jews as the intolerant bullies, unwilling to transcend what the ACLU characterized as prejudice and ill will, to allow a competing religion to have equal expression. Despite the one-sided nature of the ACLU's characterization, the organization was willing to raise money on the theme, as it positioned to champion Islam against Jews, Protestants, and Catholics.

On November 2, 2010, the citizens of Oklahoma voted overwhelmingly in favor of State Question 755, known as the "Save Our State" amendment to the Oklahoma Constitution, which was approved by the legislature. Specifically, the constitutional amendment prohibited Oklahoma judges from using international law as the basis for their decisions, banning specifically the ability of judges to rely on Islamic sharia law in deciding cases. The language of the Oklahoma House of Representatives resolution specifically amended the state constitution to require Oklahoma courts to rely on federal and state laws when deciding causes; it specifically prohibited Oklahoma courts from looking at international law or sharia law when rendering decisions.

The proposal to outlaw sharia law in Oklahoma passed the Oklahoma legislature with an 82–10 vote in the House of Representatives and a 41–2 vote in the Senate.[26] The amendment passed with more than 695,000 Oklahomans, just over 70 percent of the total vote, voting to pass it. With the passage of the amendment, Oklahoma became the first state in the Union to ban Islamic law. Oklahoma, a state with a population of approximately 3.7 million people, had a Muslim population that numbered between 15,000 and 30,000 people at the time this constitutional amendment was passed.[27]

Muneer Awad, the director of the Oklahoma chapter of the Council on American-Islamic Relations (CAIR), almost immediately brought a federal lawsuit seeking to block the implementation of the amendment. CAIR, whose headquarters is in the nation's capital, describes itself as "America's largest civil liberties and advocacy group." CAIR argues that its mission "is to enhance the understanding of Islam, encourage dialogue, protect civil liberties, empower American Muslims, and build coalitions that promote justice and mutual understanding."[28] World Net Daily (WND) has documented FBI evidence that points to the origin of CAIR as a front group for the Muslim Brotherhood and its offshoot Hamas. CAIR sued WND for the publication of a best-selling exposé, *Muslim Mafia: Inside the Secret Underworld That's Conspiring to Islamize America*.[29] The lawsuit is ongoing as this book is being written.[30]

In Oklahoma, the ACLU joined CAIR in the lawsuit, arguing the Oklahoma amendment violated Awad's rights under both the free exercise and the establishment clauses of the First Amendment.[31] In November 2010, following passage of the antisharia amendment, but before it took effect, Oklahoma City federal judge Vicki Miles-LaGrange issued an injunction enjoining enforcement of the amendment, concluding there was a "substantial likelihood" that the ban violates the establishment clause.[32] On November 29, 2010, Judge Vicki Miles-LaGrange of the Federal District Court in Oklahoma issued a preliminary injunction prohibiting the Oklahoma State Election Commission from certifying the vote on State Question 755, thereby enjoining the constitutional amendment from taking effect until the district court had a chance to hear the appeal and render a decision.[33]

On May 10, 2011, CAIR and the ACLU together filed a brief with the US Court of Appeals. "This amendment is nothing more than a blatant attempt to subvert the Constitution by enshrining anti-Muslim bigotry into state law," said Daniel Mach, the director of the ACLU Program on Freedom of Religion and Belief, at a press conference held to announce the filing of the jointly drafted CAIR-ACLU brief. "This brief and the court's previous ruling make clear that our Constitution does not tolerate using state laws to target religious minorities," said CAIR staff attorney Gadeir Abbas at the press conference.[34]

The ACLU noted that Awad was deeply concerned not only that the law was discriminatory but also that it would prevent Oklahoma courts from "recognizing personal legal documents that incorporate his beliefs," such as his last will and testament. "As a citizen of Oklahoma, it is appalling to think that my state representatives regard my belief system and that of other Muslims as a threat," said Awad. "This law singles us out for no reason, and cuts us off from the protections of the law against discrimination that are granted to all other faiths." The ACLU also argued that the law could prevent Oklahoma courts from "respecting international commitments, honoring global business agreements, and recognizing international adoptions and marriages conducted overseas."[35]

In an ACLU analysis of the Oklahoma law, the ACLU asks the following questions: "Are all faiths equal under the law? Does the fundamental right to worship in this country depend on the approval of the majority?"[36] The analysis dismissed the argument of the Oklahoma state's attorney that the law does not target a particular amendment but instead mentions sharia law only as an illustration or a clarification. "The government should never play favorites with religion, and Oklahoma's 'Save Our State Amendment' does just that," the ACLU argued. "It tramples the free exercise rights of a minority faith, and sends a powerful, clear message that Muslims are religious and political outsiders in their own state. Whatever its arguments on appeal, Oklahoma can't escape the basic fact that in the U.S., we simply don't put religious liberty up for a vote."[37]

The ACLU-CAIR brief filed with the US District Court made clear that plaintiff Muneer Awad is an American citizen, born in Ann Arbor, Michigan, and is "a devout, lifelong Muslim." It further pointed out that Awad "lives his life in accordance with a set of religious principles set forth in the Quran, the Muslim Holy Book, and the teachings of the Prophet Mohammed, which are collected in religious guides called 'Hadiths.'" The ACLU-CAIR conceded that no single document exhaustively defines sharia law. "Rather, the meaning and requirements of Sharia law are subject to individual and communal interpretations and thus differ from region to region, across denominations, and among individual Muslims," the brief admitted. It also argued that a central tenet of sharia is that Muslims live in accordance with the law of the nation in which they reside, one reason sharia differs from region to region. Still, the ACLU-CAIR brief stressed that obeying sharia law would not place Awad at odds with also following Oklahoma law. "Thus, as Mr. Awad practices his religion, following U.S. and Oklahoma law is paramount to living a virtuous and faith-abiding life," the brief stressed.[38]

This case most likely will be appealed to the Supreme Court, testing whether the First Amendment requires that state courts in the United States must apply sharia law to Muslims, even in disputes that involve state law. While CAIR and the ACLU present the case as one involving religious discrimination, it is obvious sharia law cannot be expected to conform to Oklahoma law in all cases. Obviously, if sharia law and Oklahoma civil and criminal law were completely identical, Muslims would not want to establish sharia law as the law applicable to them as religious believers. If CAIR and the ACLU win, which set of laws will be considered to be superior to the other? An extreme case might involve honor killings, in which the murder of a child by a parent may be deemed justifiable under sharia law if the child is judged by the parent to have violated Islamic law, particularly in the case of sexual mores. If justified under sharia law, would a decision in the Oklahoma case involving State Question 775 mean a parent killing a child in an Islamic honor killing could not be prosecuted under Oklahoma state criminal law?

In many countries, including Great Britain, Muslims have used an incremental approach to supplanting the secular laws of the nation with the religious law of Islam. Muslims readily admit that sharia law is not a codified legal structure but a series of maxims and principles that are applied differently around the world, in part depending upon how strictly orthodox the religion is practiced in any particular locale. Fundamentally, however, the demand to be judged by sharia law is a threat to the sovereignty of the country itself. Using an incremental approach, the demand to be judged under sharia law is typically followed by the Muslim demand to be judged by Islamic courts. In the final analysis, if Muslims reject the authority of a nation's secular courts over their own religious sharia law courts, Islam will in effect have become a state-established religion, as least as far as processes of civil and perhaps even criminal adjudication are involved.

That the ACLU will support the use of sharia law in the secular legal processes of the United States is now apparent. How far the ACLU will go in supporting sharia law remains to be seen. But even if the ACLU realizes the potential hypocrisy of its position, it is doubtful it would be sympathetic to Christian and Jewish demands to utilize the law of Christ as expressed in the New Testament or the law of Yahweh as expressed in the Torah and various books of the Old Testament to adjudicate civil and criminal legal disputes involving Christian and Jewish believers. While the ACLU thinks it is somehow appropriate for Muslims to assert that sharia law has supremacy over believers in Islam, the ACLU would undoubtedly insist that Christians and Jews have agreed to submit themselves to the law of the land when they decided to be Americans first and Christians or Jews second.

In a seperate but related case on December 16, 2008, Judge Keith Rollins in Douglasville, Georgia, arrested forty-year-old Lisa Valentine, a Muslim woman known also by her Islamic name, Miedah, for her refusal to take off her head scarf at a security point when she entered the municipal courthouse, thus violating a stated policy of allowing no headgear in court. Rollins ordered Valentine held for ten days in jail, where she was forced to remove her head scarf, but she was released later that evening, after CAIR entered the case to protest, and the head scarf was returned to her. "It was very humiliating," Valentine told the *Atlanta Journal-Constitution*, once she returned home. "I wear my hijab faithfully and for no reason, I was asked to take it off. It was unreal." According to the newspaper report, Judge Rollins had ordered other women to remove their religious head scarves. One woman, Sabreen Abdul Rahman, age fifty-five, said she was asked to take off her head scarf when she went to the same municipal courtroom the week before. The newspaper reported: "'I can't. I'm Muslim,' she mouthed silently to the bailiff, who then removed her from the courtroom." Another woman, Halimah Abdullah, age forty-three, said she spent twenty-four hours in jail in November 2007 after Rollins held her in contempt of court for refusing to release her head scarf.[39]

According to the Associated Press, Valentine's husband, Omar Hall, said his wife was at the municipal court to accompany her nephew to a traffic citation hearing. At the metal detector in the court's security area, a bailiff allegedly told her she had to remove the head scarf. Hall said Valentine, an insurance underwriter, told the bailiff that she had been in courtrooms before and continued to wear her hijab. She also insisted that removing the head scarf would be "a religious violation." According to the Associated Press report, Valentine responded with an expletive to the bailiff's insistence she would still need to remove the head scarf and then turned to leave the municipal courtroom building. The bailiff reportedly handcuffed her and took her to the judge's chambers. "I just felt stripped of my civil, my human rights," Valentine told the Associated Press, after she was released.[40]

"On December 16, 2008, I accompanied my nephew to the Douglasville Municipal Courtroom," Valentine explained to the ACLU.

> As we approached the security desk, the officer told me that I was not allowed in the courthouse with my headscarf on. I am a practicing Muslim woman who wears a headscarf (*hijab*) daily when out in public. As I explained this to the officer, she told me, it didn't matter, that the judge did not allow any type of headgear in the courtroom. In disbelief

I asked how can that be? This is my constitutional right. Not allowing me access to the courthouse is discrimination. The officer remained adamant that I would not be allowed in the courthouse even after I expressly conveyed to her that the wearing of the headscarf is an expression of my faith. I told her that it was [ridiculous] and proceeded to leave.[41]

Valentine confirmed that the bailiff took her to the judge's chambers, and the judge sentenced her to ten days in jail for contempt of court. "After being booked, fingerprinted, and disrobed I was chained to other detainees, men and women alike," Valentine continued in her statement published by the ACLU.

Thankfully, I did not have to spend a full night in jail. Thanks to the numerous phone calls from family members, (my husband especially), members of CAIR, the Department of Justice and other organizations I was released later in the evening. Maybe it's hard for some people to understand how I can compare to having to remove my headscarf in public to being disrobed. Wearing the *hijab* is an expression of my faith and it is a practice that I have adhered to for over 13 years. My headscarf is as much a protective piece of clothing as a shirt or pants or any other article of clothing that one may find embarrassing to be without.[42]

In reaction to Valentine's arrest, CAIR called upon the US Department of Justice to investigate a series of incidents in which Muslim women in Georgia were prevented from entering courtrooms. "We ask the Department of Justice to investigate these troubling incidents to determine whether the women's civil or religious rights were violated," said CAIR national communications director Ibrahim Hooper in a press release. "Judges have the right [to] set standards of dress and behavior in their courtrooms, but those standards should not violate the constitutional right to free exercise of religion or block unencumbered access to our nation's legal system." CAIR sent a letter to the Georgia attorney general following the incident, charging that the judge had violated the Georgia Code of Judicial Conduct, Title III of the Civil Rights Act of 1964, as well as First and Fourteenth Amendment "rights to freedom of religion and equal protection under the law."[43]

On July 27, 2009, the ACLU announced that the Supreme Court of Georgia's Committee on Access and Fairness in the Courts had adopted a policy presented by the ACLU of Georgia that clarified Islamic religious head scarves can be worn in Georgia courthouses. "We are thrilled that the Georgia Judicial Council has decided to adopt this policy, thereby ensuring that no one in Georgia will ever have to choose between their fundamental right to free expression of religion and their right to gain access to a courtroom," said Azadeh Shahshahani, the ACLU of Georgia National Security/ Immigrants' Rights project director, who had attended a meeting on June 10, 2009, with the Committee on Access and Fairness in the Courts and presented the policy. "This is a step in the direction of ensuring that the guarantee of religious freedom is assured to all Georgia residents, regardless of faith."[44]

The head scarf policy adopted for the municipal courthouse in Douglasville specified that head coverings would be permitted to be worn into the courtroom for medical or religious reasons. Any person wearing a head covering would still have to undergo initial screening by a metal detector and any additional screening that might be necessary. "With respect to individuals wearing a head covering for religious or medical reasons who have been arrested and/or detained, said individuals will only be required to remove their head coverings while they are in a private area under the supervision of an officer of the same gender, out of view of any people of the other gender, including officers of the other gender," the policy specified. "At no time will the arrested or detained person be required to have a head covering off while publicly visible or visible to people of the opposite gender."[45]

Once the Georgia head scarf policy was altered, CAIR and the ACLU need not worry that once inside the courtroom the Muslim woman wearing her head scarf might have to risk being offended by any depiction of the Ten Commandments or any symbol of Judeo-Christian religious beliefs, such as a crucifix or Star of David, being in evidence anywhere in the courtroom. Possibly someone in the courtroom might happen to be wearing jewelry bearing a crucifix or Star of David, but if so, that privilege had not been obtained through the intervention of the ACLU. When has the ACLU ever sued any government body to secure the right for a woman in the public space to wear on her person any symbol of Judeo-Christian beliefs?

The ACLU has issued a major policy statement on "Discrimination Against Muslim Women" that devotes considerable attention to the issue of head scarves. "Many Muslim women, although by no means all, practice *hijab* in accordance with their religious beliefs: these women may wear a headscarf, also known as *hijab* or *khimar*, and loose-fitting clothing when they are in public and when they are in the presence of men who are not part of their immediate family," the ACLU policy statement began. "Some women additionally cover much of their face with a covering known as *niqab*." The ACLU pointed out that "Muslim women, like all people in the United States, have the right to practice their religion." The ACLU says the concern is that Muslim women who wear distinctive Islamic clothing may have their rights infringed: Muslim women "have been harassed, fired from jobs, denied access to public places, and otherwise discriminated against because they wear *hijab*. Because of their visibility, Muslim women who wear *hijab* face particular exposure to discrimination and have increasingly been targets for harassment in the aftermath of September 11."[46]

Clearly, the ACLU wants to evoke themes from the civil rights movement to frame as *discrimination* the issue of how Muslims are treated. The ACLU's goal is to draw a moral equivalence between the way Muslims are treated and the way, for instance, African Americans were treated before the era of civil rights legislation and court cases that have distinguished the United States since the 1950s. Yet the questions may not necessarily be the same. Today in the United States, a civil rights crime would occur if a private citizen or a public official tried to prevent an African American from getting a driver's license because of the color of his or her skin. But is the issue identical if a Muslim woman demands to cover all her face except her eyes before her driver's license photograph is taken? In the civil rights movement, the point was that race did not justify different treatment but instead demanded equal treatment before the law. However, when the issue is Islam, the ACLU's point is that religion demands different treatment before the law, such that Muslims will be exempted because of religious reasons for practices and behaviors in public that do not conform with the majority.

Do we really believe Muslims must be treated differently from Christians and Jews? What the ACLU seems to want is not separation of mosque and state but for the state to intervene to protect Islam on a favored basis.

⌁

Political commentator Ed Lasky has noted the ACLU "twists itself into a pretzel shape, trying to justify opposing all state funding" for religion, except when Muslims "want foot baths in schools and other public facilities for religious reasons."[47]

The University of Michigan in Dearborn, Michigan, began noticing pools of water accumulating on the floor in some restrooms—only to realize that 10 percent of the students are Muslims and the sinks were being used as part of the ritual ablutions required before Muslim students' five-times-a-day prayer. After discussions with the Muslim Students' Association, the university decided to install foot-washing stations (at a cost of twenty-five thousand each) in several restrooms. But as the *New York Times* reported, this was only one of many accommodations being required for Muslim students.[48] How about serving *halal* food in cafeterias and scheduling classes and vacations around Muslim holidays? Maybe public schools should create Islamic prayer rooms, complete with prayer rugs and separate sections for men and women, all in accordance with Muslim religious practices!

The newspaper reported the issue was particularly difficult for the ACLU. "Our policy is to object whenever public funds are spent on any brick and mortar component of religion," Kary Moss, director of the Michigan Civil Liberties Union told the *Times*. "What makes this different, though, is that the footbaths themselves can be used by anyone, don't have any symbolic value and are not stylized in a religious way. They're in a regular restroom, and could be just as useful to a janitor filling up buckets, or someone coming off the basketball court, as to Muslim students." Moss further stretched the case by arguing the maintenance staff was worried about the hazard of wet floors. "We were also aware that if the university said students could not wash their feet in the sink anymore, that could present a different civil liberties problem, interfering with Muslim students' ability to practice their religion."[49]

This is occurring while Christian schoolteachers in Florida are being forced to hide in closets to pray after a controversial court order. "Under an order crafted by the ACLU, school employees in Santa Rosa School District must act in an 'official capacity' whenever they are at a 'school event'— including breaks, after-school events on or off campus, and at private events held on campus," according to a report in *World Net Daily*. Liberty Counsel, a nonprofit law firm, together with Christian Educators Association International, sought to overturn the legal order that has resulted in school officials being charged with contempt—for daring to pray. WND reported that, according to Liberty Counsel, school officials were strictly prohibited from showing agreement with anyone "communicating with a deity," such as "bowing the head" or "folding hands." Christian employees of the public schools in the Santa Rosa School District in Florida have testified the court order has "literally driven them to hide in closets" to avoid contempt charges because they were praying.[50]

The ACLU hypocrisy is clear: public school prayer is criminalized, with court orders establishing fines and even jail time for offending Jewish and Christian school employees, including teachers who dare to pray while at school or while involved in a school-related activity. Yet the ACLU argues to legitimate prayer rooms established for Muslim students in state-funded universities. Again, the ACLU charges that not providing prayer rooms could discriminate against Muslims, but the problem is that Muslims will claim discrimination unless they are allowed to behave differently from Christians and Jews—allowed to practice Islam openly in schools funded by the taxpayers, while Christians and Jews are forced to hide to avoid punishment if they want to bow their heads to say a silent prayer.

WND has also reported on seventh-grade students in the Byron Union School District in California, who pretend they are Muslims as part of a history and geography class. In a twenty-two-page ruling in 2003, US District Judge Phyllis Hamilton said the Excelsior Middle School in Byron, California, was not violating rules requiring separation of church and state because the purpose of the instruction was not to instruct the students in Islam but to teach them about the Muslim culture. The Islamic simulations at Excelsior were outlined in the state-adopted textbook, *Across the Centuries*, published by Houghton Mifflin, which prompts students to imagine they are Islamic soldiers and Muslims on a pilgrimage to Mecca.[51] Generally, parents do not have the right to prevent their children from being exposed to various topics in public school just because the parents find the topics objectionable.[52]

"While public schools prohibit Christian students from reading the Bible, praying, displaying the Ten Commandments, and even mentioning the word 'God,' students in California are being indoctrinated into the religion of Islam," Richard Thompson, chief counsel for the Thomas More Law Center told WND, on the filing of an appeal. "Public schools would never tolerate teaching Christianity in this way. Just imagine the ACLU's outcry if students were told that they had to pray the Lord's Prayer, memorize the Ten Commandments, use such phrases as 'Jesus is the Messiah,' and fast during Lent." Predictably, the ACLU did not intervene in the case to defend sensitive atheist parents worried their children might be exposed to Islam taught by the public school as a religion.[53]

On October 2, 2006, the US Supreme Court decided not to hear an appeal by Christian students and their parents in a case arguing that a Contra Costa County school engaged in unconstitutional religious instruction when teaching students about Islam by having them recite Islamic prayers.[54] The decision left intact a ruling by the Ninth US Circuit Court of Appeals in San Francisco that decided in favor of the Byron Union School District in eastern Contra Costa, on the case involving the seventh-grade social studies course teaching about Islam at Excelsior Middle School in Byron, which was discussed previously.

Yet if the Supreme Court had deigned to apply the *Lemon* test to the Ninth Circuit Court's decision in *Eklund v. Byron Union School District*, it is hard to imagine how the case would have passed the three-pronged test. Despite the school district's protestation that the only goal was to teach Muslim history and culture, how can that culture be separated from the religion of Islam?

By the nature of the religion, Islam seeks to establish a religious state. Isn't that the point when Muslims seek to be ruled by sharia law instead of by the secular law of the nation? Separation of church and state may be a principle the ACLU wants Christianity and Judaism to live under in the United States, but separation of mosque and state truly is not the point of Islam, at least not of Muslim fundamentalists.

It is tempting to speculate that the ACLU supports Islam on a basis that is discriminatory against Christianity and Judaism on the theory that the enemy of my enemy is my friend. Even if we cannot finally explain why the ACLU favors Islam, the duplicity of the organization when it comes to Islam is apparent. Unspoken is the ACLU's presumption in requiring toleration of Islam that Islam itself is a tolerant religion.

Truthfully, the vast majority of Christians and Jews would not give much thought about tolerating Islam if it were not for the underlying fear that the ultimate goal of Islam is to move in slowly and gain a position of respect and equality in any given society—all in preparation for Islam gaining ascendency, so as to exclude ultimately all other religions. So, too, underlying the controversy over the Ground Zero Mosque was the concern that extremist Muslims were responsible for 9/11 in the first place. Nonetheless, to even articulate such a thought would be an act of hate speech, or so the ACLU would claim.

Repeatedly, the ACLU asks Americans to put aside the thought that Islam has extremist elements that drive many of the demands Muslims make on the secular states within which they live. But the concern remains that Islam, even in its less extreme forms, is only marginally accommodating of other religions.

Nor can we completely eliminate speculation that the ACLU supports

Islam because it knows Islam shares the religious intolerance at the heart of ACLU-supported First Amendment cases. If the ACLU succeeds in creating a public square removed from the God of Christians and Jews, how far behind is removing Christianity and Judaism from the hearts and minds of today's believers?

The ACLU as an organization has intervened in disputes to protect Islam in the identical or near-identical fact situations where it would have intervened to oppose Christians and Jews. The ACLU has also attempted to establish the support of Islam as politically correct, and that any step taken to restrain Islam in the public sphere is an act of discrimination, motivated by hate. In direct contrast, the ACLU argues that keeping Christianity and Judaism out of the public sphere is an act required by the Constitution, motivated by a constitutional obligation to make sure the United States never establishes Christianity or Judaism as a state religion.

6

THE ASSAULT
ON THE FAMILY

Every day should be National Day of Appreciation for
abortion providers.

—BRIGITTE AMIRI, REPRODUCTIVE
FREEDOM PROJECT[1]

The truth is, an attack on God ultimately necessitates an attack on
the family, something Far-Leftists have realized since the days
of Karl Marx. The challenge to the traditional family is fundamentally a challenge to educating children in the Judeo-Christian beliefs
as professed in the Bible. Nothing illustrates better the ACLU assault on
God than the organization's support of abortion. By grabbing the ability to
indoctrinate children in the public schools with the values of the lesbian-
gay-bisexual-transgender (LGBT) agenda—all done in the name of civil
liberties and identity rights—the ACLU has set a course to undermine the
Judeo-Christian values underlying the Constitution. Despite the ACLU's
protests that the only goal of the group is to protect the Constitution, the

group is dead set on creating a godless public square, containing godless public schools, peopled by godless LGBT families that have no use for Judeo-Christian values or the Bible.

➝

The ACLU has established March 10 as the National Day of Appreciation for Abortion Providers, commemorating the date on which Michael F. Griffin murdered Dr. David Gunn in 1993 outside the abortion clinic in Florida where Gunn worked. After shouting, "Don't kill any more babies," Griffin shot Gunn three times in the back as Gunn was getting out of his car in the clinic's parking lot.[2] In 1999, six years after Gunn's murder, the ACLU commemorated the day by renewing the organization's commitment "to protecting a woman's fundamental right to choose—and access—abortion." In a statement that praised abortionists as "heroes of the pro-choice movement," the ACLU noted that twenty-six years after *Roe v. Wade*, "the reality of a woman's right to choose abortion rests on the courage and compassion of doctors and clinic workers." The statement affirmed the organization stood in awe of the determination of abortion doctors and clinic workers "to provide this essential medical service in the face of malice, threats and all-too real danger."[3]

In the same 1999 press release, the ACLU boasted the organization was "at the forefront of the struggle for reproductive rights since its inception in 1920" and was then "the only pro-choice legal organization" with a presence in all fifty states. The ACLU also noted it had founded the Reproductive Freedom Project in 1974 "to coordinate the legal, legislative, and public defense of the endangered rights secured by *Roe v. Wade*." Janet Benshoof headed the ACLU's Reproductive Freedom Project from 1977 to 1993, armed with an annual budget of approximately $2 million and a staff of seventeen employees. Abortion has been called the top priority of the ACLU, evidenced by claims by ACLU leaders that the organization handles some 80 percent of the abortion rights litigation cases nationwide. Benshoof's radical pro-abortion stance was evidenced by her admonition that pro-choice activists should march on courtrooms where abortion cases were being heard, with the intent of applying mob pressure on the judiciary.[4]

"Benshoof's extremism is tolerated by her superiors because the question is not a difficult one for the ACLU," argues William A. Donohue, president since 1993 of the Catholic League for Religious and Civil Rights. "It's a matter of a woman's right to choose, not a conflict between her right to abort and the right of someone else to live." Donohue points out that the ACLU vilifies anti-abortion protesters because they are seen not as analogous to the civil rights protesters of the 1960s but as "lunatic fascists out to destroy freedom."[5] But when it comes to anti-abortion protesters being able to exercise their First Amendment rights, the ACLU is nowhere to be seen, not even when Racketeer Influenced and Corrupt Organizations Act (RICO) charges are leveled to put pro-life advocates in jail. Donohue points out that Benshoof was behind the ACLU suggestion that abortion clinics might want to use RICO to stop anti-abortion protests.[6]

The ACLU's policy is reducible to "abortion on demand," the argument that any woman should be able to ask a doctor to terminate a pregnancy at any stage of the pregnancy, including when the head of the baby is emerging from the womb in the process of being delivered full term.[7] According to BlackGenocide.org, 1,876 African American babies are aborted every day in the United States on average. Further, while minority women constitute only about 13 percent of the female population ages fifteen to forty-four in the United States, they undergo approximately 36 percent of the abortions.[8] Philosopher and journalist Michael Novak pointed out in 2009 that of the 47 million children aborted since the US Supreme Court issued the *Roe v. Wade* decision in 1973, an estimated 16 million African American babies were aborted in a population then of some 33 million African Americans in the United States.[9] If these babies had been allowed to live, the black population in the United States would be almost 50 percent larger than it is today—about 63 million instead of the 42 million African Americans reported in the 2010 US Census—perhaps as much as 20.4 percent of the population, instead of 13.6 percent.[10]

Interestingly, the Scopes trial and the ACLU's passionate support of abortion trace back to the same intellectual roots in Darwin's theory of evolution. Margaret Sanger, the founder of the organization that today is Planned Parenthood, began her crusade for abortion on the theme of eugenics, drawing heavily on Darwin's concept that the human race is an evolving species. Her journal, the *Birth Control Review*, was filled with articles advocating the elimination of the "unfit"—including persons with mental and physical disabilities—to produce a superior race of humans. Her slogan, "Birth Control: To Create a Race of Thoroughbreds," appealed to the type of racist thinking that gave rise to Hitler's propaganda and the resultant racial purification violence of the Holocaust.

"Margaret Sanger aligned herself with the eugenicists whose ideology prevailed in the early twentieth century," wrote Tanya L. Green in "The Negro Project: Margaret Sanger's Eugenic Plan for Black Americans." The idea was that if the "unfit" could be induced to abort their children, the process of natural selection would be advanced by human intervention—all part of a grand plan to make sure only the fittest were allowed to be born. "Eugenicists hoped to purify the bloodlines and improve the race by encouraging the 'fit' to reproduce and the 'unfit' to restrict their reproduction. They sought to contain the 'inferior' races through segregation, sterilization, birth control and abortion," Green noted.[11]

Sanger's writing was filled with a mix of popular ideas of the day drawn from early sexual psychology and Darwinism. She advocated that women separate sex from childbearing, so they preserved the "right" to have an abortion when childbearing did not suit their economic or psychological needs. Her views were extreme, to the point almost any reason expressed by a woman justified abortion, even that of inconvenience. In her 1922 book, *The Pivot of Civilization*, Sanger wrote that eugenics "shows us that we are paying for and even submitting to the dictates of an ever increasing, unceasingly spawning class of human beings who never should have been born at all—that the wealth of individuals and of states is being diverted from the development and the progress of human expression and civilization."[12]

Her writings strongly attacked Christianity, often expressing a vehement anti-Catholicism. While protesting that she did not mean to attack the Catholic Church, Sanger nonetheless objected that the pope assumed authority over non-Catholics by characterizing abortion as immoral. "The question of bearing and rearing children we hold is the concern of the mother and the potential mother," Sanger wrote in *The Pivot of Civilization*. "If she delegates the responsibility, the ethical education, to an external authority, that is her affair. We object, however, to the State or the Church which appoints itself as arbiter and dictator in this sphere and attempts to force unwilling women into compulsory maternity."[13]

In the final analysis, Sanger understood that birth control and abortion separated sex from the family and procreation. If sex was liberated such that the consequences of pregnancy could be avoided, Sanger could advance her evolutionary goals by promoting sexual revolution. The result, she believed, was that the combination of birth control and abortion would produce more children from the "fit" and fewer children from the "unfit."

The theme of sexual freedom traces back to Freud's attack on religion as a human invention designed to suppress human sexual behavior in the drive to create civilization; the theme of sexual freedom is also evident in Marx's view that religion, as an opiate of the masses, suppresses sexual appetites—a theme William Z. Foster openly articulated in his book *Toward Soviet America*. The attack on the family ultimately flows from the enlightenment attack on sexual mores, a theme Communist supporters like Roger Baldwin understood. Not surprisingly, the ACLU continues to advocate the teaching of Darwinian evolutionary theory in schools, to the exclusion of teaching intelligent design theories, just as the ACLU champions abortion, to the exclusion of supporting the rights of the unborn. Advocates of abortion, like Margaret Sanger, provided the ACLU the intellectual underpinning for the argument that abortion serves a socially useful purpose, much as contemporary atheists like Dawkins and Hitchens provided the intellectual underpinning for arguing that belief in God is a dangerous construct of reality that impedes the scientific progress of the human endeavor. So, the ACLU advances the right of a woman to demand an abortion much like the ACLU supports the right of an atheist to be in a godless public square. Ignored in the process are the rights of the unborn to live and the rights of Judeo-Christian believers in God to express their religion openly—rights that our Founding Fathers would have seen as placed by God in human nature.

Sanger's Negro Project, launched in 1939, represented a concerted attempt to build birth control clinics in black areas across the country. The underlying goal was to keep down the rising number of African Americans by reducing African American birthrates throughout the rural South as well as in the urban cities of the North. By placing birth control centers in or near black communities, Sanger sought to convince African Americans that by having fewer babies more carefully spaced in a family, they would enjoy an improved standard of health that would be measured in a reduction in maternal and infant deaths. Sanger's letters of the time outline a plan to convince black religious leaders to preach the virtues of birth control. The tone of the letters conveys a thinly disguised racism aimed at attacking the reproductive practices of black Americans.

In a 1939 letter to Dr. Clarence J. Gamble, prominent for creating the soap-manufacturing company Proctor and Gamble, Sanger wrote: "We do not want word to go out that we want to exterminate the Negro population, and the minister is the man who can straighten out that idea if it ever occurs to any of their more rebellious members."[14] Sanger supporters argue that the purpose of the Negro Project was not to practice race control against African Americans but to alleviate poverty in African American populations by reducing the number of African American children born, utilizing the techniques of birth control and abortion. At the time the letter was written, Gamble was then serving as Southern director for Sanger's Birth Control Federation of America, a predecessor to Planned Parenthood.

"Statistics which show that the greatest number of children are born to parents whose earnings are the lowest, that the direst poverty is associated with uncontrolled fecundity emphasize the character of the parenthood we are depending upon to create the future of the race," Sanger wrote in *The Pivot of Civilization*. She even objected to charities helping the poor, simply because the charitable aid increased the longevity of their offspring. "A distinguished American opponent of Birth Control some years ago spoke of the 'racial' value of this high infant mortality rate among the 'unfit,'" she continued. "He forgot, however, that the survival-rate of the children born of those overworked and fatigued mothers may nevertheless be large enough, aided and abetted by philanthropies and charities, to form the greater part of the population of to-morrow."[15]

Railing against Sanger, Rev. Jesse Lee Peterson has repeatedly attacked the racial policies of Planned Parenthood. "The undiscussed truth is that Planned Parenthood still operates in line with these ideas today," he wrote in his book *From Rage to Responsibility*. "Planned Parenthood clinics—and abortion clinics generally—are frequently located in inner cities where they can prey on poor minority women, and receive public funds for doing so."[16] Peterson charged that Sanger never did intend for abortion to be widespread among the white population but instead saw abortion as a way of "improving" the population by inducing the minority poor to destroy their offspring. Peterson also pointed out that packaging abortion as "a woman's right to choose" ignores the father's rights, as well as the rights of the unborn child. "But men do not choose to become fathers," he wrote in *From Rage to Responsibility*. "In fact, women—through electing either to obtain or not to obtain an abortion—choose *for* men whether men will become fathers."[17]

Yet Sanger's logic remains alive and well, if only slightly modified by modern social science perspectives. In the 2005 bestseller *Freakonomics: A Rogue Economist Explores the Hidden Side of Everything*, University of Chicago economist Steven Levitt, who fancies himself a solver of everyday life riddles, postulates that abortion was responsible for the observed drop in the crime rate in the United States during the 1990s. When a woman does not want to have a child, "she usually has a good reason," Levitt and his coauthor, Stephen Dubner, postulated, sounding very much like Margaret Sanger's musings of the 1920s. "She may be unmarried or in a bad marriage. She may consider herself too poor to raise a child. She may think her life is too unstable or unhappy, or she may think that her drinking and drug use will damage the baby's health. She may want a child badly but in a few years, not now."[18] Levitt and Dubner never pause to consider these may be good reasons to indulge in abstinence in order to avoid pregnancy altogether, but that consideration does not appear to calculate in their moral universe. Levitt and Dubner argued that what was missing in the decades of children after *Roe v. Wade* was the children who stood the greatest chance of becoming criminal, identified in their analysis as the children who were unwanted by their mothers, for whatever reason.

Even though their observation was at best a correlation, the authors drew a causal conclusion: "Legalized abortion led to less unwantedness; unwantedness leads to high crime; legalized abortion, therefore, led to less crime."[19] Conveniently, Levitt and Dubner ignored the economic strength of the Clinton years and the improvements that had been made in law enforcement technology and manpower in the 1990s as contributing causes. They were interested in establishing an abortion-crime causal implication so as to provide a social justification for mothers deciding to terminate their pregnancies in abortion. In the moral universe inhabited by Levitt and Dubner, killing babies was okay as long as crime statistics remained low. We have yet to see whether crime rates will rise in the aftermath of the global economic recession that began in 2008. But even if a prolonged global downturn occasions increased crime rates, Levitt and Dubner are unlikely to issue a new edition of *Freakonomics* in which they admit their error. Or to engage in reductio ad absurdum, why not just abort all babies? That might eliminate crime altogether.

The ACLU in court has argued abortion as a matter of rights, not social utility. Yet arguments that abortion reduces crime add a utilitarian aspect to the ACLU's cause. Again, the point is that if the science begins to turn against the ACLU's position, the ACLU's thinly disguised political preferences become more vulnerable. We saw this with regard to the Darwinian evolutionary theory versus intelligent design. To the extent well-established contemporary scientists reject Darwin, the ACLU's support of Darwinian evolutionary theory is undermined. Similarly, the battle against the ACLU on abortion needs to proceed by contesting the rights of the unborn as a counterbalance against the unbridled rights of a woman to choose. But this is not the only front on which the battle must be fought. If abortion can be shown to be dysfunctional to important social and economic goals the society embraces, the ACLU's presumption that abortion serves a socially useful purpose is challenged, weakening the argument overall that abortion is acceptable because it has no adverse social consequences. In this context, the work of the late social scientist and US senator Daniel Patrick Moynihan merits reexamination.

When serving as assistant secretary of labor heading the Office of Policy Planning and Research in 1965, Daniel Patrick Moynihan wrote the report *The Negro Family: The Case for National Action*.[20] In what is commonly known as the "Moynihan Report," Moynihan cautioned that government programs, such as Aid to Families with Dependent Children, could actually induce families on government assistance to break up. He was concerned that nearly a quarter of all African American families were dissolved and nearly a quarter of all African American births were illegitimate. Although Moynihan did not mention abortion in his report, had he foreseen *Roe v. Wade* and the impact of abortion on the dissolution of the family, Moyihan would have had grounds to be concerned that Supreme Court approval of abortion, even without government funding of abortion, could be seen as another government policy that could contribute to the breakup of the family.

Statistics on children born out of wedlock and children born to teenagers are alarming to those of us concerned with preserving the family in America. Of all 1995 births to African American women, 66 percent were to unmarried women (i.e., women who had never married or were widowed or divorced at the survey date). This is three times as high as that reported by white women, 19 percent, and twice as high as that reported by Hispanic women, 28 percent.[21] In 2008, the rate of births to unmarried women was 72.5 per 1,000 women for the black community, compared to 48.2 for the white community.[22] In 2008, the rate of births to black teenage mothers was about twice that for white teenage mothers: 63.4 births to teenage mothers per 1,000 women in the black community, compared to 37.8 in the white community.[23]

The statistics on abortions by race are equally hard to find, most likely because the higher rates among African Americans are not politically correct to report. According to the Kaiser Family Foundation, in 2008, 40.2 percent of all reported abortions were to African American women, even though African Americans constituted less than 14 percent of the population—meaning that African Americans were disproportionately likely to seek abortions.[24]

In writing his controversial report, Moynihan warned that the disintegration seen in the African American family was a prelude to the phenomenon reaching equal proportions in the majority family. Again, abortion is only one factor in a complex set of factors contributing to the disintegrating status of the family in America. Central to the argument of this book is that an attack on the Judeo-Christian tradition necessarily becomes an attack on the family. Central to the Judeo-Christian tradition is the idea that marriage is a relationship between one man and one woman, with the primary purpose being procreating and raising children. Marx correctly understood that Judeo-Christian nations would never convert to communism unless the family structure could be broken up. Detaching sex from procreation is achieved nowhere more directly than through abortion. The point is that an ACLU with its historical and intellectual roots in communism was predestined to attack the family as certainly as the organization was predestined to attack Judeo-Christian prayer in the schools and to push for removal from the public square of all references to the God of Jews and Christians.

Nowhere in the ACLU's unshakable support of abortion does the notion of God enter the equation. Moreover, by characterizing abortion as a civil liberty, couched in the concept of a woman's right to choose, the ACLU has managed to transform the concept of abortion from the killing of an unborn human being to a pro-choice freedom libertarians would understand, even if there is no right to an abortion specified anywhere in the Bill of Rights. In his book *The Marketing of Evil: How Radicals, Elitists, and Pseudo-Experts Sell Us Corruption Disguised as Freedom*, journalist David Kupelian graphically points this out: "What if reporters and editors cut through the high-flying rhetoric of civil rights and constitutional freedom and women's health and brought the issue down to little, perfectly formed human babies—three thousand of them every day, the same number of people as perished on 9-11—being painfully ripped apart, suctioned, chemically burned, sliced up, or decapitated?"[25]

Kupelian speculates what would happen if the *New York Times* aggressively and relentlessly published with saturation coverage dozens of front-page stories on abortion, in a manner similar to how the newspaper covered the Abu Ghraib prison scandal under the administration of President George W. Bush. "Can there be any doubt as to the result?" Kupelian asks. "Americans would see the truth once again, and the realization of the horror of abortion would, as it did for centuries before this generation, seep into and eventually permeate the public consciousness." With intensive media exposure of the truth of what abortion involves, Kupelian believes the American public would once again return to seeing abortion as "grossly immoral, barbaric and criminal."[26]

According to the ACLU website, the organization has created an LGBT Project with the mission to create "a society in which lesbian, gay, bisexual and transgender people enjoy the constitutional rights of equality, privacy and personal autonomy, and freedom of expression and association."[27] The ACLU goal is to make LGBT sexual behavior and lifestyles equivalent to race—that is ordinary human characteristics like skin color that people are born with and, as such, have a right to exhibit and experience without being subject to discrimination based on that characteristic. In other words, today it is illegal to discriminate—in education, jobs, housing, and a host of other arenas—against a person simply because that person is African American or Asian or whatever skin color. Tomorrow, the ACLU would like to make it illegal to discriminate against a person who is lesbian, gay, bisexual, or transgender. "This means an America where LGBT people can live openly, where our identities, relationships, and families are respected, and where there is fair treatment on the job, in schools, housing, public places, health care, and government programs," the ACLU's LGBT page proclaims. "The Project brings impact lawsuits in state and federal courts throughout the country—cases designed to have a significant impact on the lives of LGBT people."[28] The current head of the ACLU nationwide is Anthony Romero, the first openly gay person to head the ninety-plus-year-old organization.[29]

With the passage of the Defense of Marriage Act (DOMA) in 1996, the US Congress defined marriage in federal law as a legal union between one man and one woman. DOMA, in effect, removed the right to define marriage from the states, since the Fourteenth Amendment could be applied to demand the states comply with the federal definition. The ACLU-backed case most likely to reach the US Supreme Court is *Perry v. Schwarzenegger*, a case that arose out of California's complicated legal situation in which Proposition 8, a statewide referendum to amend the state's constitution, overturned a state supreme court decision that had allowed same-sex marriages in California. Interestingly, the two attorneys joining together to challenge Proposition 8 on US constitutional grounds are Ted B. Olson, a Republican constitutional lawyer and the former solicitor general under President George W. Bush, and David Boies, the Democratic trial lawyer who was Olson's opposing counsel in the US Supreme Court case deciding the outcome of the Florida recount in the 2000 presidential contest between George W. Bush and Al Gore. As Margaret Talbot reported in *New Yorker* magazine, the team of Olson and Boies has mounted an ambitious case that attempts to short-circuit the incremental, "state-by-state strategy" that leading gay-rights organizations have typically pursued in the same-sex marriage controversy. "The Olson-Boies team hopes for a ruling that will transform the legal and social landscape nationwide, something on the order of *Brown v. Board of Education* in 1954 or *Loving v. Virginia*, the landmark 1967 Supreme Court ruling that invalidated laws prohibiting interracial marriage."[30]

The ACLU has been active in the case, submitting amicus briefs in *Perry v. Schwarzenegger* at various state and federal courts as the case winds its way up the federal appeals process, with the ACLU arguing that DOMA and Proposition 8 violate the US Constitution. Ultimately, the ACLU wants to eliminate gender discrimination, so LGBT couples can not only marry but also adopt children and become foster parents. "Our work debunks myths about the undesirability of same-sex couples raising children," the ACLU proclaims. "The ACLU challenges policies and laws that prevent qualified and caring LGBT people from foster parenting or adopting kids. We also strive to challenge laws or practices that interfere in custody and visitation relationships between LGBT parents and their children."[31] In February 2011, the U.S. Court of Appeals for the Ninth Circuit sided with the ACLU in the renamed case *Perry v. Brown*, ruling California's 2008 amendment banning same-sex marriage is unconstitutional.[32]

Even more fundamentally, the ACLU attacks not only gender discrimination but also the very nature of gender itself. In a 1967 case involving the Los Angeles police clamping down on the performances of Sir Lady Java, a transgender woman, at the Red Foxx Club, the ACLU position was, "The [way] in which the freedoms of lesbian, gay, bisexual and transgendered people are limited is rooted in the same stereotypical and tightly bound notions of gender (including gender roles, attributes assigned to either gender, and the expression of gender identity)."[33] The ACLU battle is against characterizing any type of gender-based sexual activity or lifestyle behavior as deviant, regardless how bizarre the sexual activity or lifestyle behavior may appear to the majority community.

The range of cases the ACLU has pursued in advocating its LGBT agenda is illustrative in understanding the range of the organization's concerns:

- In 2005, the Wisconsin state legislature passed a law prohibiting
  doctors from prescribing hormone treatment or sex-change
  operations for inmates in state prisons. The ACLU sued, relying on
  the testimony of medical experts that blocking people from access
  to hormone treatment after they have been on the treatment can
  cause life-threatening damage. The ACLU also sued that the state
  law was a violation of the Constitution's equal protection clause as
  well as the guarantee against cruel and unusual punishment to bar
  transgender prison inmates from access to "individualized medical
  care." On August 5, 2011, the Seventh Circuit Court of Appeals
  struck down the 2005 Wisconsin state law, ruling it violates the
  Constitution.[34]

- On May 10, 2011, the ACLU of Illinois together with the national
  ACLU filed a lawsuit to allow transgender individuals who had not
  had gender-change surgery to correct the gender marker on their
  birth certificates. The ACLU argued that it was unconstitutional for
  the Division of Vital Records of the Illinois Department of Public
  Health to change the gender on the birth certificates of transgender
  persons only if those persons had successfully completed gender-
  change surgery. "Illinois long ago recognized the importance
  for transgender people to have a birth certificate that accurately
  describes who they are," said John Knight, director of the LGBT
  Project at the ACLU of Illinois. "We've been telling the department
  for two years that its arbitrary surgery rules clash with the medical
  standard of care for transgender people and make it impossible
  for most transgender people to correct the gender on their birth
  certificates. We took them at their word when they said they would
  make an appropriate change, but all we've seen is more delay. It's
  time that they did something to fix that."[35]

- Under pressure from the ACLU of Utah Foundation, Inc., the
  Washington County School District agreed in March 2010 to allow
  the formation of "Gay-Straight Alliances" (GSAs), noncurricular
  student clubs focused on educating students about gay and lesbian

students with the goal of "promoting tolerance of all people regardless of sexual orientation or gender identity." Previously several high school principals in the school district refused to allow GSAs on their campuses, and several school administrators in the district explicitly discouraged faculty from acting as advisers to GSAs. "To the extent we can avoid lengthy litigation by surfacing early in the process to educate school and district administrators about their constitutional obligations under the First Amendment, we prefer that," said ACLU legal director Darcy Goddard. "Most educators seem to understand the need to create a safe and tolerant environment for all students, regardless of their sexual orientation, political views, religion, race, or any other factor."[36]

• On May 19, 2008, the ACLU of Kentucky filed suit on behalf of five families charging that segregating classes by sex in Breckinridge County Middle School is unconstitutional. "The Breckinridge County sex-segregated classrooms are not only unlawful because they deny boys and girls equal opportunities in education, these kinds of experimental programs are also misguided in that they distract from efforts that we know can improve all students' education like improved funding, smaller classes, more parental involvement and better trained teachers," said Emily Martin, deputy director of the ACLU Women's Rights Project. The ACLU lawsuit argued that Breckinridge County Middle School's sex-segregated classes are unconstitutional under the Fourteenth Amendment's equal protection clause, Title IX of the Educational Amendments of 1972, the Equal Educational Opportunities Act, and the state sex equity law. The ACLU suit charged that different textbooks covering different academic material at different rates were used in the classes for boys and the classes for girls. The organization decided to sue when the Breckinridge County Middle School administrators decided to assign students to all-male, all-female, or coeducational classes, without allowing the students and parents to choose. The father of Nikki Anthony, one of the girls affected, objected that his daughter could not participate in math classes with boys. "Real life doesn't put boys in one room and girls in another," Nikki Anthony said. "I don't think it's fair that the smartest boys in my grade can't take math with me or that I can't take English with them."[37]

- The ACLU championed the Florida case of Martin Gill and his partner of more than two years, who have been raising two foster children brothers since 2004. Gill took the children, believing they were suffering from neglect, a decision a Florida judge affirmed in 2006 when terminating the parental rights of the biological parents. The Gill case challenged a law banning gays and lesbians from adopting—the only such law in the United States—that the state legislature voted more than three decades ago, after a campaign led by Anita Bryant in the 1970s.[38] The ACLU has argued that nationwide some six to fourteen million children live with at least one gay parent. With millions of children remaining under state care because of a shortage of adoptive and foster parents, the ACLU has argued that home environments with lesbian and gay parents are "as likely to successfully support a child's development as those with heterosexual parents."[39] The ACLU has also brought lawsuits against state laws that limit the visitation rights of LGBT parents on the theory that "a best interest of the child" standard applies and "a person's sexual orientation cannot be the basis for ending or limiting parent-child relationships unless it is demonstrated that it causes harm to a child—a claim that has been routinely disproved by social science research."[40] On September 22, 2010, Florida's Third District Court of Appeals decided in the Gill case that Florida's law banning adoption by gay people has no rational relationship to the best interests of children. The state of Florida decided not to appeal the ruling.[41]

The next frontier for the ACLU will be to champion the teaching of the LGBT agenda in public schools. The Unified School District in Alameda,

California, a suburb of San Francisco and Oakland, decided in 2009 to implement a new curriculum aimed at addressing bullying of LGBT students, with the express goal of establishing respect and sympathy for LGBT students. According to the school district decision, compulsory lessons about the LGBT community will be taught to children as young as five years old. Angry parents have objected that the real goal of the school district is to indoctrinate children to transform attitudes that heterosexual sex and the view of marriage as between one man and one woman discriminate against LGBT-favorable attitudes of sex and marriage. "I believe these children are far too young to be learning about what these issues mean," a mother of three children who attend elementary school in Alameda told Fox News. "These are adult issues and they are being thrust upon the children." Attorneys for the school district explained to Fox News that parents will have no legal right to remove their children from class when the LGBT lessons are being taught.[42]

The ACLU promotes "making public schools safe and bias-free for LGBT students." According to the LGBT Youth & Schools page on the ACLU website, "No one should have to be afraid being gay in school. [LGBT] youth should have the freedom to be open (or not) about their identity and ideas in schools and government facilities. The ACLU LGBT Project strives to protect their right to be safe and visible, and to have their identity embraced rather than belittled or erased."[43] How far from here is it for the ACLU to target for legal action any student, teacher, or administrator who opposes the LGBT agenda for religious reasons?

Are those who dare to believe homosexuality violates God's law criminals? The ACLU would have us believe that any student, teacher, or administrator who believes homosexuality is a sin is no different from someone who would deny to African Americans equal access to voting, housing, or employment opportunities. Clearly, no student should be subject to bullying in any public school. Yet if the ACLU is successful in advancing the LGBT agenda in the public schools, those who support heterosexual sex and same-sex marriage for religious reasons will be categorized as bigots by definition. Truthfully, what the ACLU seeks is not only to remove every trace of the Judeo-Christian God from the public schools but also to remove from the public schools any student, teacher, or administrator who believes homosexuality and the LGBT agenda are contrary to Judeo-Christian religious beliefs as taught in the Bible.

Those who think the LGBT agenda could never be extended to include sexual activity as bizarre as bestiality should pause to examine the New York City–recommended sex education curriculum developed by the Department of Education. On October 24, 2011, the *New York Post* reported on the curriculum after obtaining an advance copy of the workbook prepared for the sex curriculum by the Department of Education.[44] Workbook assignments included having high-school students go to stores to jot down condom brands, prices, and features, such as lubrication. Teens were also asked to research routes from school to a clinic that provides birth control and sexually transmitted disease (STD) tests and to write down the clinics' confidentiality policies.

The workbook also refers students to resources such as Columbia University's website Go Ask Alice! The list of sexual topics explored on this site is mind-boggling—exploring in detail sexual variations far beyond the average person's experience, such that after spending any time on the website, the discussion of what most people would consider sexual perversions ranges far beyond bestiality to fringe sexual practices even more bizarre in their nature. But once introduced to the website, underage minors and teens are free to explore topics that would take most adults into unexplored areas guaranteed to shock the majority of first-time readers. Go Ask Alice! is not age-restricted and does not require registration or a password to enter. Anyone, including a child old enough to navigate the Internet on his or her own, is free to read the website at will. Once the public schools make sure students are aware the website exists, word of mouth among students of all ages can be expected to spread the news that the site exists and is not forbidden to view. Even more pernicious, that the website is hosted on a Columbia University website gives Go Ask Alice! a patina of erudition, despite the salacious nature of the website's sexual content. Fortunately, the website does not have pictures or videos, meaning that those accessing it have to be literate in order to peruse the contents. While this might exclude kindergarten and prekindergarten students, precocious elementary school children advancing rapidly in reading skills will be able to access and surf Go Ask Alice! knowledgably. That the site will be sexually titillating, especially to a sexually inexperienced audience, will undoubtedly add to the allure for young readers.

~

Catholic League president William A. Donohue, in his book *The Politics of the American Civil Liberties Union,* described the ACLU as *"the* liberal defender of pornography in the United States." Donahue argued that the ACLU "simply has monopolized the defense of pornographers everywhere. Its reason: Pornography is free speech covered by the First Amendment—a constitutional right."[45]

While the ACLU has consistently maintained that child pornography should be a crime, the ACLU has defended the dissemination of child pornography once it has been manufactured. A case in point is the US Supreme Court Case *Ashcroft v. Free Speech Coalition,* 535 U.S. 234 (2002), in which the ACLU filed an amicus brief.[46] This case challenged the Child Pornography Prevention Act of 1996, with the ACLU arguing that the prohibition of any photograph, film, video, picture, or computer-generated image of what appears to be a minor engaged in sexual activity but did not actually portray a minor engaged in sexual activity, was vague and overbroad. The Supreme Court agreed. Moreover, because no minors were actually used in the production of virtual or computer-generated images, the Supreme Court could not find harm in the actual production of the image.

In a related case, *Aschroft v. ACLU,* 535 U.S. 564 (2002), the ACLU challenged the constitutionality of the Child Online Protection Act of 1998 that attempted to put in place barriers, such as blocking or filtering software and age verification procedures related to credit cards, with the goal of blocking children from viewing pornographic material on the Internet. The ACLU again objected, arguing the statute violated First Amendment rights to view pornographic material, while there were less restrictive alternatives to prevent children from viewing pornography. Again, the Supreme Court agreed.[47]

In yet another amicus brief filed in *United States v. American Library Association*, 539 U.S. 194 (2003), the ACLU argued that First Amendment free speech rights prevented public schools and libraries receiving federal funding from installing blocking or filtering software designed to prevent minors from viewing pornography.[48] Here the Supreme Court disagreed, ruling that the Children's Internet Protection Act of 2000 was constitutional and that public schools and libraries receiving federal funding could install filtering or blocking software to prevent minors from viewing online pornography. The ACLU expressed disappointment over the decision. "Although we are disappointed that the Court upheld a law that is unequivocally a form of censorship, there is a silver lining," said Chris Hansen, an ACLU senior staff attorney. "The Justices essentially rewrote the law to minimize its effect on adult library patrons."[49] The court's ruling allowed librarians to disable the software on the request of an adult user and the presentation of a legitimate reason about why the adult user wanted the Internet site unblocked.

What is clear from these cases is that for the ACLU, the free speech right of adults to produce and view pornography is paramount, while all attempts to protect children from being exploited by pornographers or from viewing pornography have to be limited, weighted against the First Amendment rights the ACLU wants to preserve for pornographers and adult consumers of pornography.

So far the ACLU has been unsuccessful in contesting the right of adults to possess child pornography. In 2007, former ACLU executive Charles Rust-Tierney, then aged fifty-one, of Arlington, Virginia, admitted to investigators that he had downloaded child pornography videos and images onto CD-ROM disks from child pornography Internet sites. Rust-Tierney was arrested on February 23, 2007, while he was still a member of the Virginia ACLU board of directors.[50] The *Washington Post* reported that Rust-Tierney used a computer in his eleven-year-old son's bedroom to view pornography that included the sexual torture of children.[51]

Rust-Tierney, who had served as president of the Virginia ACLU chapter for years, was also distinguished for pursuing a case in federal courts to forbid Loudoun County public libraries from equipping computers with filters to protect children from viewing pornography. This case filed by the Virginia Chapter of the ACLU was a component of the ACLU's national campaign to oppose the Children's Internet Protection Act of 2000, a campaign that culminated with *United States v. American Library Association*. At the trial, Rust-Tierney testified as president of the ACLU's Virginia chapter that libraries must provide "universal access to information." The ACLU prevailed in the Virginia case, and Rust-Tierney demanded $460,000 in attorneys' fees to reimburse the ACLU of Virginia, which would be paid by taxpayers. Rust-Tierney and the ACLU of Virginia were disappointed, however, when the federal judge in the case awarded the ACLU only $37,000 in legal fees. Loudoun County and the state of Virginia decided to accept the loss and pay the fees rather than risk additional costs in a prolonged appeal.[52]

On September 7, 2007, the *Washington Post* reported Rust-Tierney was sentenced to seven years in federal prison for buying child pornography the prosecutors had labeled sadistic and masochistic.[53]

Those pursuing the LGBT agenda have been open in explaining the public relations launched in the late 1980s with the goal of changing the attitudes of the majority community from hostile to sympathetic. The ACLU has been able to fight the LGBT battle in the courts largely because gay rights activists have waged a systematic public relations campaign to change US public attitudes toward LGBT lifestyles. The point is that the ACLU can succeed in its radical leftist legal agenda only if public attitudes shift to accept the lifestyle behavior the ACLU pursues as part of the organization's political agenda. This holds across the spectrum of ACLU political causes. The ACLU cases attacking God in the public schools and in the public arena would not have been possible unless the US society had become more secular in nature.

Similarly, ACLU cases seeking to establish legal abortion in the United States depended upon first desensitizing the US society against the death of the unborn fetus inherent in the act of abortion. The same logic holds with regard to the ACLU attack on sexual mores.

Gay rights activists Marshall Kirk and Hunter Madsen laid bare their tactics in their book *After the Ball: How America Will Conquer Its Fear and Hatred of Gays in the 90's.* "It's time to learn from Madison Avenue, to roll out the big guns," Kirk and Madsen wrote. *"Gays must launch a large-scale campaign—we've called it the Waging Peace campaign—to reach straights through the mainstream media.* We're talking about propaganda."[54] Citing Sigmund's Freud's observation that "groups are subject to the truly magical power of words," Kirk and Madsen urged gays to talk about homosexuality openly, frequently, and positively. Under the principle that constant talk builds the impression that public opinion is divided and that a sizable block accept or even practice homosexuality, they advised, "The main thing is to *talk about gayness until the issue becomes thoroughly tiresome.*"[55] They suggested that gays should portray themselves as victims in need of protection, "so that straights will be inclined by reflex to adopt the role of protector."[56] They urged that the message be kept simple— gay rights—calculating that potential protectors needed to perceive that homosexuals had a just cause.

Kirk and Madsen critiqued a series of advertisements designed to promote homosexuality, rating each ad according to the following eight-point criteria:

1. Communicate; don't just express yourself.
2. Appeal to ambivalent skeptics.
3. Keep talking (desensitize, don't shock).
4. Keep message simpleminded: gay rights.
5. Portray gays as victims, not aggressors.
6. Give potential protectors a just cause.
7. Make gays look good.
8. Make victimizers look bad.

The authors criticized one ad because "it showcases a couple that reinforces an unappealing stereotype—suggesting, perhaps, two leathery old dykes from tobacco road who bark at each other with gin-cracked voices, and who first met at a motorcycle roundup."[57] Another ad—this one showing two male sailors in uniform locked in an intimate kiss—the authors criticized because instead of "offering potential friends the ideal of Love as a just cause worth defending, this ad offers the ideal of Gay Lust, which isn't half so compelling or legitimate to straights. Overall, the ad's effect is not to desensitize, jam, or convert: it merely reinforces revulsion and inflames homohatred. Not recommended."[58] The authors liked an ad with a photo of a gay man smiling. The ad, captioned "Someone You'd Like to Know," was scored positively for employing the following strategy: "Strategy: *Conversion*. Compensate straights' lack of familiarity with gay people by presenting them with 'solid citizens'—likable individuals who defy uncomplimentary stereotypes. The interviewee talks about his conventional gay life in a relaxed, low-key, matter-of-fact way, undercutting several myths as he talks."[59]

The public relations strategy the authors proposed carefully avoided any explicit discussion of what sexual practices gays, lesbians, bisexuals, and transgender individuals actually want viewed as normal, for risk of offending a majority heterosexual audience by providing too much information. Instead, the authors merely advise against a list of rather explicitly discussed behaviors they characterize as "homosexual misbehaviors"—practices that range from aggressive homosexual sex displayed in public to openly practiced homosexual promiscuity involving multiple partners and seemingly little or no emotional attachment. "Self-indulgent, self-destructive behavior is lamentable enough when it occurs, so to speak, 'within the family,' but when Brother Gay trots out his unsavory shenanigans for the consumption of the general public, the rest of us are dragged down with him," the authors admonished.[60] But a successful public relations campaign professionally managed with the right messages properly delivered, the authors envisioned, could not only turn public opinion positive toward homosexuality but also prove lucrative in the process. "If the ads project a new, resolutely positive, all-American image with which most gays can identify, we think that, in no time, millions will be so eager to perpetuate these good works that they'll begin to donate money to our appeals on TV as though their social salvation depended on it. Which it does," the authors advised with great anticipation.[61]

The sexual revolution that began with Freud, advanced with Hugh Hefner and *Playboy* magazine in the 1950s, and was propelled by the 1960s revolutionaries and antiwar activists is nothing new in human history. Beyond the LGBT Project, what form of sexuality will the ACLU champion next? Are we to turn to the libertine practices of civilizations like ancient Greece and ancient Rome to debate the question of which sexual frontier the ACLU will next champion? In ancient Rome and Greece, pederasty was commonplace and polygamy rare. Yet what is the moral or legal basis on which the ACLU could argue that the LGBT agenda is a civil liberty, while denying that pederasts and polygamists do not have the right to openly profess and practice their sexual proclivities? In other words, if practices such as birth control and abortion on demand successfully separate sex from procreation, can there be any limit placed on a sexual practice that is deemed deviant?

If all sexual practices are argued to be equivalent behavior resulting from impulses tracing back to birth, then no sexual practice, regardless how extreme or bizarre, can be ruled to be learned or an aberration of human nature. This is the fundamental power of Freud and Marx. If God is merely an idea created by human beings, or if atheistic views are to prevail, then no God exists to set limits on acceptable human practices. If moral behavior is determined by allowing individuals with rights to engage in behavior those rights presume, then what moral bound is there to lust?

Why stop with the pedophilia agenda or the polygamist concept of family? If pederasts and polygamists have rights, then what about those who practice bestiality or necrophilia? On what basis would these behaviors be ruled out of bounds? How possibly can organizations like the ACLU argue that the rights of beasts or the rights of the dead are a sufficiently conflicting state interest justifying restraints on the sexual impulses of those so inclined to indulge in these particular lusts? Or will the ACLU argue the dead have sexual rights but unborn humans in the womb have no rights? In the final analysis, the pagan agenda provides no moral compass for regulating sexual preferences.

Now homosexuals have openly bragged that a cleverly crafted public relations campaign is a major reason the LGBT agenda is today increasingly being considered favorably. What prevents pederasts, pedophiles, polygamists, as well as those who practice bestiality and necrophilia, from designing public relations campaigns of their own? At a certain point, Kirk and Madsen are probably right that the public will tire of the entire discussion and simply give up, preferring to turn a blind eye to all forms of sexual behavior found distasteful. At that point, sexual behavior is reduced to being little more than a fashion, much like a change of clothes, with no moral implications left worth serious thought or contemplation.

Arguments deriving from moral relativism lose the ability to assert certain behaviors must be proscribed because those behaviors violate natural right. Unless moral relativists are willing to practice hypocrisy, they are bound by logic to see one form of sexual impulse as morally equivalent to another. The ACLU today struggles with the line between how far the organization is willing to go to support pedophilia or to oppose child pornography. This mirrors the progression in the ancient world from the time when heterosexuality was considered normal to the period when homosexuality was considered unobjectionable, to the era when pederasty was considered common. The problem is that following the logic of civil rights divorced from a concept of God and natural right, the ACLU loses the ability to draw logical moral lines in which this type of behavior is considered an acceptable if not approved civil liberty while that type of behavior is designated as aberrant, psychologically disturbed, or possibly even a crime.

The record shows that after attempting to redefine LGBT sexual relations as normal, the ACLU next undertook to defend the free speech rights of NAMBLA, the North American Man-Boy Love Association, an organization seeking to legalize consensual sex between adult men who engage in pederasty with underage boys.

One of the most controversial ACLU cases in recent years involved the ACLU supporting the First Amendment free speech rights of NAMBLA. The $200 million civil lawsuit claimed "educational" content on the group's website encouraged two pedophiles, Salvatore Sicari and Charles Jaynes, to commit the 1997 murder of ten-year-old Jeffrey Curley of Cambridge, Massachusetts. They were convicted and are serving life sentences for it.

The two men abducted Jeffrey while he was playing outside his home, luring him into their vehicle with the promise of a new bicycle. After a stop at a public library where they accessed NAMBLA's website, they proceeded to take the boy across state lines to New Hampshire, where Jaynes had an apartment. There, the two men attempted to sexually assault the young boy. When Jeffrey fought back, Sicari and Jaynes choked him to death with a gasoline-soaked cloth. Then they molested the body and later placed his corpse in a cement-filled container they threw into the Maine River.

In a wrongful death and civil rights lawsuit filed in the United States District Court for the District of Massachusetts, Jeffrey's parents sought to block NAMBLA from continuing to publish information encouraging sexual relations between men and boys, in the hope of stopping other pederasts from committing the type of gruesome murder their son suffered. According to the Curleys' suit, Jaynes was a member of NAMBLA, registered under an alias, at the time of the slaying. ABC News reported that the Curleys' lawsuit also alleged NAMBLA literature presenting techniques to seduce children sexually as well as techniques to avoid police investigations of pedophilia charges was found in Jaynes's car and apartment.[62]

The ACLU of Massachusetts entered the case on the side of NAMBLA. John Roberts, the executive director of the ACLU of Massachusetts, was reported saying, "There was nothing in those publications [of NAMBLA] or Web site which advocated or incited the commission of any illegal acts, including murder or rape. NAMBLA's publications advocate for changes in society's views about consensual sex between adults and minors. This advocacy is political speech protected by the First Amendment."[63] John Reinstein, the legal director of the ACLU of Massachusetts, added, "Regardless of whether people agree with or abhor NAMBLA's views, holding the organization responsible for crimes committed by others who read their materials would gravely endanger important First Amendment freedoms."[64]

NAMBLA is "not just publishing material that says it's OK to have sex with children and advocating changing the law," said Larry Frisoli, the Cambridge attorney who argued the case in federal court for Jeffrey Curley's parents.[65] The NAMBLA manual, Frisoli maintained, "is actively training their members how to rape children and get away with it. They distribute child pornography and trade live children among NAMBLA members with the purpose of having sex with them." As evidence for his accusations, Frisoli cited a NAMBLA publication *The Survival Manual: The Man's Guide to Staying Alive in Man-Boy Sexual Relations.* Frisoli characterized the publication as the Rape and Escape Manual, arguing, "Its chapters explain how to build relationships with children. How to gain the confidence of the children's parents. Where to go to have sex with children so as not to get caught. . . . There is advice, if one gets caught, on when to leave America and how to rip off credit card companies to get cash to finance your flight. It's pretty detailed." In his diary in 1996, one year before the murder of Jeffrey Curley, Jaynes wrote he had reservations about having sex with children until he discovered NAMBLA.[66]

In 2008, lawyers for Robert and Barbara Curley filed papers in US District Court ending their civil lawsuit against NAMBLA, after a judge ruled that the one witness who was prepared to testify that NAMBLA influenced Jaynes to commit rape and murder was not competent to testify. Susan R. Wunsch, a staff attorney for the ACLU of Massachusetts, told the *Boston Globe* the case never had merit. Wunsch conceded that Jaynes did belong to NAMBLA for a year before the murder, but she argued there was nothing illegal about the NAMBLA magazines Jaynes obtained. She further argued the NAMBLA magazines, which the Curly lawsuit alleged Jaynes viewed before the murder, were available in some bookstores and on the group's website. "There never was any evidence that NAMBLA was connected to the death of Jeffrey Curley," Wunsch told the newspaper. "It's been our view for the last eight years, it's been the First Amendment that's been the defendant in this case. In America, there's freedom to publish unpopular ideas, and that's what this case was about."[67]

When the controversy came to allowing an admitted homosexual into the Boy Scouts of America, the ACLU predictably opposed the Boy Scouts.

The US Supreme Court case, *Boy Scouts of America et al. v. Dale*, 530 U.S. 640 (2000), involved an adult, James Dale, who was thrown out of the Monmouth Council of the Boy Scouts of America in New Jersey because of his avowed homosexuality. Dale had distinguished himself as a member of the Boy Scouts, where he had been admitted to the Order of the Arrow honor camping society and earned the Eagle Scout badge, Scouting's highest honor that only 3 percent of all Boy Scouts achieve. He was fired as an assistant scoutmaster of the Matawan, New Jersey, troop in 1990, when he was twenty years old, after the *Newark Star-Ledger* profiled him in print as the copresident of the Gay and Lesbian Alliance at Rutgers University.[68] He filed suit against the Boy Scouts in 1992, after he applied for an adult leadership position with the Boy Scouts of America and was rejected in writing, with the Boy Scouts explaining to him that his homosexuality was contrary to the organization's values.[69]

The New Jersey Supreme Court upheld Dale's claim, arguing that New Jersey's public accommodations law applied to the Boy Scouts because of its broad-based membership solicitation and its connection with public entities. Given this, the New Jersey Supreme Court ruled the Boy Scouts violated New Jersey's public accommodations law by revoking Dale's membership based on his homosexuality.

The US Supreme Court reversed the ruling of the New Jersey Supreme Court by ruling that the New Jersey public accommodations law did not apply and that the Boy Scouts had a constitutional right under the First Amendment freedom of association to exclude gay members because opposition to homosexuality is part of the organization's message.[70] "We are not, as we must not be, guided by our views of whether the Boy Scouts' teachings with respect to homosexual conduct are right or wrong," wrote Chief Justice William Rehnquist, delivering the majority 5–4 decision of the court. "[P]ublic or judicial disapproval of a tenet of an organization's expression does not justify the State's effort to compel the organization to accept members where such acceptance would derogate from the organization's expressive message."[71]

The ACLU supported Dale by submitting an amicus brief to the Supreme Court on his behalf. Almost immediately after the Supreme Court announced its decision, the ACLU commented that the ruling "will have only a limited impact on civil rights nationwide." Characterizing the ruling as "damaging but limited," the ACLU emphasized that the decision would not apply very far beyond groups like the Boy Scouts. "Anti-gay groups did not get the 'free pass' they were looking for to dismantle civil rights laws that provide equal protection to lesbians and gay men," said Matt Coles, director of the ACLU Lesbian and Gay Rights Project. "This ruling is limited to groups that exist for the purpose of expressing views and ideas." The ACLU portrayed the Boy Scout opposition to homosexuality as a form of "identity discrimination," a term the ACLU has used in the LGBT agenda to mask the word *sexual* in arguing sexual discrimination should be the equivalent of racial discrimination, age discrimination, or gender discrimination. "The Court has essentially said that freedom of speech gives an organization the right to discriminate on the basis of an individual's identity, rather than a message that is in conflict with the group's views," Coles continued.[72]

Alan Sears, the CEO and general counsel of the Alliance Defending Freedom, formerly the Alliance Defense Fund—an organization established to counter the influence of the ACLU—and Craig Osten, a vice president of the Alliance Defending Freedom, disagreed with the ACLU on the importance of the *Boy Scouts v. Dale* case in their book *The Homosexual Agenda: Exposing the Principal Threat to Religious Freedom Today*. Sears and Osten argued that the case had ramifications for all private organizations, including churches, such that had the Supreme Court decided in favor of Dale, churches and other private organizations would have lost their right to determine their own criteria for leadership and related hiring practices: "Why? Because churches and religious organizations could also be subject to public accommodation laws like New Jersey's because they invite others from the general public to attend and join, just like the Boy Scouts," Sears and Osten wrote. "The only possible way for churches to avoid this would be to just let the members in and lock the door and leave those who need to hear the gospel out in the street."[73] Sears and Osten also pointed out that the Supreme Court decision set off a wave of protest from radical LGBT activists, including threats by sympathetic city and county governments to throw the Boy Scouts out of their public, tax-funded meeting places, and a round of booing from the delegates at the 2000 Democratic National Convention when the Boy Scouts presented their colors at the gathering.[74]

Contrasting the ACLU position in the case involving the murder of Jeffrey Curley and the exclusion of James Dale from the Boy Scouts leaves no doubt regarding the ideological position of the ACLU. The goal of the ACLU is to replace the notion that heterosexual relations between men and women are within God's order with the concept that sex among human beings is a malleable concept, and with the LGBT deserving equal constitutional protection as conventional marriage. President George W. Bush, in arguing for the necessity of a constitutional amendment to elevate the Defense of Marriage Act from congressional action to constitutional protection, argued that after more than two centuries of American jurisprudence and millennia of human experience, "a few judges and local authorities are presuming to change the most fundamental institution of civilization," namely, the family.[75]

The record shows the ACLU will protect the presumed First Amendment rights of the North American Man-Boy Love Association to publish an agenda that justifies pederasty—even if that means destroying the Boy Scouts of America, because the Boy Scouts refused to roll over and accept the ACLU's LGBT agenda.

7

THE FAR-LEFT
ACLU JUGGERNAUT

The ACLU has, in fact and in effect, been taken over by the hard left.

—MICHAEL MYERS, FORMER
ACLU BOARD MEMBER[1]

In a segment of *The O'Reilly Factor* broadcast in January 2006, Bill O'Reilly took on the ACLU, after the ACLU took out three attack full-page ads in the *New York Times*, charging that President George W. Bush broke the law with National Security Agency (NSA) phone taps and "is as bad as Richard Nixon."[2]

O'Reilly branded the ACLU as "the attack dog in the secular progressive jihad to change the culture and political landscape in America." His proof for that assertion was to document the "moneymen" behind the ACLU. The top ACLU donor, O'Reilly noted, has been "Far-Left businessman" Peter Lewis, the force behind Progressive Insurance, headquartered in Cleveland, Ohio, who has given the ACLU about $25 million since 2001—a sum

O'Reilly characterized as "a colossal amount of money." O'Reilly charged that Lewis "wants legalized drugs, a libertine society." Right behind Lewis is George Soros, who has donated more than $5 million to the ACLU since 2001. O'Reilly characterized Soros as "another Far-Left fanatic" and a "pal" of Lewis. As the primary funder behind MoveOn.org, Soros "routinely coordinates with the ACLU."[3]

The third in the triad singled out by O'Reilly as ACLU moneymen was Anthony Romero, "another Far-Left guy, who actively opposes most traditional beliefs." Romero was a Ford Foundation executive while that organization contributed some $7 million to the ACLU. Since 2001 Romero has served as the first openly gay executive director of the ACLU. O'Reilly drew the connection, arguing, "It's no surprise Romero is currently running the place." O'Reilly's conclusion was clear: "So when you combine Lewis and Soros and Romero, you have three radical Americans who are bent on changing this country. And all this nonsense about protecting rights is a ruse."[4]

Romero's credentials with the political Left in the United States are sterling. He worked for both the Rockefeller Foundation in addition to the Ford Foundation. In 2005, *Time* magazine named Romero one of the twenty-five most influential Hispanics in America. "Romero, 40, the ACLU's first Hispanic—and also its first openly gay—executive director, was raised in housing projects in the Bronx, N.Y.," noted *Time*. "Despite being U.S. citizens, his Puerto Rican parents labored under the sort of stigma illegal immigrants often face. In an era in which many immigrants feel besieged by the Patriot Act, Romero says his background gives him a special empathy. 'We bring who we are to our job,' he says. 'When you have seen prejudice, you understand that we aren't finished, that we're still perfecting this American experiment.'"[5]

Romero has had a rocky tenure as ACLU executive director. Around 1:00 a.m. on June 26, 2011, the East Hampton police arrested Romero on a DWI charge, after he was observed driving his 2005 convertible Mini Cooper erratically. Evidently another driver became so disgusted with Romero's slow and erratic driving that he called police on his cell phone.[6] The arresting officer reported that Romero "appeared drunk; his breath smelled of alcohol, his eyes were bloodshot and glassy, his speech was slurred and he was unsteady on his feet." Romero reportedly had to use his car for support to keep his balance when police asked him to step out of his car. He refused to perform field sobriety tests, including a breath test.[7] The *New York Post* reported that Romero had been celebrating the passage of New York's gay marriage law and he refused to take a Breathalyzer test because "his criminal defense attorney friends generally counseled against doing so."[8]

In a glowing article published in 2009, the *New York Times* had reported that Romero lives in Jersey City, but spends his weekends in the Hamptons. "I've got a little place on an old horse farm out there that's divided into a property association and about 30 or so cottages," Romero told the *Times*. "The fields are rented out to a polo player who has 15 horses, and in between coffee and brunch in the morning, I'll feed the horses, if they're out."[9] Attorney Wendy Kaminer, a dissident former ACLU national board member, writing in *The Atlantic*, noted that ACLU president Susan Herman informed the national board of Romero's DWI charge only after the *New York Post* reported the incident on August 10, weeks after it occurred.[10] Despite the DWI charge and his unwillingness to be forthright with ACLU management, Romero retained his position as ACLU executive director. Nor was there any indication his $329,206 annual salary[11] was reduced, either for his irresponsible behavior or for his failure to be forthright with the ACLU board regarding it. In the final analysis, Romero would not be dismissed, not as long as the ACLU money machine continued rolling along.

The ACLU operates two distinct operations: the American Civil Liberties Union, simply known as the ACLU, a 501(c)4 nonprofit organization that focuses on legislative lobbying; and the ACLU Foundation, a 501(c)(3) nonprofit organization that conducts the group's litigation activity.[12] Of the two, the ACLU Foundation is by far the greater, operating in 2010 on approximately $74.8 million revenue, compared to $30.8 million revenue for the ACLU.[13] Contributions to the ACLU 501(c)(4) are generally not tax deductible, whereas contributions to the ACLU Foundation 501(c) (3) are typically tax deductible. Unlike a 501(c)(3), a 501(c)(4) can support or oppose political candidates, provided that doing so is not the group's primary activity. The ACLU 501(c)(4) is a membership organization, and contributors have to be members to get an ACLU card.

ACLU supporters may contribute to one or both of the ACLU or the ACLU Foundation. The website for the ACLU of Pennsylvania, for instance, instructs the following: "Many donors choose to make their larger tax-deductible gifts to the ACLU Foundation, but also continue to make smaller gifts to the ACLU in order to maintain their 'card-carrying' membership status with the ACLU and to support our important lobbying efforts."[14] Since 2006, the ACLU has reported a membership of approximately five hundred thousand contributors.[15] Despite the importance of individual enrollment to the organization, the ACLU Foundation, the larger of the two ACLU organizational structures and the one most directly involved with litigation, relies primarily on large donors, in some years getting 60 percent or more of its funding from grants from wealthy individuals and foundations.

Since November 1952, the national ACLU has operated out of its head-quarters office in New York City. The ACLU operates one or more separate offices in each of the fifty states, plus Puerto Rico and the District of Columbia. Each state operates independently, as a separate ACLU chapter, with its own management and staff of attorneys. The state chapter revenues add considerably to the ACLU war chest, with large states favorable to the ACLU capable of adding millions to the national ACLU total fund-raising effort. For instance, in 2009–10, the ACLU Foundation of California, the 501(c)(3) litigation arm of the organization, reported operating income and expenses of approximately $7 million, while the ACLU of Northern California, the 501(c)(4) lobbying organization, reported operating income and expenses of $1.5 million.[16] While funding sources and amounts vary from chapter to chapter, about half the donations in the state chapters come from individual contributions, with the remainder being from large donations and grants, ACLU investments, and attorney fees that are awarded when the ACLU wins cases.[17] Approximately two hundred ACLU staff lawyers and thousands of volunteer attorneys handle ACLU litigation each year, making the ACLU clearly one of the largest legal advocacy groups in the country.

On September 15, 2010, the ACLU celebrated its ninetieth anniversary by announcing the organization had just completed its largest fund-raising in the group's history, an effort designated the Leading Freedom Forward campaign that gathered $407 million in contributions over the previous five years—a campaign that resulted in $150 million in cash gifts and $250 million in pledged gifts, including a $12 million contribution and an additional challenge grant from the George Soros–backed Open Society Foundation. To celebrate the victory, Peter Lewis sponsored a gala celebration on Ellis Island, and Mayor Bloomberg declared September 15 to be ACLU Day in honor of the milestone. The ACLU announced a major goal of the campaign was "to substantially increase the ACLU's grassroots presence and effectiveness from coast to coast by significantly increasing the programmatic and instructional capacity of its state affiliates."[18]

Critics of the ACLU, such as the American Civil Rights Union (ACRU), founded by California conservative Robert B. Carleson, speculated that the ACLU's goal in the Leading Freedom Forward campaign was to raise hundreds of millions of dollars to "threaten law suits, and file law suits, in towns and states where ACLU views are least popular. And in each case, it will seek attorneys [sic] fees and costs when it badgers a potential defendant into submission, or when it prevails in court."[19] The ACRU indicated that the ACLU planned to pump these funds into states where its fund-raising is not as successful. The ACLU press release announcing the success of the fundraising effort acknowledged that resources would go disproportionately to Florida, Texas, New Mexico, Montana, Mississippi, Michigan, Eastern Missouri, Tennessee, and Arizona. "The litigation is intended to pay for itself, by funds extracted from local and state taxpayers, either because the potential defendants cave under pressure, or because courts order such payments from public coffers," the ACRU critics concluded.[20]

Particularly objectionable to ACLU critics is the degree to which it uses federal law—particularly what is known as the Civil Rights Attorney Fees Act, Title 42 U.S.C. Chapter 21, Subchapter 1, Section 1988—to have taxpayers pay the attorneys' fees when the ACLU wins a case under the civil rights laws in state or federal courts.[21] ACLU critics, such as the American

Legion, have objected that the ACLU seeks and receives millions of dollars annually in taxpayer-paid attorneys' fees. In specific, at its national conventions in 2004 and 2006 the 2.7 million-member American Legion adopted Resolution 326, calling upon the US Congress to amend the Civil Rights Act to eliminate the authority of judges to award attorneys' fees to the ACLU.[22] The American Legion cited as objectionable the following examples:

- The ACLU received $940,000 in attorney fees when San Diego settled an ACLU lawsuit to drive the Boy Scouts out of Balboa Park.
- The ACLU received $500,000 in the famous Judge Roy Moore case demanding the removal of the Ten Commandments from his Alabama courthouse.
- Portland Public Schools were ordered to pay the ACLU $108,000 in a case brought by an atheist who objected to the Boy Scouts being allowed to recruit in public schools; additionally, Portland spent $232,000 defending the case.
- The ACLU has received in excess of $63,000 in attorney fees for its efforts to remove the Mojave Desert Veterans Memorial, a solitary Christian cross originally erected by veterans on what was then private land that in 1999, with legislation signed by President Clinton, was incorporated into the Mojave National Preserve.[23]

The American Legion points out that the ACLU collects from taxpayers attorneys' fees at $350/hour in civil rights cases the ACLU wins, even when the ACLU attorneys involved are volunteers who charge the ACLU no fees for their services.[24] The ACLU all too well appreciates that Section 1988 is the back door to an indirect tax subsidy the ACLU has learned to use as a club against towns, school boards, and local communities that dare to oppose in court the ACLU's radical agenda for transforming America into a godless society. As we saw in the previous chapter, that club wielded by the ACLU includes forcing towns, school boards, and local communities to accept an extreme sexual agenda that our Founding Fathers never would have imagined could be imposed on the God-loving America they thought they were creating.

In 1994, a group of prominent Christian leaders, including James Dobson, founder of Focus on the Family, and the late D. James Kennedy, founder of Coral Ridge Ministries, founded Alliance Defending Freedom (ADF), formerly the Alliance Defense Fund to create a legal advocacy group capable of confronting and defeating the godless ideological agenda of the ACLU. The 2010 IRS Form 990 filed by the ADF reveals it had total revenue in 2010 totaling $35 million.[25] As of 2011, the ADF employed a total of 139 full-time members at its Team Resource Center in Scottsdale, Arizona, and at its Regional Service Centers nationwide. As of 2011, the ADF employed 42 full-time attorneys, with more than 2,100 ADF-allied attorneys affiliated nationwide. The group's media guide points out that ADF-allied attorneys have been trained at or qualified for the ADF Legal Academy. As of December 2011, the ADF estimated that ADF-affiliated attorneys provided nearly $136 million in pro bono/dedicated legal service. More than 1,000 law students representing some 140 law schools have graduated from the ADF Blackstone Legal Fellowship, an in-depth summer internship program that "helps equip these students to assume leadership positions to shape the future of American law."[26]

Though the ACLU dwarfs the ADF in terms of the number of years in operation, the size of the group's annual revenue, and the number of attorneys on staff or available as volunteers, the ADF can still claim several important Supreme Court victories in its relatively short history:[27]

1. *Arizona Christian School Tuition Organization v. Winn*, 563 U.S. _____ (2011)

The US Supreme Court ruled that a group of "offended taxpayers" represented by the ACLU lacked standing in a case the ACLU intended to use to block tax revenue from going to religious schools. Specifically, the case involved an Arizona public school tuition tax credit that allows parents to choose the best educational option for their children, including allocating their tax credits to direct the state to award scholarships to religious schools.

"Today's decision ignores precedent, defies logic and undermines the role of the courts in preserving the core constitutional principle that government may not subsidize religion," said Steven R. Shapiro, legal director of the ACLU.[28]

Justice Elena Kagan, a liberal appointed to the Supreme Court by Barack Obama, dissented from the majority opinion of the Supreme Court, claiming the majority decision would diminish the meaning of the First Amendment's establishment clause. "Sometimes, no one other than taxpayers has suffered the injury necessary to challenge government sponsorship of religion," Kagan wrote, arguing that the offended Arizona taxpayers should have been granted standing to challenge the Arizona tax credit tuition plan.[29] "Today's holding therefore will prevent federal courts from determining whether some subsidies to sectarian organizations comport with our Constitution's guarantee of religious neutrality."[30] To support her argument, Kagan obviously could not document that the words *religious neutrality* appear anywhere in the Constitution or the First Amendment.

2. *Salazar v. Buono*, 559 U.S. _____ (2010)

The ADF declared "a major win" for America's World War I veterans and religious liberty, when the majority of the Supreme Court allowed a memorial cross to stand in the Mojave Desert in California. The ACLU represented Buono, a former Park Service employee who claimed to visit the Mojave Preserve on a regular basis, even after he left Park Service employment. One of the dissenting opinions was filed by Justice John Paul Stevens, joined by two of the Supreme Court's most liberal members—Justice Ruth Bader Ginsburg, formerly ACLU general counsel, and Obama appointee Sonia Sotomayor, the Supreme Court's first Hispanic justice. "A Latin cross necessarily symbolizes one of the most important tenets upon which believers in a benevolent Creator, as well as nonbelievers, are known to differ," Stevens wrote.[31] "In my view, the District Court was right to enforce its prior judgment by enjoining Congress' proposed remedy—a remedy that was engineered to leave the cross intact and that did not alter its basic meaning. I certainly agree that the Nation should memorialize the service of those who fought and died in World War I, but it cannot lawfully do so by continued endorsement of a starkly sectarian message."[32]

3. Gonzales v. Carhart, 550 U.S. 124 (2007)

The US Supreme Court, in a 5–4 decision, ruled the nationwide ban on partial-birth abortions imposed by the 2003 Partial-Birth Abortion Act does not violate the Constitution. Justice Anthony Kennedy, writing the majority decision, affirmed for perhaps the first time since *Roe v. Wade* that the "State's interest in promoting respect for human life at all stages in the pregnancy" could outweigh a woman's "exercise of the right to choose" whether or not she should have an abortion.[33] Expectedly, Justice Ginsburg voiced strong disagreement. "Retreating from prior rulings that abortion restrictions cannot be imposed absent an exception safeguarding a woman's health, the Court upholds an Act that surely would not survive under the close scrutiny that previously attended state-decreed limitations on a woman's reproductive choices," Ginsburg wrote in her dissent.[34] The ADL and the ACLU submitted amicus briefs to the Supreme Court in the case.

4. Van Orden v. Perry, 545 U.S. 677 (2005)

The US Supreme Court, in a 5–4 decision, upheld the constitutionality of a Ten Commandments display on the grounds of the Texas Capitol complex. The victory was muted in that on the same day, the Supreme Court also decided *McCreary County, Kentucky v. ACLU of Kentucky*, 545

U.S. 844 (2005), also a 5–4 decision, in which the Supreme Court held Ten Commandments displays in two Kentucky county courthouses were unconstitutional. The swing vote was Justice Stephen Breyer, who saw a distinction between the two cases. Four justices—Rehnquist, Scalia, Kennedy, and Thomas—would have upheld the displays in both cases; and four justices—Stevens, O'Connor, Souter, and Ginsburg—would have invalidated both displays.

Evidently, Justice Breyer was impressed that the Texas Ten Commandments monument had been there for forty years, while the Kentucky displays were of recent origin. Breyer also concluded that the Texas monument served a secular purpose, while the Kentucky displays had an expressly religious purpose.[35] "Here [on the Texas State Capitol grounds] the tablets have been used as part of a display that communicates not simply a religious message, but a secular message as well," Breyer wrote in his separate concurring opinion in *Van Orden v. Perry*. "The circumstances surrounding the display's placement on the capitol grounds and its physical setting suggest that the State itself intended the latter, nonreligious aspects of the tablets' message to predominate. And the monument's 40-year history on the Texas state grounds indicates that that has been its effect."[36]

5. Good News Club v. Milford Central Schools, 533 U.S. 98 (2001)

This case involved an ADF follow-up to a previous victory scored in the 1995 case *Rosenberger v. Rector and Visitors of the University of Virginia*, in which the US Supreme Court stopped discrimination and ordered equal access when a Christian university newspaper was denied funding provided other groups. Following the Rosenberger decision, the ADF launched its nationwide Equal Access Project, encouraging other school groups to organize for the expression of religious beliefs. In *Good News Club v. Milford Central Schools*, the US Supreme Court ruled that the sponsors of the Good News Club, a private Christian organization for children ages six to twelve, were denied their free speech rights under the First Amendment when the Milford Central School District in New York denied the group's request to hold the club's after-school meetings in the school. Milford had denied the request, arguing that the Good News Club had plans to sing religious songs, hear Bible lessons, memorize scripture, and pray, which constituted religious worship prohibited by the school district's community use purpose.

Justice Clarence Thomas, delivering the opinion of the court, ruled that denying the club the use of a "limited public forum" in the school facilities because the club's message was religious constituted viewpoint discrimination. He further held that the club's use of the school facilities did not violate the establishment clause because the club's activities "do not constitute mere religious worship, divorced from any teaching of moral values."[37] Milford had compromised its position by acknowledging in lower court proceedings that it would have allowed a group to use the facilities to present Aesop's fables to impart moral values to children and that it had allowed the Boy Scouts to use the facilities to foster the character development of young men. The ACLU filed an amicus brief in the case.

Supporters of the ACLU often point to the "trial" the ACLU board of directors held on the evening of May 7, 1940, at the City Club of New York, in which founding member and board member Elizabeth Gurley Flynn was thrown out of the ACLU for being a member of the Communist Party USA. Corliss Lamont, the radically leftist philosopher who served as an ACLU director from 1932 to 1954, published in 1968 a transcript of the proceedings in which he identified Roger Baldwin as the moving force behind Flynn's expulsion from the ACLU. Why did the ACLU change its mind on Flynn? "There were two major reasons," Lamont explained. "First, the Nazi-Soviet non-aggression pact in August, 1939, the outbreak of World War II in September and the Soviet invasion of Finland in November led to increasing tensions among Americans, and to renewed hostility towards the Soviet Union and Communists in general." He lamented that these factors created within the ACLU board an influential group that "was more interested in fighting *against* Communists than *for* civil liberties." The second reason was that the House Committee on Un-American Activities had alleged the ACLU was a Communist front organization.[38]

After Elizabeth Gurley Flynn was expelled, the ACLU passed the Resolution of 1940 that proclaimed it was inappropriate for anyone to serve on ACLU governing committees "who is a member of any political organization which supports totalitarian dictatorship in any country"; that is, the Communist Party. Historian Paul Kengor commented that Baldwin perhaps grew "tired of being misled and lied to—duped—by his own officers and 'liberal' 'friends.'" By the early 1950s, Baldwin required that all ACLU officers and board members take a non-Communist oath. "Baldwin came to see that any ACLU member who held allegiance to a totalitarian dictatorship could not truly be serious about civil liberties," Kengor wrote. "But Lamont and others—including I. F. Stone, several editors at *The Nation*, and several professors from Columbia—publicly objected to this attempted 'purge' by the ACLU."[39] Lamont ultimately resigned from the ACLU and worked with a competing organization, the National Emergency Civil Liberties Committee.[40]

What the ACLU actually accomplished was not to scrub the organization of Communists, but merely to require Communists operating within the organization to be more circumspect about their ideological leanings. Even after Flynn was expelled, Communists remained within the ACLU ranks. Notably, in the 1950s, Communist Party operative Frank Wilkinson, who in the 1950s was active in launching the National Committee to Abolish the House Committee on Un-American Activities, remained on the board of the Southern California ACLU. In the 1950s, Wilkinson, then a Los Angeles housing official, was jailed for refusing to tell the House Committee on Un-American Activities whether he was a Communist.[41] As late as 1997, the ACLU awarded Wilkinson the Earl Warren Civil Liberties Award.[42] Even today, the expulsion of Elizabeth Gurley Flynn remains very controversial within the ranks of the ACLU, with many agreeing with Lamont that the decision to expel Flynn was equivalent to the red-baiting blacklisting that the ACLU accused Senator Joe McCarthy of doing in the 1950s. In 1976, the ACLU reinstated Flynn posthumously.

It does not take much investigation to find causes that both the ACLU and the Communist Party USA openly support. The Occupy Wall Street movement that gained momentum in October 2011 is a good example. "As the Occupy Wall Street movement gains steam, the NYCLU [ACLU of New York] is standing beside the demonstrators and defending their right to speak their minds," Donna Lieberman, NYCLU executive director, proclaimed on the group's website. "Teams of NYCLU staff and volunteers regularly visit the movement's headquarters at Zuccotti Park to distribute our Know Your Rights information and engage the demonstrators on their experiences with the NYPD." Lieberman pledged to hold the police accountable for any misconduct.[43]

"I bring greetings and solidarity from the Communist Party," John Bachtell, an Illinois-based community organizer and Communist Party USA board member told the Occupy Chicago protest on Sunday, October 16, 2011. "We are here, marching side-by-side. We'll sleep here. We'll be with this movement 'til the very—'til we make all the changes that we know we have to make."[44]

The Communist Party USA itself warmly embraced Occupy Wall Street. "We greet the Occupy Wall St. movement as it spreads throughout our country from large cities to small towns, led by youth and joined by people of all ages and backgrounds, giving voice to deep anger at extreme economic inequality," the Communist Party USA website proclaimed. "The time has come to put people before profits."[45]

Interestingly, the ACLU did not offer to support the free speech or assembly rights of the Tea Party movement, and the Communist Party USA did not endorse Tea Party political goals and motivations. The Occupy Wall Street movement is squarely anticapitalist, arguing for redistribution of income, expanded government, and redistribution of economic power in favor of workers and unions. Not surprisingly, these themes are nothing more than hard-line Communist objectives, worked over with liberal Democratic public relations rebranding.

The transformation of the ACLU from an openly Communist organization to an organization that secretly advanced the Communist agenda
was made primarily for public relations purposes. Fundamentally, the
Communists within the ACLU who morphed into progressives and liberal
Democrats never abandoned the class warfare fundamental to Marx and
Lenin. Hijacking the progressivism of a Teddy Roosevelt from its populist
roots, the Communists in the ACLU early on found they could advance
their revolutionary goals faster and more effectively by simply appearing to
champion civil liberties, instead of openly proclaiming the atheistic materialism at the core of its revolutionary class-warfare beliefs.

Perhaps no one issued the warning more clearly than W. Cleon Skousen
in his 1958 book *The Naked Communist*. Beginning with an embrace of science, the Far-Left could advance its materialistic atheism with an urbane
sophistication designed to make Bible-reading Christians and Jews look out-
of-date and old-fashioned. The following two paragraphs from that book
shows Skousen clearly understood that communism, by its very nature, was
always the enemy of religion:

> The strategy of the materialists was to appropriate to themselves the
> toga of "science" and to take credit for all scientific accomplishments.
> Then they determined to ridicule and rationalize away all of the things
> which they opposed by pronouncing them "unscientific." Thus they
> attacked the Bible, called themselves higher critics, and attempted to
> explain it away. They explained the worship of God as being merely the
> effort of man to project the qualities of his own better nature into some
> fictitious superior being. They called Jesus Christ an itinerant preacher
> whose life and writings were effeminate and weak. They ridiculed the
> possibility of resurrection. They denied the immortality of human life
> or the existence of the spirit or soul.
>
> They said that man was nothing but a graduate beast and that
> human life—especially the other man's life—was no more sacred than

that of a centipede, a caterpillar, or a pig. As Marx and Engels boasted in their *Manifesto*: Our program "abolishes eternal truths; it abolishes all religion and all morality . . . it therefore acts in contradiction to all past historical experience."[46]

Skousen warned that a major premise of communism is *"that all religion must be overthrown because it inhibits the spirit of world revolution."*[47] He cautioned that the founders of communism "were not satisfied to have their disciples merely ignore religion." Instead, Communists felt it was "highly essential that religion be methodically replaced with militant atheism."[48] So, the Scopes trial was not incidental to the growth and development of the ACLU. The attack that Clarence Darrow launched on William Jennings Bryan and the Bible was central to the objectives of the Communists founding the organization. So, too, the determination of the ACLU to remove God from the public schools and to create a godless public square is not a strategy the ACLU has pursued to expand civil liberties in America; instead, the War on God waged by the ACLU is a war the ACLU had to win if the organization was to have any chance of realizing the Communist dreams of its founders. The atheism at the core of the theory of evolution is the same atheism at the center of the ACLU's secret goal to belittle God in America, with the goal of replacing Judeo-Christian morality and religious beliefs with the moral relativism and pagan sexuality at the heart of the LGBT agenda.

William Z. Foster, examined in an earlier chapter as a founding member of both the Communist Party USA and the ACLU, expressed his open embrace of communism in his 1932 book *Toward Soviet America* and in his 1951 book *Outline Political History of the Americas*.[49] In chapter 6 of the 1951 book, Foster described the church in the American colonies not in terms of a faith that drove the vision of our Founding Fathers to create a constitutional republic designed to preserve unalienable rights granted by God, but in class warfare terms—as a coconspirator with the European ruling classes that sought to exploit the wealth of the Western Hemisphere and oppress the colonialists in the process. "The Church, in both its Protestant and Catholic phases, was part and parcel of the European ruling classes that set out to conquer, rule, and exploit the western hemisphere and its peoples," Foster wrote. "The special role of the Church, in all its sections, in the conquest and exploitation of the colonial Americas, was twofold: first, it provided a moral and religious cover for the many barbarities that were committed in the course of the whole life of the colonies; and, second, it paralyzed the resistance of the people by capturing their minds with a benumbing ruling-class-inspired religion."[50]

Skousen warned that Communists would not advance their ideology openly. Instead, Communists would take the stealth route, presenting themselves to the American public as "progressives" and liberal Democrats—populists rather than Socialists. "But how many Americans would recognize a Communist without his label?" Skousen asked.[51] His answer, unfortunately, was that few Americans would be able to see Communists for who they truly are. "We are fighting for freedom but allowing some of our boys and girls to grow up believing in things which turn out to be Communist concepts."[52] His greatest concern was that the Communist stealth agenda would ultimately succeed. "Without his ever knowing it, a young American is thereby trained to be a potential Red ally." This, Skousen characterized as "the great secret weapon of Communism."[53]

Fundamentally, Skousen devoted much of his adult career to exposing communism for the lie it is:

> It is interesting, however, that the economics of Communism are primarily for propaganda purposes. The idea of sharing the wealth appeals to the masses. However, when the Communists took over in Russia you will recall that the first thing they did was impose upon the Russian people a form of economics which we got rid of back in the feudal days. It is a system where a privileged few dispense the necessities of life to the serfs who work for them and rely upon them for protection and leadership.[54]

More than half a century ago, Skousen was prescient about where the United States would be today. In *The Naked Communist*, he detailed the stealth agenda he expected Communists would pursue:

- "Get control of the schools."
- "Use them as transmission belts for socialism and current Communist propaganda."
- "Soften the curriculum."
- "Get control of teachers' associations."
- "Put the party line in textbooks."
- "Eliminate all laws governing obscenity by calling them 'censorship' and a violation of free speech and free press."
- "Break down cultural standards of morality by promoting pornography and obscenity in books, magazines, motion pictures, radio, and TV."
- "Present homosexuality, degeneracy and promiscuity as 'normal, natural, healthy.'"
- " Infiltrate the churches and replace revealed religion with 'social' religion."
- "Discredit the Bible and emphasize the need for intellectual maturity which does not need 'a religious crutch.'"
- "Eliminate prayer or any phase of religious expression in the schools on the ground that it violates the principle of 'separation of church and state.'"
- "Discredit the American Constitution by calling it inadequate, old-fashioned, out of step with modern needs, a hindrance to cooperation between nations on a worldwide basis."
- "Discredit the American Founding Fathers. Present them as selfish aristocrats who had no concern for the 'common man.'"
- "Discredit the family as an institution."
- "Encourage promiscuity and easy divorce."
- "Emphasize the need to raise children away from the negative influence of parents."
- "Attribute prejudices, mental blocks and retarding of children to suppressive influence of parents."[55]

Read today, this list looks remarkably like a summary of the ideological agenda the ACLU has pursued since the *Everson* decision in 1947.

"The ACLU is flush with money," former ACLU board member Michael Myers told Fox News host Bill O'Reilly on his show on January 6, 2006. "It has a lot of money, and not just from Peter B. Lewis and not just from George Soros. It has a lot of money."[56]

Being flush with cash is not necessarily an advantage for the organization, according to Myers. "It's all about fundraising, and the lefty loony agenda of Anthony Romero, its term executive director," Myers told O'Reilly's audience. "The ACLU has, in fact and effect, been taken over by the hard left."[57]

"So there you have it, ladies and gentlemen," O'Reilly summarized the interview with Myers. "The ACLU is no longer about liberties, or the Constitution, or the regular folks. It is about imposing a radical agenda on America. And you can take that to the bank."[58]

The controversy over ACLU fund-raising techniques dates back to July 31, 2004, when Adam Liptak reported in the *New York Times* that Anthony Romero, with the full knowledge or approval of the ACLU board, registered the ACLU for a federal charity drive that required the ACLU to certify in writing that the organization would not knowingly employ people who were on government watch lists, including the government's no-fly terrorist watch list.[59] "We oppose 'no fly' lists," ACLU board member Michael Myers told the newspaper. "Now we have a 'no hire' list that we've signed onto. We're in the midst of an organizational cultural crisis of enormous size."[60] For many leftist supporters of the ACLU, Romero's decision brought back what had become ugly memories of the decision by the ACLU to kick Elizabeth Gurley Flynn off the board because she was a member of the Communist Party USA and to institute what amounted to a "loyalty oath" demanding board members to pledge they did not belong to any organization that espoused or otherwise supported totalitarian government.

Romero affirmed to the *New York Times* that he had signed an agreement with the US government that the ACLU would not knowingly employ individuals or contribute funds to organizations found on lists created by the federal government, the United Nations, and the European Union. The certification Romero signed specifically referred to three lists maintained by the Justice, State, and Treasury Departments, including one called for by the Patriot Act, the antiterrorism law the ACLU had previously opposed. The *New York Times* further quoted Mara T. Patermaster, director of the charity program run by the Office of Personnel Management, the federal government's human resources office. Patermaster explained that Romero could not simply use as a defense that he and the ACLU intended to ignore the lists. "We expect that the charities will take affirmative action to make sure they are not supporting terrorist activities," she said. "That would specifically include inspecting the lists. To just sign a certification without corroboration would be a false certification." The *Times* reported that the Combined Federal Campaign, a charity drive for federal employees and military personnel, raised a total of $250 million in 2003, and that the ACLU had received some $470,000 from the program in that year.[61]

On August 1, 2004, the day after Liptak's article appeared in the *New York Times*, the ACLU withdrew from the federal charity drive, foregoing the $500,000 the group had expected to receive from the program in 2004. Backtracking, Romero told the newspaper the ACLU would not have signed the funding agreement "if we thought we had to check our employment records against a government blacklist."[62]

The controversy over Romero's eagerness to raise funds reached new heights when, on December 18, 2004, Stephanie Strom published another exposé on the ACLU in the *New York Times*. Strom revealed that the ACLU was using sophisticated computer technology to collect a wide range of information about its members and donors, and that this fund-raising aggressiveness had ignited a bitter debate within the ACLU management hierarchy.[63] Daniel S. Lowman, vice president for analytical services at Grenzebach Glier & Associates, a Chicago-based firm specializing in providing philanthropic management consulting, was using Prospect Explorer software, a sophisticated neural network analysis tool, to compile background information on members and donors, including estimates of each individual's net worth and assets, holdings in public corporations, and history of contributions to philanthropic interests.

Strom quoted Wendy Kaminer, then an ACLU board member, on her concerns. "It is part of the A.C.L.U.'s mandate, part of its mission, to protect privacy," Kaminer told the newspaper. "It goes against A.C.L.U. values to engage in data-mining on people without informing them. It's not illegal, but it is a violation of our values. It is hypocrisy." Michael Myers was equally incensed. "If I give the A.C.L.U. $20, I have not given them permission to investigate my partners, who I'm married to, what they do, what my real estate holdings are, what my wealth is, and who else I give my money to," Myers said.[64]

The newspaper further reported that the ACLU's fund-raising methodology had drawn the interest of the New York attorney general, who had begun investigating whether the ACLU had violated promises to protect the privacy of members and donors. Evidently, then New York attorney general Eliot Spitzer addressed a letter to Romero, informing the ACLU that his office was conducting an inquiry into the matter. The *New York Times* article also revealed that Romero had advised the Ford Foundation, his former employer, to follow the Patriot Act in composing language for its grant agreements, in an effort to make sure that none of its money inadvertently ended up underwriting terrorist activities. The ACLU, the newspaper disclosed, had accepted sixty-eight thousand dollars from the Ford Foundation under these terms. The ACLU board voted in October 2004 to return the money and to reject further grants from the Ford Foundation and the Rockefeller Foundation, which evidently used similar language in grant agreements.[65]

In September 2006, a group of more than thirty longtime donors, former board and staff members, and lawyers who had come together to form a new organization, Save the ACLU, began pressing for the ouster of the group's leaders. "It's a home for A.C.L.U. loyalists who have been shut out of the organization," Ira Glasser, the executive director of the ACLU for twenty-three years (1978–2001), told the *New York Times*.[66] "We're a protest group, trying to get the board to exercise its fiduciary and governing responsibility in a way that it has not. We're loyal to the existing organization and above all to the principles it is intended to advance." ACLU spokesperson Emily Whitfield defended the organization by pointing to the organization's growth under the leadership of Anthony Romero: "Our programs, both legal and legislative, have never been stronger. And then there's the phenomenal growth of the A.C.L.U., where we've nearly doubled our staff, our revenues are higher, membership and donations are higher, and that, to us, tell us where we are right now, in terms of our organization. We're proud of it."[67]

Glasser's criticism was particularly troubling, since as ACLU executive director, Glasser had handpicked Romero to be his successor. "He's totally ill-suited for this job," Glasser told *New York* magazine reporter David France in February 2007. "He lies, and he covers up for his lies. Anybody who tries to call him on this, he threatens and attacks personally. He's got some of his own board members scared of retaliation against them or their local affiliates. And the rest of the board is suffering from some sort of willful blindness." Glasser rejected Whitfield's suggestion that Romero's faults should be overlooked because he had been successful in growing the organization rapidly. "If people stop paying attention to us because they think we're hypocrites, five years from now the organization—I don't care if it's five times as big—won't be as effective as it was half as big," Glasser said.[68]

After Wendy Kaminer left the ACLU board in 2009, she wrote a scathing book-length attack of the organization under Romero's leadership, *Worst Instincts: Cowardice, Conformity, and the ACLU*.[69] "Eventually, at the ACLU, money became less a temptation than a mark of success, and even rectitude," she wrote. "How could the ACLU be wrong if it was getting rich?"[70] Kaminer was offended not only that by agreeing to the watch lists, Romero had agreed to limit advocacy speech but also that Romero had signed the agreements with the federal charity program and the Ford Foundation without informing the ACLU board of his decision to do so. "Imagine the pope endorsing abortion rights," Kaminer said in disdain. "Imagine the head of the NRA secretly supporting a prohibition on handguns or the head of a gay-rights group quietly opposing gay marriage. Romero's covert approval of the watch lists was a similar betrayal—which the board declined to condemn, or when given the chance, immediately correct."[71]

Her ultimate judgment on ACLU hypocrisy regarding case selection under Romero was equally harsh: "Once the nation's leading civil liberties group and reliable defender of everyone's speech rights, the ACLU is becoming just another human-rights, social-justice advocate that reliably defends the rights of liberal speakers."[72]

In driving this point home, Kaminer has noted the hypocrisy of the ACLU in refusing to defend a high-school student's right to wear a T-shirt condemning homosexuality, while paying particular attention to cases in which it represented students wearing pro-gay—as well as anti-Bush—T-shirts. The Alliance Defending Freedom—not the ACLU—represented Tyler Chase Harper, the high-school student who was disciplined in 2004 for wearing a T-shirt declaring his religious objections to homosexuality, when he sued the school district. Kaminer lamented the judge's decision in the Harper case. "In a patronizing, anti-libertarian decision in which Judge Stephen Reinhardt stressed the imagined feelings of gay students, the Ninth Circuit rejected Harper's First Amendment claims." The ACLU, Kaminer noted, was reluctant to support Harper strictly because of the content of his speech. "Despite its professed commitment to religious liberty, for example, the ACLU tends to absent itself from cases on college campuses involving the associational rights of Christian school groups to discriminate against gay students, in accordance with their rights."[73]

In the final analysis, Kaminer criticized the ACLU for engaging in a hypocritical pursuit of money in order to prosecute a one-sided Far-Left agenda. She charged the ACLU engaged in this hypocrisy even when the fund-raising activity violated ACLU fundamental principles and necessitated a public relations campaign to cover up the abuse. Curiously, Kaminer's attack on the ACLU from the political Left sounded remarkably like Bill O'Reilly's attack on the ACLU from the political Right. "Of course the ACLU hasn't definitively abandoned its defense of speech,"

Kaminer concluded. "Large, national organizations change incrementally. But people should no longer depend on the ACLU to defend what they preach (especially at a cost), if it disapproves of what they practice."[74]

In October 2011, the Obama administration cut funding for a Catholic Church campaign against human trafficking reportedly because the US Conference of Catholic Bishops refused to fund abortions.

Sister Mary Ann Walsh, director of media relations for the US Conference of Catholic Bishops, said in a press release there "was no reason" given by the Department of Health and Human Services for rejecting the conference's application for a new grant at the end of September 2011. She also said the bishops' Migration and Refugee Services work had been "well regarded." Yet in a letter to the US Catholic hierarchy addressed September 29, 2011, New York then archbishop (now cardinal) Timothy M. Dolan, president of the US Conference of Catholic Bishops, warned the Obama administration was "requiring that Migration and Refugee Services provide the 'full range of reproductive services' to trafficking victims and unaccompanied minors in its cooperative agreements and government contracts." Dolan indicated that the "full range of reproductive services" was a veiled reference to contraception and abortion. Dolan further noted the new federal government followed "exactly the position urged by the American Civil Liberties Union (ACLU) in the ongoing lawsuit challenging the constitutionality of MRS's [Migration and Refugee Services'] contracts."[75]

The controversy dates back to 2009, when the ACLU of Massachusetts sued the US Conference of Catholic Bishops, claiming that federal funding through the Trafficking Victims Protection Act to the Catholic group was unconstitutional because the group would not aid or refer program participants for services, such as contraception and abortion, that violate church teachings. "Human trafficking is basically a form of modern-day slavery," said Brigitte Amiri, staff attorney with the ACLU Reproductive Freedom Project, in a 2009 ACLU press release.[76] "There are many organizations that are deeply committed to assisting trafficking victims; our government should ensure that these organizations can provide the full range of needed services, including reproductive health care." The ACLU press release indicated the federal government distributes funds through the Trafficking Victims Protection Act to cover the needs of more than fourteen thousand individuals, mainly women, who are brought into the United States annually and are exploited for their labor, predominantly in the commercial sex industry. The ACLU press release also stressed that many trafficking victims experience extreme violence and sexual assault at the hands of the traffickers, while some become pregnant as a result of rape, and others contract sexually transmitted diseases.

"For more than two years, the Bush administration has sanctioned the United States Conference of Catholic Bishops' blatant misuse of taxpayer dollars," said Daniel Mach, director of litigation for the ACLU Program on Freedom of Religion and Belief, in the 2009 ACLU press release.[77] Since 2006, Health and Human Services had awarded the US Conference of Catholic Bishops grants ranging from $2.5 million to $3.5 million under the Trafficking Victims Protection Act. "We are asking the court to stop this misuse of taxpayer dollars to protect the health and safety of trafficking victims," said Sarah Wunsch, staff attorney with the ACLU of Massachusetts. "Trafficking victims need comprehensive and compassionate care to gain their freedom and lead safe and healthy lives."[78]

Sister Mary Ann Walsh objected to the HHS decision to cut funding, saying the decision was unfair, demanding that the group had a right to know how the decision was made. "The contract pointed out that 'preference' would be given to those who offer 'the full range of legally permissible gynecological and obstetric care,' which is a codeword for artificial contraception, sterilization and abortion," Walsh told a reporter for CNSNews.com. Walsh suggested the HHS decision was a direct attack on the religious beliefs of the US Conference of Catholic Bishops. She pointed out that the group's Migrant and Refugee Services had worked with 163 organizations ranging from the Salvation Army to the YMCA to Lutheran family service to help more than 2,700 victims.[79] The ACLU of

Massachusetts lawsuit against the US Conference of Catholic Bishops has yet to be decided by the federal courts.

In response to the HHS decision, Archbishop Dolan formed the Ad Hoc Committee for Religious Liberty,[80] citing some Obama administration policy decisions and the passage of a gay marriage law in New York, measures aimed at restricting religious freedom.[81] Dolan charged:

1. The Department of Health and Human Services (HHS) is seeking to force private health care providers to carry contraceptive and sterilization services.

2. HHS wants to force the USCCB's Migration and Refugee Services to provide "the full range of reproductive services."

3. The federal government is seeking to force international relief programs to offer reproductive health services.

4. The Department of Justice is attacking the Defense of Marriage Act, arguing that support for marriage as existing between one man and one woman is a form of bigotry.

5. The Justice Department is attacking a religious liberty known as the "ministerial exception"; it insulates religious employers from state encroachment.

6. New York State recently legalized gay marriage, providing a very narrow religious exemption.

"This is welcome news," Catholic League president William Donohue said. "Our bishops are preparing for war." Donohue noted the Obama administration intends to utilize its rigid pro-abortion policy as a means of damaging the Catholic Church financially.[82] In his book *Twilight of Liberty: The Legacy of the ACLU*, Donohue argued that the ACLU has also pursued a policy of seeking to strip the Catholic Church of its tax exemption.[83] Donohue further noted that the ACLU has argued that allowing the Catholic Church to maintain its tax exemption allows the church to follow political policy objectives, such as condemning abortion, with an unfair advantage. Donohue said that the Obama administration—unable to remove the Catholic Church's tax-exempt status—has now sought to punish the Catholic Church financially because it refuses to bow to the Obama administration's determination to provide federal funding for what amounts to abortion on demand. In so saying, Donohue implied the ACLU in this instance is acting as little more than a legal operative for the Obama administration.[84]

In 1970, in *Walz v. Tax Commission of the City of New York*, 397 U.S. 664 (1970), the US Supreme Court upheld the constitutionality of tax exemptions granted to religious organizations under the establishment clause of the First Amendment. Yet the protection is not absolute. A church can lose its tax exemption if the courts find the church has crossed the line into political advocacy by lobbying activities. The ACLU filed an amicus brief in the case, arguing the grant of property tax exemptions to religious organizations for religious purposes is a violation of the establishment clause of the First Amendment.[85]

Removing the tax-favored status of churches is the last bastion in the battle that atheists have waged for decades to separate church and state. None less than Madalyn Murray O'Hair realized the importance of money to winning the war she waged against God. A pauper before her Supreme Court victory, Madalyn became wealthy writing books, going on TV and radio talk shows—she was the first guest Phil Donahue had on his television show in the 1970s—and touring the nation, all the while making sure her audience knew the post office box where checks could be sent. Immediately after her Supreme Court case removing Bible reading from the public schools, Madalyn ordered her lawyer to sue the city of Baltimore—her residence and the location of the public schools she'd sued in *Murray v. Curlett*—to prevent Baltimore from exempting churches from property and other taxes.[86]

In 1968, speaking on her radio show about the New York City decision to impose property taxes on churches, Madalyn was enthusiastic. "New

York City Budget Director Frederick O'R. Hayes and Mayor Lindsay are both now stating that for the first time in the history of New York, taxes will be applied against—hold on to your pews—churches, synagogues, and other religious institutions," she told her listeners. "Why not put the churches on a free enterprise system and let them pay full taxes wherever they practice?"[87]

Madalyn lost her case, *Murray v. Goldstein* (1963), but the setback did not reduce her determination to attack the tax preferences she saw as a public subsidy for religion. As noted previously, in 1970, the Supreme Court addressed the issue in *Walz v. Tax Commission of the City of New York,* 397 U.S. 664 (1970). Still wanting to speak her mind, Madalyn filed an amicus brief to the Supreme Court in *Walz.* In that case, the Supreme Court held that tax exemptions do not violate the establishment clause of the First Amendment. Undaunted by the ruling, Madalyn and her husband, Richard O'Hair, in 1970 formed their own church, Poor Richard's Universal Life Church. The Associated Press quoted Madalyn and Richard at the press conference launching their church as admitting they had organized the church for tax purposes. "From here on," Madalyn told the press, "we're going to take every exemption. We are not going to pay any taxes on telephones. We're not going to pay any tax on our airline tickets. We're going to operate just as all churches do. . . . Now the churches have told us a million times over and so has the federal government that atheism is a religion so we're going to accept this."[88]

The ACLU is a Far-Left juggernaut precisely because the organization is well funded. None less than Madalyn Murray O'Hair understood the final battle over the future of Jewish synagogues and Christian churches in America could well be fought over tax status. The ACLU can be expected to fight hard to remove any and all tax advantages that Judeo-Christian religious groups and organizations yet maintain because the ACLU realizes legal battles are frequently won or lost as a function of the financial resources available to the litigants. That the preservation of religious freedom for Judeo-Christian faith organizations may come down to a matter of money shows how far from the original intent of the Founding Fathers the United States has come as a nation. The Founding Fathers intended the First Amendment to establish religious freedom in America as sacrosanct—not vulnerable to legal attack by any person or organization, regardless how well funded. Today, the ACLU is free to wage its War on God, knowing the ACLU has the financial advantage. Today in an America where the ACLU can be expected to appear in court at least with an amicus brief supporting any plaintiff who attacks Judeo-Christian religious freedom in court, the importance of money in defense of God is a reality Judeo-Christian faith groups and their supporters cannot afford to ignore. Fortunately, many groups are coming on the scene, fighting side-by-side with the Alliance Defending Freedom. Among the groups that are joining the battle are the American Center for Law and Justice, the Pacific Justice Institute, and the Liberty Institute. Turning the tide against the ACLU will not be easy, but with leadership that is emerging, turning the tide is now beginning to appear possible.

Conclusion

GOD FIGHTS BACK

At such a time in history, we who are free must proclaim
anew our faith. This faith is the abiding creed of our
fathers. It is our faith in the deathless dignity of man,
governed by eternal moral and natural laws.

—PRESIDENT DWIGHT D. EISENHOWER, INAUGURAL ADDRESS[1]

We conclude the book as we began it—with the conviction that God did not inspire our Founding Fathers to create the United States as a land of religious freedom, only to see subsequent generations squander away that precious religious freedom because a group of politically motivated lawyers funded by the ACLU fought nearly unopposed a sophisticated, ideological War on God. The only way the ACLU will win victory in its War on God is if warriors for God fail to engage to defend their right to live and profess their religious and moral views openly. For decades, the Bad Samaritan of the ACLU has beaten and robbed the First Amendment's statement of religious freedom to the point that Judeo-Christian believers have been left lying by the side of the road, as if abandoned to die. Americans were bequeathed "a land of the free and a home of the brave" by our forefathers, who founded this nation as a refuge where those wishing to profess openly their faith in God could do so without fear. It is time for Judeo-Christian Good Samaritans to come forward to defend our faith and reestablish the open presence of God in our lives, our schools, and our communities. The point of this book is that the hour is late, but the battle is not yet lost.

"The ACLU's attempt to silence religious expression over the years has known no rational bounds," wrote Alan Sears and Craig Osten, two of the guiding lights behind the Alliance Defending Freedom. "The climate of fear and intimidation that has been created through its systematic attacks on people of faith has grown to such an extent that many public officials have developed a knee-jerk response to anything 'religious.'"[2] Having won key decisions regarding prayer in the schools and the presence of God in the public arena, the ACLU has made the sexual agenda its cutting-edge battlefield. If the ACLU wins its War on God, our founding documents— including the Declaration of Independence, the Constitution, and the Bill of Rights—will not be worth the parchment on which they were written.

What type of world does the ACLU envision for the future of America? "Our precious freedoms—of speech, at least public religious speech, of association, of worship, of living our faith—will have all but vanished," Sears and Osten caution. "The ACLU's vision of freedom—the public sale and prime-time display of hard-core pornography; the legalization of child pornography, public profanity and blasphemy; the redefinition, and per-haps abolition, of marriage; the silencing of the church and ministries on moral issues such as homosexual behavior; and legalized, unlimited abor-tion and euthanasia—will be manifest."[3]

For decades the ACLU appeared in court alone, to advance its godless agenda without serious challenge. But today, thanks to the faith groups that founded advocates for God in court, the ACLU can no longer expect to show up in court unopposed. We must be committed to opposing the ACLU's godless agenda at every court case of significance, dogging the ACLU even when the ACLU tries to bully a town, county, pastor, or church into submission, just by the threat of legal action. Even though groups like the Alliance Defending Freedom, the American Center for Law and Justice, the Pacific Institute, and other groups are relatively new organizations and small by the standards of the ACLU staff and balance sheet, legal advocates for God can demand their day in court to argue for a Judeo-Christian view of the First Amendment. With the legal advocates for God now on the scene, God need no longer lack legal representation in court.

On January 14, 1988, President Ronald Reagan issued a proclamation articulating the concept of personhood, a concept designed to fight back the pro-abortion forces behind *Roe v. Wade.*

Eloquently, Reagan reminded America that among the unalienable rights affirmed by the Declaration of Independence is the right to life. "That right to life belongs equally to babies in the womb, babies born handicapped, and the elderly or infirm," Reagan proclaimed. "That we have killed the unborn for 15 years does not nullify this right, nor could any numbers of killings do so." Then Reagan importantly tied the concept of personhood for the unborn to the Fifth and Fourteenth Amendments. "The unalienable right to life is found not only in the Declaration of Independence but also in the Constitution that every President is sworn to preserve, protect, and defend," he pointed out. "Both the Fifth and Fourteenth Amendments guarantee that no person shall be deprived of life without due process of law."[4]

By so framing the concept of personhood, Reagan fully realized he was building a legal defense for the unborn that ultimately could and should prevail at the Supreme Court. The Fifth Amendment specifically states that no person shall be deprived of life, liberty, or property, without due process of law; the Fourteenth Amendment specifically extends the Fifth Amendment to the states by specifying that "nor shall any State deprive any person of life, liberty, or property, without due process of law." Ronald Reagan knew the precise legal impact of his strategy, when he declared:

> Now, therefore, I, Ronald Reagan, President of the United States of America, by virtue of the authority vested in me by the Constitution

and the laws of the United States, do hereby proclaim and declare the unalienable personhood of every American, from the moment of conception until natural death, and I do proclaim, ordain, and declare that I will take care that the Constitution and laws of the United States are faithfully executed for the protection of America's unborn children.[5]

The importance of this tactic cannot be overestimated. The majority of the court in deciding that abortion was constitutional relied in *Roe v. Wade* on a "right to privacy" that included a woman's right to terminate her pregnancy, even though that right is nowhere specified in the Constitution. In direct contrast, as President Reagan pointed out, the right to life is articulated in the Declaration of Independence, such that the right to life can safely be presumed to be fundamental to the unalienable, God-given rights our founding documents were crafted to protect. Once the unborn are considered "persons" within the meaning of the Declaration of Independence, the Fifth Amendment, and the Fourteenth Amendment, the only possible conclusion is that abortion must be outlawed as unconstitutional. Once the unborn are considered "persons" within the meaning of the Declaration of Independence, the Fifth Amendment, and the Fourteenth Amendment, pro-choice arguments no longer have any constitutional claim to primacy, and abortionists by necessity lose the argument.

The right to privacy upon which the Supreme Court based the *Roe v. Wade* decision was truly hypothecated—created out of whole cloth—under the Warren Court in the 1965 decision *Griswold v. Connecticut*, 381 U.S. 479 (1965). As we would expect, the ACLU submitted amicus briefs in both *Roe v. Wade* and *Griswold v. Connecticut*.

The *Griswold v. Connecticut* case involved Estelle Griswold, the executive director of the Planned Parenthood League of Connecticut at that time, who was found guilty and fined one hundred dollars under a Connecticut statute that prevented giving instruction and medical advice as a means of preventing conception. Justice William O. Douglas, delivering the majority opinion of the court to reverse Griswold's conviction, ruled that the First Amendment creates a "penumbra where privacy is protected from governmental intrusion."[6] Dissenting from the majority opinion, Justice Hugo Black argued there was no explicit mention of privacy specified as a right under the Declaration of Independence, the Constitution, or the Bill of Rights. "I like my privacy as well as the next one, but I am nevertheless compelled to admit that government has a right to invade it unless prohibited by some specific constitutional provision," Justice Black wrote.[7] In his dissent to *Roe v. Wade*, Justice William Rehnquist commented, "To reach its result, the Court necessarily has had to find within the scope of the Fourteenth Amendment a right that was apparently completely unknown to the drafters of the Amendment."[8]

The point is that Judeo-Christian groups, seeking to fight back against the ACLU, will have to argue legal theories such as the concept of personhood as effectively as the ACLU has used an implied right to privacy that was never specified in the Constitution if we are to displace the linchpin theory on which the ACLU arguments in favor of abortion have been founded.

"2011 has been a banner year for abortion opponents," wrote Simon van Zuylen-Wood, a researcher-reporter for the *New Republic*. "Thus far, 87 state laws restricting abortion have been enacted, the most in any year since *Roe v. Wade*. But one rogue wing of the pro-life movement sees no reason to celebrate: the budding 'personhood movement,' which wants to turn abortion into homicide by methodically amending state constitutions to define conception as the beginning of a person's life." Correctly, Simon van Zuylen-Wood understood that the personhood movement was designed to challenge "*Roe's* premise outright."[9] Dan Becker, a leader in the personhood movement, defines *personhood* as "the recognition by our culture and our government that each individual human life has an 'unalienable' right to life from its earliest biological beginning." Becker continues to explain that this right to life "extends to natural death, regardless of one's disability, gender, race, dependency or manner of conception." He asserts the unalienable right to life "comes from God by virtue of the fact that we have been created in His image and are thus imbued with a unique worth and dignity not found in the rest of creation."[10]

Importantly, the personhood objective is being fought on the state level. The goal is to get a statewide vote amending the state constitution to outlaw abortions. "I do not believe the Constitution requires States to permit abortion, but neither do I believe that it invalidates state laws that permit abortion," Supreme Court Justice Antonin Scalia pointed out in a 2009 interview. "Upholding such a state law does not make me a participant in any 'evil'—even if it goes against my religion. It is not I who am performing or requiring that abortion; I am simply applying the law which permits a woman to have an abortion if she chooses."[11] As we saw earlier, the First Amendment required only that "Congress shall make no law . . . ," but said nothing about the states. At the time the Bill of Rights was ratified, a number of states had established religions, a question the First Amendment left open. Scalia is suggesting here that state constitutional amendments may take precedence to prevent abortions, effectively overruling *Roe v. Wade*. Also under the Ninth and Tenth Amendments, funding abortions was not a power specifically delegated to the federal government. So under what constitutional authority does the federal government mandate abortion policies over the states? The point is that warriors for God need to have a constitutionally based argument and that the legislative/judicial strategy designed to advance religious freedom under the First Amendment needs to be calculated to have a reasonable probability of success.

In the verbal arguments before the US Supreme Court in *Roe v. Wade*, Justice Potter Stewart drew the obvious and necessary conclusion in questioning legal counsel seeking to establish a right to abortion: "If it were established that an unborn fetus is a person within the protection of the Fourteenth Amendment, you would have almost an impossible case here, would you not?" Sarah Weddington, the pro-abortion legal counsel Stewart was questioning in *Roe*, conceded the point: "I would have a very difficult case."[12] Justice Stewart agreed, "You certainly would."[13]

The importance of the personhood argument is that pro-life forces are working to find an argument based on the Constitution—in this case, a person's right to life as specified in the Declaration of Independence—that

counters the hypothetical right to privacy pro-choice forces used to fashion the legal basis of the *Roe v. Wade* decision. In fighting the ACLU, we
should not expect it will be enough for legal advocates for God simply
to show up in court to oppose the ACLU. Advocates for God must also
show up in court well funded, with legal arguments that have a sufficiently
sound basis in constitutional law to win the battle in court.

As noted in the previous chapters, the ACLU's constitutional reasoning can
be successfully defeated in court is amply demonstrated by the case *ACLU v.
Mercer County, Kentucky*, a case brought before the US Court of Appeals for
the Sixth Circuit that involved posting a display of the Ten Commandments
in a courthouse.[14] On October 9, 2001, Carroll Rousey, a Mercer County
resident, requested a display entitled "Foundations of American Law and
Government" be posted in the Mercer County Courthouse. The display
included the Mayflower Compact; the Declaration of Independence; the
Ten Commandments; the Magna Carta; "The Star-Spangled Banner";
the National Motto, "In God We Trust"; the Preamble to the Kentucky
Constitution; the Bill of Rights; and Lady Justice.

The Mercer County Fiscal Court allowed Rousey to hang the display
after learning that the Kentucky General Assembly had recently passed a
resolution authorizing the inclusion of the Ten Commandments in displays
of formative, historical documents on government property. Rousey framed
and hung the display at his own expense. Shortly thereafter, Bart McQueary,
a member of the ACLU and a resident of Mercer County, brought a legal
suit against the county, seeking an injunction to have the display removed
because it contained a version of the Ten Commandments, violating the
establishment clause of the First Amendment.

Writing the opinion of the US Court of Appeals for the Sixth Circuit,
Judge Suhrheinrich delivered the conclusion of the three-judge panel hearing the case, ruling that the display lacked a religious purpose and further
that it did not endorse religion. The circuit court thus allowed the display

containing the Ten Commandments to remain in place in the Mercer County Courthouse. Judge Suhrheinrich's opinion is interesting not just for denying the ACLU its victory, but by the solid rebuke against the ACLU that the court expressed in the language of the decision.[15]

The ruling noted that were the court simply to focus on the perception of observers, every religious display would be deemed unconstitutional, as long as some passerby perceived a government endorsement of religion in the display. Moreover, the court dismissed the ACLU's perception of the Ten Commandments display, arguing that the ACLU was a biased observer. "Thus, we find unavailing the ACLU's own assertions that it finds the display offensive and that the display 'diminishes [its] enjoyment of the courthouse,'" Judge Suhrheinrich wrote. "Religion does not become relevant to standing in the political community simply because a particular viewer of a government display feels uncomfortable." The ACLU, Judge Suhrheinrich felt, was a *particularly* biased observer: "Our concern is that of the reasonable person. And the ACLU, an organization whose mission is 'to ensure that . . . the government [is kept] out of the religious business,' does not embody the reasonable person." As support for this contention, Judge Suhrheinrich footnoted a page from the ACLU website that has since been removed.[16]

"The ACLU's argument contains . . . fundamental flaws," he continued. "First, the ACLU makes repeated reference to 'the separation of church and state.' This extra-constitutional construct has grown tiresome. The First Amendment does not demand a wall of separation between church and state."[17]

With these sentences, Justice Suhrheinrich brushed aside the application of Jefferson's letter to the Danbury Baptists as irrelevant, precisely because the phrase "wall of separation between church and state" appeared nowhere in the Constitution or the Bill of Rights—the same defect inherent in *Roe v. Wade* where the decision that abortion is legal depends on some implied right to privacy that likewise is not expressed in any of the founding documents, including the Declaration of Independence, the Constitution, and the Bill of Rights.

Judge Suhrheinrich then went on to assert: "After all, [w]e are a religious people whose institutions presuppose a Supreme Being."[18]

➤

"Liberals believe that it is unconstitutional for citizens to act on their moral judgments, such as the view that homosexuality is wrong, in their dealings with fellow citizens," ambassador Alan Keyes wrote in 2000. "They believe that the state has the right collectively to dictate conscience on these points—and on a civil rights pretext force citizens to accept what is contrary to their religious conscience."[19]

Keyes correctly observed that the political Left wants to bend the Constitution so the coercive force of law can be brought to bear down on anyone who dares disagree with its radical interpretation of what's right and what's wrong.

"The clearest instance of this tyranny now occurs in the service of the radical homosexual agenda," Keyes continued. "Liberals pretend that what is at issue in our society now is what people do in the privacy of their bedrooms. But when liberals attempt to use the government to force the Boy Scouts to have homosexual Scoutmasters, the issue is not what goes on in the privacy of somebody's bedroom, but what will be imposed as a matter of law upon the consciences of those whose religious beliefs cannot countenance homosexual practices."[20]

Joseph Farah, founder and CEO of World Net Daily, agreed, arguing the United States is in the throes of a clash of cultures today in which traditional Jewish and Christian views are under attack as never before. "I do not seek to deny homosexuals any of their God-given, unalienable civil rights," Farah wrote. "Neither do the Boy Scouts. Rather, it is the homosexual political activists who seek to undermine the institutions that represent the bedrock of freedom, of self-government, of individual rather than group rights."[21] What concerned Farah was that the hard Left was gaining in the culture war, assisted by its establishment press allies, its federal government, its foundation allies, and a public relations message

refined over decades and delivered today through popular devices as ubiq-
uitous as the laptop computer and the smartphone.

"It's time to reframe the debate," Farah insisted. "That's the only way
our civilization, as we know it, can survive. It's time to tell the truth. It's
time to stand up for decency."

Farah acknowledged the stakes are high. "I guess it's time to add me
to the enemies list . . . unequivocally, unabashedly, unashamedly," he concluded, in the final analysis. "The Boy Scouts personify the kind of world
in which I would like to live and raise my family. If this is the new dividing
line in our society, let the barricades be erected. I'm not retreating—not
another inch."[22]

How long will God be left to lie by the side of the road, battered and abandoned by the Bad Samaritan of the ACLU? Has the United States already
become such a secular state that the jackals of the mainstream media must
hector any book such as this that dares to treat the Judeo-Christian tradition seriously? Are we approaching the day when a godless president and a
secular Congress will pack the Supreme Court with enough former ACLU
activists that the practice of faith in America will be relegated to the cellar,
such that Christians and Jews who dare profess their faith openly risk fines,
legal penalties, and possibly even imprisonment?

These are serious questions in an era where the ACLU has largely succeeded in removing God from the public square in the name of protecting
First Amendment religious freedom. The Bad Samaritans of the ACLU
have now had decades since the 1920s to impose upon America a twisted
interpretation of the First Amendment that ends up identifying us as intolerant bigots because we continue to have faith in God and adhere to the
traditional values of Judeo-Christian beliefs. With God largely removed
from our public schools and our public squares, no American should be
surprised if God abandons the United States. Reading the Bible, we are at
a loss to find a single people or civilization that turned their back on God,

only to be rewarded for doing so. The day the Supreme Court bans God from all but private expressions of faith in America will mark the day this nation loses its freedom and begins its inevitable decline. "One nation without God" is not a formula under which the United States can be expected to long endure or prosper.

If we are to avoid descending once again into the dark depths of moral depravity from which this time in human history there may be no easy or certain recovery, the faithful among us who have taken God's Word to heart must remain determined to proclaim openly that Word in this land, regardless of what legal challenges and personal consequences we may face in doing so. As Good Samaritans, we resolve, here and now, to come to the defense of God in the courts. To be certain, defeating the ACLU in court will require highly skilled legal advocates for God determined to counter the ACLU in each and every case the ACLU supports in court. Equally important, legal advocates for God must go even farther, being willing to initiate court challenges, as a strategy to overturn wrongful constitutional precedents set over the past few decades by a secular Supreme Court that has refused to defend God or interpret the First Amendment as our Founding Fathers meant it to be interpreted.

If our Founding Fathers were right in proclaiming that religious freedom is an inalienable right placed by God in human nature, no state shall ever permanently succeed in removing God completely from the human mind, the human heart, and from the prayers of believers – not even a nation as powerful and revered for religious freedom as the United States of America once was. We reject the ACLU because we reject a social destiny where broken families without fathers are the norm, a culture destiny in which every form of pornography and sexual aberrant behavior is defined as a personal entitlement, and a religious destiny where God's name in school or the public square may only be uttered if the expression is profane. The ACLU must not be allowed to win this battle, not in this nation where our Founders so clearly charged us not to lose the religious freedom bestowed upon us.

In conclusion, we must dedicate ourselves to restore to this land the true freedom of religious expression God and our Founding Fathers intended for us, and we must do so not only for ourselves, but also for our children, and for generations of the yet unborn. With the publication of this book, let the word go forward throughout the land proclaiming that now is the time for Good Samaritans to come forward to demand the ACLU be resisted and scorned, so that God may be rescued from the side of the road and be restored to the center of America, the place where God rightfully belongs.

NOTES

Preface: Protecting Faith, Preserving Liberty

1. W. Cleon Skousen, *The 5000 Year Leap: The 28 Great Ideas that Changed the World* (Malta, ID: National Center for Constitutional Studies, 1981), 4th Principle, 75.
2. Luke 6:30.

Chapter 1: The War on God

1. "Joint Press Availability with President Obama and President Gul of Turkey," Cankaya Palace, Ankara, Turkey, April 6, 2009, Office of the Press Secretary, the White House, http://www.whitehouse.gov/the_press_office/ Joint-Press-Availability-With-President-Obama-And-President-Gul-Of-Turkey.
2. Ibid.
3. 103rd Congress, An Act to Designate Certain Lands in the California Desert as Wilderness, January 25, 1994, http://www.wilderness.net /NWPS/documents/PublicLaws/PDF/103-433.pdf.
4. "Plan Your Visit," Mojave, National Park Service, US Department of the Interior, National Park Service, www.nps.gov/moja/planyourvisit /index.htm. The size of the Mojave National Preserve is noted by Justice Anthony Kennedy in writing the majority opinion of the court in *Salazar v. Buono*, 559 U.S. ____ (2010).
5. Robert Barnes, "For Couple, Memorial Became a Mission," *Washington Post*, September 28, 2009, www.washingtonpost.com/wp-dyn/content /article/2009/09/28/AR2009092803125.html.
6. Ethan Cole, "Mojave Desert Cross Stolen; Supporters Outraged," May 11, 2010, http://www.christianpost.com/news/mojave-desert -cross-stolen-supporters-outraged-45115/.
7. Barnes, "For Couple, Memorial Became a Mission."

8. ACLU, "ACLU Sues Federal Government over Christian Cross in Mojave National Preserve," press release, ACLU.org, March 22, 2001, www.aclu.org/religion-belief/aclu-sues-federal-government-over-christian-cross-mojave-national-preserve.

9. Adam Linkner, "How *Salazar v. Buono* Synthesizes the Supreme Court's Establishment Clause Precedent into a Single Test," *Emory International Law Review* 25 (2011), http://www.law.emory.edu/fileadmin/journals/eilr/25/25.1/Linkner.pdf.

10. ACLU, "ACLU Sues Federal Government Over Christian Cross in Mojave National Preserve."

11. Ibid.

12. Ibid.

13. Ibid.

14. Ibid.

15. Tim King, "Oregon Man Battles to Remove Historic Mojave Desert Cross Honoring War Dead," Salem-News.com, June 3, 2009, www.salem-news.com/articles/june032009/desert_cross_6-1-09.php; Robert Longley, "Government Loses Latest Battle over the 'Mojave Cross,'" About.com, April 24, 2005, usgovinfo.about.com/od/rightsandfreedoms/a/mojavecross.htm.

16. Longley, "Government Loses Latest Battle over the 'Mojave Cross.'"

17. Ibid. See also US Court of Appeals for the Ninth Circuit, *Buono v. Kempthorne*, filed September 6, 2007, http://www.ca9.uscourts.gov/datastore/opinions/2007/09/05/0555852.pdf.

18. David G. Savage, "U.S. Supreme Court Takes Up Case of Cross in National Park," *Los Angeles Times*, February 24, 2009, articles.latimes.com/2009/feb/24/nation/na-supreme-court-cross24.

19. *Salazar v. Buono*, 559 U.S ____ (2010), http://www.supremecourt.gov/opinions/09pdf/08-472.pdf.

20. Ibid.

21. Robert Barnes, "Supreme Court Overturns Objections to Cross on Public Land," *Washington Post*, April 29, 2010, www.washingtonpost.com/wp-dyn/content/article/2010/04/28/AR2010042801949.html.

22. *Salazar v. Buono*, 559 U.S ____ (2010), http://www.supremecourt.gov/opinions/09pdf/08-472.pdf.

23. Robert Jablon, "Thieves Steal Controversial Mojave Cross," Associated Press, May 11, 2010, www.marinecorpstimes.com/news/2010/05/ap_mojave_cross_theft_051110/.

24. Daniel B. Wood, "Mojave Cross Theft Shows Planning, Veterans Groups Vow to Rebuild," *Christian Science Monitor*, May 11, 2010,

www.csmonitor.com/USA/2010/0511/Mojave-cross
-theft-shows-planning-veterans-groups-vow-to-rebuild.

25. Ben Goad and Dug Begley, "Mojave Cross Replaced, Then Removed,"
    Press-Enterprise, May 21, 2010, PE.com, http://usconstitutionalfreepress
    .wordpress.com/2010/05/21/mojave-cross-replaced-then-removed/.

26. Bob Unruh, "Will Supremes Call Out the Bulldozers?" World Net Daily,
    October 7, 2009, www.wnd.com/?pageId=112209.

27. Brian Montopoli, "'Ten Commandments Judge' Ray Moore to Run for
    President," CBS News, March 28, 2011, www.cbsnews.com/8301
    -503544_162-20048033-503544.html.

28. ACLU, Brief for Respondents, *McCreary County, Kentucky, et al. v.
    American Civil Liberties Union of Kentucky, et al.*, 545 U.S. 844 (2005),
    http://www.lc.org/attachments/TenCommACLU_BriefMerits.pdf.

29. *McCreary County, Kentucky, et al. v. American Civil Liberties Union of
    Kentucky, et al.*, 545 U.S. 844 (2005), http://caselaw.lp.findlaw.com
    /scripts/getcase.pl?court=us&vol=000&invol=03-1693#opinion1.

30. ACLU, "ACLU Urges Supreme Court to Protect Religious Liberty in Ten
    Commandments Case," ACLU.org, March 2, 2005, www.aclu.org
    /content/aclu-urges-supreme-court-protect-religious-liberty-ten
    -commandments-case.

31. Ibid.

32. Ibid.

33. Michael Anthony Sells, *Approaching the Qur'an: The Early Revelations*
    (Ashland, OR: White Cloud Press, 1999).

34. Christopher Buck, "The Constitutionality of Teaching Islam: The
    University of North Carolina Qur'an Controversy," in *The State of Islamic
    Studies in American Universities* (Herndon, VA: International Institute of
    Islamic Thought, n.d.), http://christopherbuck.com/Buck_PDFs/Buck_
    Islam_2011.pdf. The legal cases against the University of North Carolina
    proceeded under *Yascovelli v. Moeser* and were unreported in that the 2002
    decisions in both the district court and the circuit court decisions were not
    published. Buck, however, details the cases and describes the decisions.

35. Carl W. Ernst, "Does the Koran Belong in Class?" letter to the editor,
    New York Times, September 3, 2002, www.nytimes.com/2002/09/03
    /opinion/l-does-the-koran-belong-in-class-688908.html.

36. John Brodie, "Koran Studies: Inquiry Isn't Indoctrination," letter to the
    editor, *Wall Street Journal*, August 23, 2002.

37. Ibid.

38. Michael Sells, "Understanding, Not Indoctrination," letter to the editor,
    Washington Post, August 8, 2002, www.library.cornell.edu/colldev

/mideast/msells.htm. Republished as Michael Sells, "Suing the Qur'an," *American Muslim*, September–October 2002, posted August 25, 2002, theamericanmuslim.org/tam.php/features/articles/suing_the_quran/.

39. Ibid.

40. Chief Justice N. Carlton Tilley Jr., memorandum opinion, *Yacovelli v. Moeser*, 324 F.Supp.2d 760 (2004), scholar.google.com/scholar_cas e?case=12430426339996681112&q=Yacovelli+v.+Moeser&hl=en &as_sdt=2,31&as_vis=1.

Chapter 2: Roots in Communism

1. Howard Zinn, *A People's History of the United States: 1492—Present* (New York: HarperCollins, 1999), 436.

2. About the ACLU, "FAQs," American Civil Liberties Union, www.aclu .org/faqs#3_6.

3. Jonah Goldberg: *Liberal Fascism: The Secret History of the American Left from Mussolini to the Politics of Meaning* (New York: Doubleday, 2008), 74, italics in original.

4. Frank Marshall Davis, *Livin' the Blues: Memoirs of a Black Journalist and Poet* (Madison, WI: University of Wisconsin Press, 1992), 277.

5. Robert C. Cottrell, *Roger Nash Baldwin and the American Civil Liberties Union* (New York: Columbia University Press, 1983), 265.

6. Ibid., 272.

7. About the ACLU, "FAQs."

8. Aaron Wildavsky, "Foreword: The Reverse Sequence in Civil Liberties," in William A. Donohue, *The Politics of the American Civil Liberties Union* (New Brunswick, NJ: Transaction Books, 1985), ix.

9. Donohue, *Politics of the American Civil Liberties Union*, 231–33.

10. Ibid., 234.

11. Debs was tried, found guilty, and sentenced to serve in the state penitentiary by the District Court of the United States for the Northern District of Ohio; his statement at the trial can be found in David Karsner, *Debs: His Life and Letters* (New York: Boni and Liveright, 1919), 28. He appealed his case; *Eugene V. Debs, Plaintiff in Error, v. the United States of America*, File No. 26,800, filed with the US Supreme Court, Term no. 714, October 1918. The Supreme Court decision was delivered March 10, 1919, and upheld the sentence and conviction; see Karsner, *Debs*, 56.

12. This paragraph is drawn from "Free Speech: Emma Goldman, 1869–1940," Jewish Women's Archive: Women of Valor, jwa.org/historymakers /goldman/free-speech.

13. Emma Goldman, "Emma Says Reds Killed Own Hopes," *Chicago*

Herald-Examiner, March 22, 1922, cited in "Article by Goldman About Her Disillusionment with the Soviet Union," Jewish Women's Archive, jwa.org/media/article-by-goldman-about-her-disillusionment-with-soviet-union.

14. Davis, *Livin' the Blues*, 263.

15. Cottrell, *Roger Nash Baldwin*, 227.

16. Ibid., 228–29.

17. Ibid., 230.

18. William Z. Foster, *Russia in 1924*, pamphlet issued by the Trade Union Educational League, 1924, Marxists Internet Archive (2006), www.marxists.org/archive/foster/1924/russ24.htm.

19. The letters in this section between the American Civil Liberties Union and the Workers Party of America are drawn from the ACLU collection in the Manuscript Division of the Library of Congress, Washington, DC.

20. Ibid.

21. Ibid.

22. Alan Sears, "The ACLU's Shocking Legacy," World Net Daily, August 25, 2005, www.wnd.com/news/article.asp?ARTICLE_ID=45959.

23. Rev. Jesse Lee Peterson, "Abortion: Black Genocide," World Net Daily, February 13, 2008, www.wnd.com/index.php?pageId=56202.

24. ACLU collection in the Manuscript Division of the Library of Congress.

25. Ibid.

26. Cottrell, *Roger Nash Baldwin*, 148.

27. Ibid., 202.

28. Ibid., 203.

29. Paul Kengor, *Dupes: How America's Adversaries Have Manipulated Progressives for a Century* (Wilmington, DE: ISI Books, 2010).

30. John Rossomando, "The ACLU's Untold Stalinist Heritage," *Daily Caller*, January 4, 2011, dailycaller.com/2011/01/04/the-aclu's-untold-stalinist-heritage/.

31. Kengor, *Dupes*, 9–10.

32. Ibid., 62.

33. As cited in Rossomando, "The ACLU's Untold Stalinist Heritage."

34. Kengor, *Dupes*, 69.

35. William Z. Foster, *Toward Soviet America* (New York: Coward-McCann, 1932).

36. Francis E. Walter, chairman, Committee on Un-American Activities, US House of Representatives, foreword to the reprinting of William Z. Foster, *Toward Soviet America* (New York: Coward-McCann, 1961), iii.

37. Foster, *Toward Soviet America*, 269.

38. Ibid., 275.

39. Ibid., 281.

40. Ibid., 307.

41. Ibid., 308.

42. Ibid., 309.

43. Fish Committee report quoted in Cottrell, *Roger Nash Baldwin*, 204.

44. Ibid.

45. J. Matt Barber, "ACLU v. Religious Liberty," *American Thinker*, March 24, 2011, www.americanthinker.com/2011/03/aclu_v_religious_liberty .html.

46. Ibid.

47. Cottrell, *Roger Nash Baldwin*, 155.

48. Marvin Olasky and John Perry, *Monkey Business: The True Story of the Scopes Trial* (Nashville: Broadman & Holman, 2005), 11.

49. Cottrell, *Roger Nash Baldwin*, 155.

50. Ibid.

51. H. L. Mencken, "Homo Neanderthalensis," *Baltimore Evening Sun*, June 29, 1925, www.positiveatheism.org/hist/menck01.htm#SCOPES1, archived in the University of Missouri-Kansas City School of Law website, "The Scopes Trial," law2.umkc.edu/faculty/projects/ftrials/scopes/scopes.htm.

52. Edward J. Larson, *Summer for the Gods: The Scopes Trial and America's Continuing Debate over Science and Religion* (New York: Basic Books, 2005), 90–91.

53. Olasky and Perry, *Monkey Business*, 110.

54. Ibid., 149–51.

55. Larson, *Summer for the Gods*, 190–91.

56. Olasky and Perry, *Monkey Business* , 160.

57. Ibid., 154.

58. Ibid., 152–53.

59. Larson, *Summer for the Gods*, 242; http://www.filmsite.org/inhe.html.

60. H. L. Mencken, "Bryan," *Baltimore Evening Sun*, July 27, 1925, archived in the University of Missouri–Kansas City School of Law website, "The Scopes Trial," positiveatheism.org/hist/menck05.htm#SCOPESC.

61. Ibid.

62. Edward J. Larson, "Scopes 75th Anniversary Broadcast," *Science Friday* with host Ira Flatow, July 21, 2000, WNYC and National Public Radio, in Olasky and Perry, *Monkey Business*, 244–66, at 245.

63. Ibid.

64. Herbert Romerstein and Eric Breindel, *The Venona Secrets: Exposing Soviet Espionage and America's Traitors* (Washington, D.C.: Regnery, 2000).

65. *Edwards v. Aguillard*, 482 U.S. 578 (1987), at 594.

66. Edward L. Bernays, *Propaganda* (New York: Liveright, 1928), 9–10, 25; http://archive.org/details/Porpaganda [*sic*].

Chapter 3: A Wall of Separation

1. Michael De Dora, "Survey Highlights Americans' Mixed Views on Church and State, Constitution," Center for Inquiry, October 19, 2010, http://www.centerforinquiry.net/blogs/show/survey_highlights _americans_mixed_views_on_church_and_state/.

2. Adam C. Calinger, "Original Intent & the Ten Commandments: Giving Coherency to Ten Commandments Jurisprudence," *Georgetown Journal of Law & Public Policy* 3 (2005): 257–93, at 265.

3. Ibid.

4. Linda D. Lam, "Silence of the Lambs: Are States Attempting to Establish Religion in Public Schools?" *Vanderbilt Law Review* 56 (2003): 911–37, at 914.

5. Ibid.

6. Ibid.

7. Calinger, "Original Intent & the Ten Commandments," italics in original.

8. Lam, "Silence of the Lambs," 916. *Everson v. Board of Education*, 330 U.S. 1 (1947), supreme.justia.com/us/330/1/case.html.

9. Thomas L. Krannawitter and Daniel C. Palm, *A Nation Under God?: The ACLU and Religion in American Politics* (Lanham, MD: Rowman & Littlefield, 2005), 71.

10. "Jefferson's Letter to the Danbury Baptists: The Final Letter, as Sent," dated January 1, 1802, archived in the Library of Congress, *Information Bulletin*, June 1998, www.loc.gov/loc/lcib/9806/danpre.html.

11. *Everson v. Board of Education*, 330 U.S. 1 (1947), 15–16.

12. Lam, "Silence of the Lambs," 917, italics in original.

13. *Everson v. Board of Education*, 330 U.S. 1 (1947), 17–18.

14. Justice Felix Frankfurter, concurring opinion, *Everson v. Board of Education*, 330 U.S. 1 (1947), 31–32.

15. Krannawitter and Palm, *A Nation Under God*, 73.

16. Daniel Dreisbach, *Thomas Jefferson and the Wall of Separation Between Church and State* (New York: New York University Press, 2002), 4–5.

17. David Barton, *Original Intent: The Courts, the Constitution, & Religion*, 3rd ed. (Aledo, TX: WallBuilder Press, 2000), 48.

18. See Matthew 22:21.

19. James Madison, "A Memorial and Remonstrance Against Religious Assessments," to the Honorable and General Assembly of the

Commonwealth of Virginia, 1785, University of Virginia website, religiousfreedom.lib.virginia.edu/sacred/madison_m&r_1785.html.

20. Christopher D. Tomlinson, "Changing the Rules of Establishment Clause Litigation: An Alternative to the Public Expression of Religion Act," *Vanderbilt Law Review* 61 (2008): 261–98, at 266.

21. *Wallace v. Jaffree*, 472 U.S. 38 (1985), 98–99, supreme.justia.com /us/472/38/case.html.

22. Ibid., 99.

23. Ibid., 107.

24. Dreisbach, *Thomas Jefferson and the Wall of Separation*, xx–xxii.

25. Bradley Tupi, "Religious Freedom and the First Amendment," *Duquesne Law Review* 45 (Winter 2007): 195–267, at 221.

26. "Jefferson's Letter to the Danbury Baptists."

27. Krannawitter and Palm, *A Nation Under God*, 72.

28. Dreisbach, *Thomas Jefferson and the Wall of Separation*, 117.

29. Ibid., 125.

30. Tomlinson, "Changing the Rules of Establishment Clause Litigation: An Alternative to the Public Expression of Religion Act," 269.

31. Samuel Walker, *In Defense of American Liberties: A History of the ACLU* (New York: Oxford University Press, 1990), 219.

32. Julie F. Mead, Preston C. Green, and Joseph O. Oluwole, "Re-examining the Constitutionality of Prayer in School in Light of the Resignation of Justice O'Connor," *Journal of Law and Education* 36 (2007): 381–406, at 382.

33. *Lemon v. Kurtzman*, 403 U.S. 602 (1971), 609, http://supreme.justia.com /cases/federal/us/403/602/case.html.

34. Josh Blackman, "This Lemon Comes as a Lemon: The *Lemon* Test and the Pursuit of a Statute's Secular Purpose," *Civil Rights Law Journal* 20 (2009–10): 351–415, at 356.

35. Krannawitter and Palm, *A Nation Under God*, 75. Here Krannawitter and Palm are adapting a thought they attribute originally to Professor Thomas G. West.

36. *Wallace v. Jaffree*, 472 U.S. 38 (1985), 472.

37. Ibid.

38. Krannawitter and Palm, *A Nation Under God*, 76.

39. *Wallace v. Jaffree*, 472 U.S. 38 (1985), http://www.law.cornell.edu/supct /html/historics/USSC_CR_0472_0038_ZC1.htmlIbid.

40. Krannawitter and Palm, *A Nation Under God*, 76.

41. Ross Schmierer, "An Attempt to Pick Up the Fallen Bricks of the Wall Separating Church and State After *Santa Fe v. Doe*," *Brooklyn Law Review* 67 (2001–2): 1291–1342, at 1291–92.

42. William A. Donohue, *The Politics of the American Civil Liberties Union* (New Brunswick, NJ: Transaction Books, 1985), 301.

43. Ibid., 310.

44. Nat Hentoff quoted in William A. Donohue, *Twilight of Liberty: The Legacy of the ACLU* (New Brunswick, NJ: Transaction Publishers, 1994), 97.

45. Alan Sears and Craig Osten, *The ACLU vs. America: Exposing the Agenda to Redefine Moral Values* (Nashville: Alliance Defense Fund, 2005), 2. The Alliance Defense Fund is now known as the Alliance Defending Freedom.

46. ACLU, Annual Report 2010, Financial Statement, page 38, at http://www.aclu.org/files/assets/annualreport_2010.pdf.

47. ACLU Form 990, http://www.aclu.org/files/pdfs/about/fy2011_acluf_990.pdf.pdf.

48. Sears and Osten, *The ACLU*, 4–5.

49. Krannawitter and Palm, *A Nation Under God*, 76.

50. Tomlinson, "Changing the Rules of Establishment Clause Litigation: An Alternative to the Public Expression of Religion Act," 262.

51. Ibid., 262–63.

52. Ibid., 263.

53. Peter A. Lillback with Jerry Newcombe, *George Washington's Sacred Fire* (Bryn Mawr, PA: Providence Forum Press, 2006), 486–89.

54. George Washington's first inaugural address, April 30, 1789, italics in original, Bartleby.com, http://www.bartleby.com/124/pres13.html.

55. George Washington's farewell address (1796), http://avalon.law.yale.edu/18th_century/washing.asp.

56. Ronald Reagan, "Remarks at a White House Ceremony in Observance of National Day of Prayer," May 6, 1982, Reagan Archives, University of Texas, http://www.reagan.utexas.edu/archives/speeches/1982/50682c.htm.

57. Lillback, *George Washington's Sacred Fire*, 397.

58. George Washington's resignation address to the Continental Congress, Annapolis, Maryland, December 23, 1783, Papers of George Washington, Alderman Library, University of Virginia, http://gwpapers.virginia.edu/documents/revolution/resignation.html.

59. Ron Chernow, *Washington: A Life* (New York: Penguin, 2010), 326.

60. James G. Wilson, *Colonel John Bayard, Anniversary Address Before the New York Genealogical and Biographical Society, February 27, 1885* (New York: Trow's Printing, 1885), http://archive.org/details/coloneljohnbayar00wils.

61. Jerry W. Knudson, *Jefferson and the Press* (Columbia: University of South Carolina Press, 2006), 1–2, 13.

62. Margaret Bayard Smith, *Forty Years of Washington Society*, ed. Gaillard

Hunt (London: T. Fisher Unwin, 1906), 13–15, books.google.com/books?
id=efw0AAAAIAAJ&printsec=frontcover&source=gbs_ge_summary_r&
cad=0#v=onepage&q&f=false.

63. Daniel Dreisbach, "The Mythical 'Wall of Separation': How a Misused
Metaphor Changed Church-State, Law, Policy, and Discourse," Heritage
Foundation, First Principles Series Report #6, June 23, 2006, www
.heritage.org/research/reports/2006/06/the-mythical-wall-of-separation
-how-a-misused-metaphor-changed-church-state-law-policy-and
-discourse.

64. Thomas Jefferson, Virginia Statute for Religious Freedom, annotated
transcript, Virginia Historical Society, http://www.vahistorical.org
/sva2003/vsrf.htm.

65. M. E. Bradford, *Original Intentions: On the Making and Ratification of the
United States Constitution* (Athens: University of Georgia Press, 1993), 99.

66. Robert L. Cord, *Separation of Church and State: Historical Fact and
Current Fiction* (Grand Rapids, MI: Baker Book House, 1988), 23–24.

67. Ibid., 214.

68. Ibid., 225.

Chapter 4: Enter the Atheists

1. Christopher Hitchens, *God Is Not Great: How Religion Poisons Everything*
(New York: Twelve, Hachette Book Group, 2007), 25, italics in original.

2. Madalyn Murray O'Hair, "History of Atheists' Fight for Radio Time,"
Program 1, KTBC Radio, Austin, Texas, June 3, 1968, in Madalyn
Murray O'Hair, *What on Earth Is an Atheist!* (New York: Arno Press,
1972), 1, italics in original.

3. Richard Tregaskis, interviewer, "Madalyn Murray," *Playboy*, October
1965, www.positiveatheism.org/hist/madplay.htm.

4. Ibid.

5. Ibid., italics in original.

6. "About RFC," Religious Freedom Coalition, www.religiousfreedomcoali-
tion.org/about/.

7. William J. Murray, *My Life Without God* (Nashville: Thomas Nelson, 1982).

8. Ibid., 7.

9. Ibid., 8.

10. Ibid., 12–13.

11. Ibid., 13.

12. Ibid., 48–49.

13. Ibid., 46–49.

14. William J. Murray III, interview with the author, October 1, 2011.

15. Murray, *My Life Without God*, 64–65.

16. Ibid.

17. Justice Tom C. Clark, delivering the opinion of the court, *School District of Abington Township, Pennsylvania v. Schempp*, 374 U.S. 203 (1963).

18. Justice Potter Stewart, dissenting opinion, *School District of Abington Township, Pennsylvania v. Schempp*, 374 U.S. 203 (1963).

19. Ibid.

20. Murray, *My Life Without God*, 89.

21. Ibid.

22. Ibid., 90.

23. Madalyn Murray, letter to the editor, *Life*, April 12, 1963, 63.

24. Ibid.

25. Justice Stewart, dissenting opinion, *School District of Abington Township, Pennsylvania v. Schempp*, 374 U.S. 203 (1963).

26. Bryan F. Le Beau, *The Atheist: Madalyn Murray O'Hair* (New York: New York University Press, 2003).

27. Howard J. Dodge, *The Big Lie: An Unmasking of Our Untruthful Religious and Political Past* (New York: Vantage Press, 1971), 25.

28. Ibid., 107.

29. Ibid., 394.

30. Ibid., 395.

31. Ibid., 456, italics in original.

32. Ibid., 419.

33. Ibid., 648.

34. Ibid.

35. Le Beau, *The Atheist: Madalyn Murray O'Hair,* 100.

36. "Reconciling Faith and Evolution in the Classroom: A Conversation with Susan Epperson, 42 Years Later," ACLU.com, December 9, 2010, http://www.aclu.org/religion-belief/reconciling-faith-and-evolution-classroom-conversation-susan-epperson-42-years-later.

37. Justice Abe Fortas, delivering the opinion of the court, *Epperson v. Arkansas*, 393 U.S. 97 (1968).

38. Justice William J. Brennan, delivering the opinion of the court, *Edwards v. Aguillard*, 482 U.S. 578 (1987).

39. Cited by Justice Brennan, *Edwards v. Aguillard*, 482 U.S. 578 (1987).

40. Justice Brennan, *Edwards v. Aguillard*, 482 U.S. 578 (1987).

41. Ibid.

42. Justice Antonin Scalia joined by Chief Justice William Rehnquist, dissenting opinion, *Edwards v. Aguillard*, 482 U.S. 578 (1987).

43. Ibid., italics in original.

44. Michio Kaku, *Parallel Worlds: A Journey Through Creation, Higher Dimensions, and the Future of the Cosmos* (New York: Doubleday, 2005), 348–49.

45. Roy Masters, *Finding God in Physics: Einstein's Missing Relative* (Grants Pass, OR: Foundation of Human Understanding, 1997), 22.

46. Hugh Ross, *Beyond the Cosmos,* the Extra-Dimensionality of God: *What Recent Discoveries in Astronomy and Physics Reveal About the Nature of God* (Colorado Springs: NavPress, 1996), 41.

47. *Darwin's Dilemma: The Mystery of the Cambrian Fossil Record*, an Illustra Media Production DVD, www.darwinsdilemma.org/.

48. Stephen C. Meyer, *Signature in the Cell: DNA and Evidence for Intelligent Design* (New York: Harper One, 2009), 19.

49. *McLean v. Arkansas*, National Center for Science Education, October 17, 2008, http://ncse.com/creationism/legal/mclean-v-arkansas.

50. Meyer, *Signature in the Cell*, 416–38.

51. Ibid., 432.

52. Ibid., 435.

53. Richard Dawkins, *The God Delusion* (New York: Houghton Mifflin, 2006), 147.

54. Ibid., 149.

55. Ibid., 153.

56. Ibid., 233.

57. Ibid.

58. Hitchens, *God Is Not Great*, 4.

59. Ibid., 27–28.

60. Ibid., 28.

61. Ibid., 78.

62. Ibid., 79.

63. Ibid., 86.

64. Ibid., 92–94.

65. Ibid., 3.

66. Le Beau, *The Atheist: Madalyn Murray O'Hair*, 135.

67. Ibid., 243.

68. About RFC, Religious Freedom Coalition.

69. Ann Rowe Seaman, *America's Most Hated Woman: The Life and Gruesome Death of Madalyn Murray O'Hair* (New York: Continuum, 2005), 11.

70. Ibid.

Chapter 5: The Godless Public Square

1. Y. M. Lichtenstein and T. Moskovits, "Justice Scalia: 'The American People Respect Religion,'" *Hamodia*, 2009, www.hamodia.com /inthepaper.cfm?ArticleID=370.

2. Leo Pfeffer, *Church, State and Freedom* (Boston: Beacon Press, 1953), 119.

3. J. David Holcomb, "Religion in Public Life: The 'Pfefferian Inversion' Reconsidered," *Journal of Law and Religion* 25 (2009–10): 57–95, at 59.
4. Pfeffer, *Church, State and Freedom*, 123.
5. Holcomb, "Religion in Public Life."
6. Ibid., 139.
7. Ibid., 147.
8. Ibid., 60.
9. Ibid., 62.
10. Richard John Neuhaus, *The Naked Public Square: Religion and Democracy in America* (Grand Rapids, MI: Eerdmans, 1984), 80.
11. Ibid., italics in original.
12. Justice George Sutherland, delivering the opinion of the court, *United States v. Macintosh*, 283 U.S. 605 (1931), http://supreme.justia.com/cases /federal/us/283/605/case.html.
13. Neuhaus, *The Naked Public Square*, 82, italics in original.
14. Ibid.
15. Justice John Paul Stevens, delivering the opinion of the court, *Santa Fe Independent School District v. Doe*, 530 U.S. 290 (2000), http://supreme .justia.com/cases/federal/us/530/290/.
16. Ibid.
17. Justice William Rehnquist, dissenting opinion, with whom Justice Antonin Scalia and Justice Clarence Thomas joined, dissenting, *Santa Fe Independent School District v. Doe*, 530 U.S. 290 (2000).
18. Ibid.
19. John Adams, Message from John Adams to the Officers of the First Brigade of the Third Division of the Militia of Massachusetts, October 11, 1798, http://oll.libertyfund.org/?option=com_staticxt&staticfile=show .php%3Ftitle=2107&chapter=161247&layout=html&Itemid=27.
20. Ralph Blumenthal and Sharaf Mowjood, "Muslim Prayers and Renewal Near Ground Zero," *New York Times*, December 8, 2009, http://www .nytimes.com/2009/12/09/nyregion/09mosque.html?pagewanted=all.
21. Morton A. Klein and Dr. Daniel Mandel, "Opposition to Mosque Near Ground Zero Not 'Islamophobia,'" *Washington Post*, September 8, 2010, newsweek.washingtonpost.com/onfaith/guestvoices/2010/09/opposition_ to_mosque_near_ground_zero_not_islamophobia.html.
22. Adam Lisberg, Barry Paddock, and Samuel Goldsmith, "Crucial Landmarks Panel Clears the Way for Ground Zero Mosque," *New York Daily News*, August 3, 2010, http://articles.nydailynews.com/2010-08-03 /local/27071657_1_landmarks-preservation-commission-landmark -protection-mosque.
23. ACLU, "NYCLU and ACLU Applaud Approval of NYC Islamic Cultural

Center for Upholding Values of Freedom and Tolerance," ACLU.org, August 3, 2010, http://www.aclu.org/religion-belief/nyclu-and-aclu -applaud-approval-nyc-islamic-cultural-center-upholding-values-freedom.

24. ACLU, "ACLU and NYCLU Statement on Controversy over New York City Islamic Center," ACLU.org, http://www.aclu.org/free-speech-religion-belief /aclu-and-nyclu-statement-controversy-over-new-york-city-islamic-center.

25. ACLU, "Sign the Petition: I Stand for Religious Freedom," ACLU. org, https://secure.aclu.org/site/SPageNavigator/Religious_Freedom_ Bloomberg?s_src=UNW100001ACT&s_subsrc=religious_freedom_ip.

26. "Sharia Law Banned: Oklahoma to Become the First U.S. State to Veto Use of Islamic Code," *Daily Mail*, November 2, 2010, http://www .dailymail.co.uk/news/article-1325986/Sharia-law-banned-Oklahoma -US-state-veto-Islamic-code.html.

27. "Don't Say We Weren't Warned," *Norman Transcript*, January 12, 2012; Joel Siegel, "Islamic Sharia Law to Be Banned in, Ah, Oklahoma," ABC News, June 14, 2010, http://abcnews.go.com/US/Media/oklahoma -pass-laws-prohibiting-islamic-sharia-laws-apply/story?id=10908521# .T7EHAI45eS0.

28. "CAIR, ACLU Urge Court to Uphold Ruling Blocking Okla. Sharia Ban," PR Newswire, May 10, 2011, http://www.bizjournals.com /prnewswire/press_releases/2011/05/10/DC99151.

29. P. David Gaubatz and Paul Sperry, *Muslim Mafia: Inside the Secret Underworld That's Conspiring to Islamize America* (Los Angeles: WND Books, 2009).

30. Joseph Farah, "CAIR: Media Darling, 1st Amendment Enemy," WND, October 4, 2011, http://www.wnd.com/2011/10/351737/.

31. "Cair Sues Oklahoma for Banning Islamic Law," WND, November 4, 2010, http://www.wnd.com/2010/11/224009/.

32. Nathan Koppel, "Oklahoma Faces Appellate Showdown over Anti-Sharia Law," *Wall Street Journal*, September 8, 2011, http://blogs.wsj.com /law/2011/09/08/oklahoma-faces-appellate-showdown-over-anti-sharia-law/.

33. John David Rausch Jr., "Political Context of the Vote on the 2010 Oklahoma International Law Amendment," http://wpsa.research.pdx .edu/meet/2012/rausch.pdf; Jonathan Turley, "Too Soon for Sharia? Tenth Circuit Rules Against Oklahoma's Anti-Sharia Law," January 11, 2012, http://jonathanturley.org/2012/01/11/too-sooner-for-sharia-tenth-circuit -rules-against-oklahomas-anti-sharia-law/. Also http://www.nytimes .com/2010/11/30/us/30oklahoma.html.

34. ACLU, "ACLU and CAIR Urge Court to Uphold Ruling Blocking Oklahoma Sharia and International Law Ban," ACLU.org, May 10, 2011,

http://www.aclu.org/human-rights-religion-belief/aclu-and-cair
-urge-court-uphold-ruling-blocking-oklahoma-sharia-and-int.

35. Ibid.

36. Daniel Mach, "Defending the Indefensible: Oklahoma Struggles to Salvage Its Unconstitutional Sharia Ban," ACLU Blog of Rights, ACLU.org, September 13, 2011, http://www.aclu.org/blog/national-security-religion-belief/ defending-indefensible-oklahoma-struggles-salvage-its.

37. Ibid.

38. The Plaintiff-Appellee Awad's Response Brief, filed in *Muneer Awad v. Paul Ziriax*, agency head, Oklahoma State Board of Elections; Thomas Prince, chairman of the board, Oklahoma State Board of Elections; Ramon Watkins, board member, Oklahoma State Board of Elections; and Susan Turpen, board member, State Board of Elections, signed by Gadeir Abbas, CAIR, Washington, DC, and Daniel Mach and Heather L. Weaver, ACLU Foundation, Washington, DC, May 9, 2011, http://www .aclu.org/files/assets/Awad_10th_Cir_Appellees_Br.pdf.

39. Moni Basu, "Douglasville: Muslim's Scarf Leads to Arrest at Courthouse," *Atlanta Journal-Constitution*, December 17, 2008, http://www.ajc.com /hotjobs/content/printedition/2008/12/17/hijab.html.

40. Associated Press, "U.S. Judge Jails Muslim Woman over Head Scarf," December 17, 2008, http://www.usatoday.com/news/nation/2008-12 -17-georgia-muslim-scarf_N.htm.

41. Lisa Valentine, "An Expression of Faith," ACLU Blog of Rights, October 6, 2011, www.aclu.org/blog/religion-belief-womens-rights/expression-faith.

42. Ibid.

43. Council on American-Islamic Relations, "Georgia Muslims Barred from Court Because of Hijab," press release, Cair.com, December 16, 2008, http://www.cair.com/ArticleDetails.aspx?ArticleID=25633&&name=n& &currPage.

44. ACLU, "The ACLU of Georgia Applauds Adoption by the Georgia Judicial Council of Policy Allowing for Wearing of Religious Head Coverings in Courthouses," ACLU.org, July 27, 2009, http://www.aclu .org/religion-belief/aclu-georgia-applauds-adoption-georgia-judicial -council-policy-allowing-wearing-reli.

45. Douglasville Municipal Court, "Headcovering Screening Policy for Court," no date, http://www.aclu.org/files/assets/valentine_ headcovering_policy.pdf.

46. "Discrimination Against Muslim Women—Fact Sheet," ACLU.org, May 29, 2008, http://www.aclu.org/pdfs/womensrights/ discriminationagainstmuslimwomen.pdf.

47. Ed Lasky, "ACLU and Public Funding for Muslim Foot Baths," *American Thinker*, August 7, 2007, http://www.americanthinker.com/blog/2007/08/aclu_and_public_funding_for_mu.html.

48. Tamar Lewin, "Universities Install Footbaths to Benefit Muslims, and Not Everyone Is Pleased," *New York Times*, August 7, 2007, http://www.nytimes.com/2007/08/07/education/07muslim.html?pagewanted=all.

49. Ibid.

50. Chelsea Schilling, "Teachers Forced to 'Hide in Closets' to Pray," World Net Daily, December 10, 2009, http://www.wnd.com/?pageId=118447.

51. "Judge Rules Islamic Education OK in California Classrooms," World Net Daily, December 13, 2003, http://www.wnd.com/2003/12/22289/.

52. Kelley R. Taylor, "Educational Role Play or Religious Indoctrination?" NAASP.org, February 2007, http://www.nassp.org/portals/0/content/55205.pdf.

53. Diana Lynne, "District Sued over Islam Studies," World Net Daily, July 2, 2002, http://www.wnd.com/2002/07/14425/.

54. Bob Egelko, "Appeal on School's Lesson in Muslim Culture Is Rejected," *San Francisco Chronicle*, October 3, 2006, http://www.sfgate.com/cgi-bin/article.cgi?f=/c/a/2006/10/03/MNG4ILH1201.DTL.

Chapter 6: The Assault on the Family

1. Brigitte Amiri, "Every Day Should Be National Day of Appreciation for Abortion Providers," ACLU Blog of Rights, March 10, 2010, http://www.aclu.org/blog/reproductive-freedom/every-day-should-be-national-day-appreciation-abortion-providers.

2. William Booth, "Doctor Killed During Abortion Protest," *Washington Post*, March 11, 1993, http://www.washingtonpost.com/wp-srv/national/longterm/abortviolence/stories/gunn.htm.

3. ACLU, "ACLU Salutes Abortion Providers on National Day of Appreciation (March 10)," press release, ACLU.org., March 8, 1999, http://www.aclu.org/organization-news-and-highlights/aclu-salutes-abortion-providers-national-day-appreciation-march-10.

4. William A. Donohue, *Twilight of Liberty: The Legacy of the ACLU* (New Brunswick, NJ: Transaction Publishers, 1994), 24–25.

5. Ibid., 25.

6. Ibid., 28.

7. "1992 Policy Guide of the ACLU," policy 263, quoted in Alan Sears and Craig Osten, *The ACLU vs. America: Exposing the Agenda to Redefine Moral Values* (Nashville: Broadman & Holman, 2005), 105.

8. "Abortion and the Black Community," BlackGenocide.org, no date, http://blackgenocide.org/black.html.

9. Michael Novak, "Notre Dame Disgrace," *National Review* Online, April 9, 2009, http://www.nationalreview.com/articles/227265/notre-dame-disgrace/michael-novak. Novak's 2009 figures are adjusted forward to reflect 2010 US Census data.

10. US Census Bureau, "The Black Population: 2010," in the series "2010 Census Briefs," www.census.gov/prod/cen2010/briefs/c2010br-06.pdf.

11. Tanya L. Green, "The Negro Project: Margaret Sanger's Eugenic Plan for Black Americans,"BlackGenocide.org, no date, http://www.blackgenocide.org/archived_articles/negro.html.

12. Margaret Sanger, *The Pivot of Civilization* (New York: Brentanos, 1922), 187.

13. Ibid., 197.

14. Sanger's letter to Clarence J. Gamble, dated December 10, 1939, is referred to in the Margaret Sanger Papers Project at New York University in the article "Birth Control or Race Control? Sanger and the Negro Project" 28 (Fall 2001), http://www.nyu.edu/projects/sanger/secure/newsletter/articles/bc_or_race_control.html.

15. Sanger, *The Pivot of Civilization*, 48.

16. Jesse Lee Peterson with Brad Stetson, *From Rage to Responsibility* (St. Paul, MN: Paragon House, 2000), 71.

17. Ibid., 75.

18. Steven D. Levitt and Stephen J. Dubner, *Freakonomics: A Rogue Economist Explores the Hidden Side of Everything* (New York: William Morrow, 2005), 137–38.

19. Ibid., 141.

20. Office of Policy Planning and Research, US Department of Labor, *The Negro Family: The Case for National Action* (Washington, DC: Government Printing Office, 1965).

21. Amara Bachu, "Fertility," in US Census Bureau, *Population Profile of the United States*, 114 (Washington, DC: US Government Printing Office, 1998), 28, http://books.google.com/books?id=QZ_KDKRV4PEC&pg=PA28&lpg=PA28&dq=Population+Profile+of+the+United+States,%E2%80%9D+Amara+Bachu,+%E2%80%9CFertility,&source=bl&ots=ZfjMuIRtZ_&sig=sl60kpt_df_XbQRLVLuHgbPcnSg&hl=en&sa=X&ei=7Yr5T_GSN4yq8ATbxMnHBg&ved=0CDgQ6AEwAA#v=onepage&q=%20%E2%80%9CFertility%2C&f=false.

22. "Births to Unmarried Women by Race, Hispanic Origin, and Age of Mother: 1990 to 2008," *The 2012 Statistical Abstract*, Table 85, U.S. Census Bureau, http://www.census.gov/compendia/statab/2012/tables/12s0085.pdf.

23. Ibid., Table 84, "Teenagers—Births and Birth Rates by Age, Race, and Hispanic Origin: 1990 to 2009."

24. "Reported Legal Abortions by Race of Woman Who Obtained Abortion by the State of the Occurrence, 2008," Kaiser Family Foundation, StateHealthFacts.org, http://www.statehealthfacts.org/comparebar .jsp?ind=468&cat=10. For population, see *Infoplease*, http://www .infoplease.com/ipa/A0922246.html, and US Census Bureau, http:// quickfacts.census.gov/qfd/states/00000.html.

25. David Kupelian, *The Marketing of Evil: How Radicals, Elitists, and Pseudo-Experts Sell Us Corruption Disguised as Freedom* (Nashville: WND Books, 2005), 187.

26. Ibid.

27. ACLU, "LGBT Rights," ACLU.org, https://www.aclu.org/lgbt-rights.

28. Local, State, and National LGBT Organizations and Groups, Center Link, http://www.lgbtcenters.org/localstatenational-groups.aspx.

29. "ACLU Pushes for Gay Marriage Nationwide," United Press International, May 11, 2009, http://www.upi.com/Top_News/2009/05/11/ACLU -pushes-for-gay-marriage-nationwide/UPI-28121242066366/.

30. Margaret Talbot, "A Risky Proposal: Is It Too Soon to Petition the Supreme Court on Gay Marriage?" *New Yorker*, January 18, 2010, http:// www.newyorker.com/reporting/2010/01/18/100118fa_fact_talbot.

31. "LGBT Rights," ACLU.org.

32. http://www.ca9.uscourts.gov/datastore/general/2012/02/07/1016696com .pdf

33. ACLU, "The Work of the ACLU: Linking Gender Identity and Gay Rights," ACLU.org, December 31, 2000, www.aclu.org /lgbt-rights_hiv-aids/work-aclu-linking-gender-identity-and-gay-rights.

34. ACLU, "*Fields v. Smith*—Case Profile," ACLU.org, August 5, 2011, www.aclu.org/lgbt-rights_hiv-aids/sundstrom-v-frank-case-profile.

35. ACLU, "ACLU Challenges Unconstitutional Illinois Requirement for Correcting Transgender Birth Certificates," press release, ACLU.org, May 10, 2011, www.aclu.org/lgbt-rights/aclu-challenges-unconstitutional -illinois-requirements-correcting-transgender-birth-cert.

36. ACLU, "Washington County School District Revises Unconstitutional Policies, Allows Formation of Gay-Straight Alliances," press release, ACLU.org, April 26, 2010, www.aclu.org/lgbt-rights/washington-county- school-district-revises-unconstitutional-policies-allows-formation-gay.

37. ACLU, "ACLU Represents Students in Challenge to Sex Segregation in Kentucky Public School," press release, ACLU.org, May 19, 2008, www .aclu.org/womens-rights/aclu-represents-students-challenge-sex -segregation-kentucky-public-school.

38. ACLU, "ACLU Seeks Immediate Florida Supreme Court Hearing for

Children and Gay Adoptive Dad," press release, ACLU.org, December 5, 2008, www.aclufl.org/news_events/?action=viewRelease&emailAler tID=3688.

39. ACLU, "Overview of Lesbian and Gay Parenting, Adoption and Foster Care," ACLU.org, April 6, 1999, www.aclu.org/lgbt-rights_hiv-aids /overview-lesbian-and-gay-parenting-adoption-and-foster-care.

40. Ibid.

41. ACLU, "In re: Gill—Case Profile," ACLU.org, January 19, 2011, www .aclu.org/lgbt-rights_hiv-aids/re-gill-case-profile.

42. Katie Landan, "Gay Curriculum Proposal Riles Elementary School Parents," Fox News, May 22, 2009, www.foxnews.com/ story/0,2933,521209,00.html.

43. ACLU, "LGBT Youth & Schools," ACLU.org, www.aclu.org/lgbt-rights /youth-schools.

44. Susan Edelman, "Parent Furor at Bawdy Sex Ed," *New York Post*, October 24, 2011, www.nypost.com/p/news/local/parent_furor _at_bawdy_sex_ed_hdtJZVpYrFFtTZeVKMbGvN.

45. William A. Donohue, *The Politics of the American Civil Liberties Union* (New Brunswick, NJ: Transaction Books, 1985), 287, italics in original.

46. ACLU, amicus brief in the case *Aschroft v. Free Speech Coalition*, 535 U.S. 234 (2002), http://www.aclu.org/files/images/asset_upload_ file431_22042.pdf.

47. *Ashcroft v. ACLU*, 535 U.S. 564 (2002), http://www.oyez.org/cases /2000-2009/2001/2001_00_1293/.

48. ACLU, "Supreme Court Hears Web-Blocking Case," ACLU.org, March 4, 2003, http://www.aclu.org/technology-and-liberty/supreme -court-hears-web-blocking-case.

49. ACLU, "ACLU Disappointed in Ruling on Internet Censorship in Libraries, But Sees Limited Impact for Adults," press release, ACLU.org, June 23, 2003, www.aclu.org/technology-and-liberty/aclu-disappointed -ruling-internet-censorship-libraries-sees-limited-impact-ad.

50. "ACLU Exec Busted for Child Porn in Court Today," World Net Daily, February 28, 2007, www.wnd.com/?pageId=40389.

51. Bill Brubaker, "Va.'s Ex-ACLU Chief Gets 7 Years for Child Porn," *Washington Post*, September 7, 2007, www.washingtonpost.com/wp-dyn /content/article/2007/09/07/AR2007090701673.html.

52. Robert Knight, "Bullying for Dollars," *Washington Times*, April 15, 2011, www.washingtontimes.com/news/2011/apr/15/bullying-for-dollars/?page=all.

53. Brubaker, "Va.'s Ex-ACLU Chief Gets 7 Years."

54. Marshall Kirk and Hunter Madsen, *After the Ball: How America Will*

Conquer Its Fear and Hatred of Gays in the 90's (New York: Doubleday, 1989), 162, italics in original.

55. Ibid., 178, italics in original.

56. Ibid., 183.

57. Ibid., 232–33.

58. Ibid., 230–31.

59. Ibid., 244–45, italics in original.

60. Ibid., 307.

61. Ibid., 263.

62. Bryan Robinson, "ACLU Represents Man-Boy Love Group," ABC News, August 31, 2001, abcnews.go.com/US/story?id=95942&page=1.

63. Ibid.

64. Quoted in Sears and Osten, *The ACLU vs. America*, 75–76.

65. All quotes in this paragraph are drawn from the following article: Deroy Murdock, "No Boy Scouts: The ACLU defends NAMBLA," *National Review* Online, February 27, 2004, http://old.nationalreview.com /murdock/murdock200402270920.asp.

66. Ibid.

67. Jonathan Saltzman, "Curley Family Drops Case Against NAMBLA," *Boston Globe*, April 23, 2008, www.boston.com/news/local/breaking_ news/2008/04/curley_family_d.html.

68. Kera Bolonik, "A Conversation with James Dale," Salon.com, July 17, 2000, www.salon.com/2000/07/17/dale/.

69. "Supreme Court Says Boy Scouts Can Bar Gay Troop Leaders," CNN Justice, June 28, 2000, articles.cnn.com/2000-06-28/justice/scotus .gay.boyscouts_1_boy-scouts-gay-troop-scout-law?_s=PM:LAW.

70. Linda Greenhouse, "The Supreme Court: The New Jersey Case; Supreme Court Backs Boy Scouts in Ban of Gays from Membership," *New York Times*, June 29, 2000, www.nytimes.com/2000/06/29/us/supreme -court-new-jersey-case-supreme-court-backs-boy-scouts-ban-gays -membership.html.

71. *Boy Scouts of America and Monmouth Council, et al. v. James Dale* 530 U.S. 640 (2000), http://www.law.cornell.edu/supct/pdf/99-699P.ZO.

72. ACLU, "U.S. Supreme Court Ruling That Boy Scouts Can Discriminate Is 'Damaging but Limited,' ACLU Says," ACLU.org, June 28, 2000, www.aclu.org/content/us-supreme-court-ruling-boy-scouts-can -discriminate-damaging-limited-aclu-says.

73. Alan Sears and Craig Osten, *The Homosexual Agenda: Exposing the Principal Threat to Religious Freedom Today* (Nashville: B & H Publishing Group, 2003), 174.

74. Ibid.

75. Timothy S. Goeglein, *The Man in the Middle: An Inside Account of Faith and Politics in the George W. Bush Era* (Nashville: B & H Publishing Group, 2011), 122.

Chapter 7: The Far-Left ACLU Juggernaut

1. Michael Myers, interviewed by Bill O'Reilly, *O'Reilly Factor*, Fox News, January 6, 2006, www.foxnews.com/on-air/oreilly/2006/01/06 /aclu-exposes-itself.

2. Ibid.

3. Ibid.; all quotes in this paragraph are drawn from this source.

4. Ibid.; all quotes in this paragraph are drawn from this source.

5. Ta-Nehisi Paul Coates, "Anthony Romero," in "25 Most Influential Hispanics in America," *Time*, August 22, 2005, www.time.com/time /specials/packages/article/0,28804,2008201_2008200_2008185,00.html.

6. Doug Auer and Selim Algar, "ACLU Was 'DWI'; Rights-Group Leader Busted on LI," *New York Post*, August 10, 2011, http://www.nypost .com/p/news/local/aclu_was_dwi_bxRkmyOJ6KTEvcvKVYoeUJ.

7. Taylor K. Vecsey, "Cops: ACLU Director Arrested on DWI Charge in June," *East Hampton Patch*, August 10, 2011, easthampton.patch.com/ articles/cops-aclu-director-arrested-on-dwi-charge-in-june.

8. Selim Algar, "Legal Pals Advised ACLU Big Not to Take Breathalyzer Test in DWI," *New York Post*, August 10, 2011, www.nypost.com/p/news /local/legal_pals_told_aclu_big_not_dwi_7bkHSONDWOOfqH8rmbghtO.

9. Alan Feuer, "Sunday Routine: Anthony D. Romero. Taking a Break from Outrage," *New York Times*, December 24, 2009, www.nytimes.com /2009/12/27/nyregion/27routine.html.

10. Wendy Kaminer, "Hypocrisy at the ACLU," *Atlantic*, August 11, 2011, http://www.theatlantic.com/national/archive/2011/08/ hypocrisy-at-the-aclu/243422/.

11. Auer and Algar, "ACLU was 'DWI.'"

12. "ACLU vs. ACLU Foundation," ACLU of Pennsylvania, http://www .aclupa.org/home/abouttheaclu/acluvsaclufoundation.htm.

13. http://www.aclu.org/files/pdfs/about/fy2011_aclu_990.pdf.pdf. The Foundation is the larger of the two legal entities. The financials come from here: http://www.aclu.org/financials-0.

14. "ACLU vs. ACLU Foundation," ACLU of Pennsylvania.

15. "Financials," ACLU.org.

16. "Financial Statements," ACLU of Northern California, ACLUnc.org, www.aclunc.org/about/financial_statements/index.shtml.

17. Ed Grabianowski, "How the ACLU Works," How Stuff Works, people.howstuffworks.com/aclu4.htm.

18. ACLU, "ACLU Announces Historic Fundraising Success, Exceeding Goal and Building Civil Liberties Infrastructure in Battleground States," ACLU.org, September 15, 2010, www.aclu.org/organization-news-and -highlights/aclu-announces-historic-fundraising-success-exceeding-goal -and-buil.

19. American Civil Rights Union, "ACLU to Raise $335 Million to Attack the US Heartland," www.theacru.org/acru/aclu_to_raise_335_million _to_a/.

20. Ibid.

21. U.S. Code, Title 42, Chapter 21, Subchapter 1, Section 1988, law.cornell.edu/uscode/usc_sec_42_00001988----000-.html.

22. "Legion Campaign Backs Anti-ACLU Bill," World Net Daily, March 4, 2006, www.wnd.com/?pageId=35083.

23. American Legion, "Americanism 2009–2010," October 2009, legion.org /documents/legion/pdf/mp_americanism.pdf.

24. "Legion Campaign Backs Anti-ACLU Bill."

25. Alliance Defense Fund, "Financial Reports," AllianceDefenseFund.org, www.alliancedefensefund.org/About/Financials.

26. Alliance Defense Fund, "Media Kit," AllianceDefenseFund.org, oldsite .alliancedefensefund.org/userdocs/adf_media_kit.pdf.

27. Alliance Defense Fund, "ADF Supreme Court Victories," in ADF's "Media Kit." A more complete listing of ADF Supreme Court cases can be found at "Supreme Court Victories," AllianceDefenseFund.org, www.alliancedefensefund.org/Home/ADFContent?cid=3197.

28. ACLU, "Supreme Court Rules Arizona Taxpayers Lack Standing to Challenge Tax Credit System Used to Award Religious-Based Scholarships," ACLU.org, April 4, 2011, www.aclu.org/religion-belief/ supreme-court-rules-arizona-taxpayers-lack-standing-challenge-tax -credit-system-used.

29. Justice Elena Kagan, dissenting opinion, with whom Justice Ruth Bader Ginsburg, Justice Stephen Breyer, and Justice Sonia Sotomayor joined, *Arizona Christian School Tuition Organization v. Winn*, 563 U.S. ____ (2011), http://supreme.justia.com/cases/federal/us/563/09-987/dissent.html.

30. Ibid.

31. Justice John Paul Stevens, dissenting opinion, with whom Justice Ruth Bader Ginsburg and Justice Sonia Sotomayor joined, *Salazar v. Buono*, 559 U.S. ____ (2010), http://supreme.justia.com/cases/federal/us/559 /08-472/dissent.html.

32. Ibid.

33. Justice Anthony Kennedy, delivering the opinion of the court, *Gonzales v. Carhart*, 550 U.S. ____ (2007), http://supreme.justia.com/cases/federal/us/550/05-380/opinion.html.

34. Justice Ruth Bader Ginsburg, dissenting, with whom Justice John Paul Stevens, Justice David Souter, and Justice Stephen Breyer join, dissenting, *Gonzales v. Carhart*, 550 U.S. 124 (2007), http://supreme.justia.com/cases/federal/us/550/05-380/dissent.html.

35. Erwin Chemerinsky, "*Van Orden v. Perry, McCreary v. ACLU*," Duke Law, www.law.duke.edu/publiclaw/supremecourtonline/commentary/vanvper. Professor Chemerinsky, Alston & Bird Professor of Law at Duke University School of Law, was counsel of record for Thomas Van Orden in *Van Orden v. Perry.*

36. Justice Stephen Breyer, separate concurring opinion, *Van Orden v. Perry*, 545 U.S. 677 (2005), http://supreme.justia.com/cases/federal/us/545/03-1500/concurrence3.html.

37. Justice Clarence Thomas, delivering the opinion of the Court, *Good News Club v. Milford Central Schools*, 533 U.S. 98 (2001), http://supreme.justia.com/cases/federal/us/533/98/case.html.

38. Corliss Lamont, ed., *The Trial of Elizabeth Gurley Flynn by the American Civil Liberties Union* (New York: Horizon Press, 1968), 20–21, italics in original.

39. Paul Kengor, *Dupes: How America's Adversaries Have Manipulated Progressives for a Century* (Wilmington, DE: ISI Books, 2010), 308.

40. Virginia Foster Durr, *Letters from the Civil Rights Years: Freedom Writer* (Athens: University of Georgia Press, 2006), 80, http://books.google.com/books?id=-lzIEnKM69IC&pg=PA80&lpg=PA80&dq=national+emergency+civil+liberties+committee+lamont&source=bl&ots=hM2DViu2hr&sig=dvuNDrZdFRWXX4WhRgBPVnrUAgw&hl=en&sa=X&ei=8cf6T6n5FIjM9QSC4uzjBg&ved=0CDMQ6AEwAA#v=onepage&q=national%20emergency%20civil%20liberties%20committee%20lamont&f=false.

41. Rick Lyman, "Frank Wilkinson, Defiant Figure of Red Scare, Dies at 91," *New York Times*, January 4, 2006, www.nytimes.com/2006/01/04/national/04wilkinson.html?_r=1&scp=3&sq=%22beverly+hills+high+school%22+attended&oref=slogin.

42. "Frank Receiving ACLU Earl Warren Civil Liberties Award, Dec. 1997, with Richard Criley in San Francisco," Frank Wilkinson Tribute, March 1, 2006, frankwilkinson.blogspot.com/2006/03/frank-receiving-aclu-earl-warren-civil.html. See also Frank Wilkinson, "Revisiting the 'McCarthy Era': Looking at *Wilkinson v. United States* in Light of *Wilkinson v. Federal Bureau of Investigation*," *Loyola of Los Angeles Law Review* 33 (2000): 681–98.

43. Donna Lieberman, NYCLU executive eirector, "Protecting Protest at Occupy Wall Street," NYCLU.org, October 6, 2011, www.nyclu.org /occupywallstreet.

44. Quoted in David Martosko, "Red, White and Angry: Communist, Nazi Parties Endorse 'Occupy' Protests,'" *Daily Caller*, October 17, 2011, dailycaller.com/2011/10/17/red-white-and-angry%E2%80%A8 -communist-nazi-parties-endorse-occupy-protests/.

45. Communist Party USA, "Communist Party Heralds Occupy Wall Street Movement," CPUSA.org, October 18, 2011, www.cpusa.org /communist-party-heralds-occupy-wall-street-movement/.

46. W. Cleon Skousen, *The Naked Communist* (Salt Lake City: Ensign Publishing Company, 1958), 292–93.

47. Ibid., 298, italics in original.

48. Ibid.

49. William Z. Foster, *Outline Political History of the Americas* (New York: International Publishers, 1951).

50. Ibid., 93.

51. Skousen, *Naked Communist*, 295.

52. Ibid., 303.

53. Ibid.

54. Ibid., 295.

55. Remarks by Representative Albert Sydney Herlong Jr., a Florida Democrat, in the US House of Representatives, January 10, 1963, placing into the record a list of "Current Communist Goals," derived from *The Naked Communist* by W. Cleon Skousen, uhuh.com/nwo/communism /comgoals.htm#Documention.

56. Bill O'Reilly, "The ACLU Exposes Itself," Fox News, January 6, 2006, www.foxnews.com/on-air/oreilly/2006/01/06/aclu-exposes-itself.

57. Ibid.

58. Ibid.

59. Adam Liptak, "A.C.L.U. Board Is Split over Terror Watch Lists," *New York Times*, July 31, 2004, www.nytimes.com/2004/07/31/us/aclu -board-is-split-over-terror-watch-lists.html?pagewanted=all&src=pm.

60. Ibid.

61. Ibid.

62. Adam Liptak, "A.C.L.U. to Withdraw from Charity Drive," *New York Times*, August 1, 2004, www.nytimes.com/2004/08/01/us/aclu-to -withdraw-from-charity-drive.html.

63. Stephanie Strom, "A.C.L.U.'s Search for Data on Donors Stirs Privacy Fears," *New York Times*, December 18, 2004, www.nytimes.com /2004/12/18/national/18aclu.html?_r=1.

64. Ibid.

65. Ibid.

66. Stephanie Strom, "Supporters of A.C.L.U. Call for the Ouster of Its Leaders," *New York Times*, September 26, 2006, www.nytimes.com /2006/09/26/us/26aclu.html.

67. Ibid.

68. David France, "Freedom to Backstab," *New York*, February 11, 2007, nymag.com/news/features/27839/.

69. Wendy Kaminer, *Worst Instincts: Cowardice, Conformity, and the ACLU* (Boston: Beacon Press, 2009).

70. Ibid., 66.

71. Ibid., 75.

72. Ibid., 129.

73. Wendy Kaminer, "The American Liberal Liberties Union," *Wall Street Journal*, May 23, 2007, online.wsj.com/article/SB117988506623111630 .html?mod=googlenews_wsj.

74. Ibid.

75. Michelle Bauman, "Administration Drops Catholic Humanitarian Work that Provoked ACLU," Catholic News Agency, October 13, 2011, www.catholicnewsagency.com/news/administration-drops-catholic -humanitarian-work-that-provoked-aclu/.

76. ACLU, "ACLU Asks Court to Stop Misuse of Taxpayer Dollars in Trafficking Victims' Program," ACLU.org, January 12, 2009, www.aclu.org/print/reproductive-freedom/ aclu-asks-court-stop-misuse-taxpayer-dollars-trafficking-victims-program.

77. Ibid.

78. Ibid.

79. Pete Winn, "HHS Withholds Grant from U.S. Conference of Catholic Bishops Apparently Because Church Opposes Abortion," CNSNews.com, October 24, 2011, cnsnews.com/news/article/hhs-withholds-grant -us-conference-catholic-bishops-apparently-because-church-opposes.

80. "U.S. Bishops Establish New Ad Hoc Committee for Religious Freedom," US Conference of Catholic Bishops, September 30, 2011, http://www .usccb.org/news/2011/11-184.cfm.

81. Letter from Most Reverend Timothy M. Dolan, Archbishop of New York, and President, US Conference of Catholic Bishops, to "My Brother Bishops," September 29, 2011, http://www.usccb.org/issues-and-action /religious-liberty/upload/dolan-letter-on-religious-liberty.pdf.

82. "USCCB Forms Religious Liberty Committee," Causa Nostrae Laetitiae, October 3, 2011, causa-nostrae-laetitiae.blogspot.com/2011/10/usccb -forms-religious-liberty-committee.html.

83. William A. Donohue, *Twilight of Liberty: The Legacy of the ACLU* (New Brunswick, NJ: Transaction Publishers, 1994), 98–99.

84. "USCCB Forms Religious Liberty Committee."

85. ACLU, "Issues and Case Summary: *Walz v. Tax Commission of the City of New York,*" December 17, 2009, http://aclu.procon.org/view.resource .php?resourceID=409#AmiciCuriae.

86. William J. Murray, *My Life Without God* (Nashville: Thomas Nelson, 1982), 95.

87. Madalyn Murray O'Hair, "Program 28, December 9, 1968, KTBC Radio, Austin, Texas: 'Religion and Taxes,'" published in Madalyn Murray O'Hair, *What on Earth Is an Atheist!* (New York: Arno Press, 1972), 144–49.

88. Bryan F. Le Beau, *The Atheist: Madalyn Murray O'Hair* (New York: New York University Press, 2003), 148.

Conclusion: God Fights Back

1. Dwight D. Eisenhower, inaugural address, January 20, 1953, http:// www.bartleby.com/124/pres54.html.

2. Alan Sears and Craig Osten, *The ACLU vs. America: Exposing the Agenda to Redefine Moral Values* (Nashville: Broadman & Holman, 2005), 194.

3. Ibid., 187.

4. Ronald Reagan, "Proclamation 5761," delivered January 14, 1988, in Washington, DC, http://www.gpo.gov/fdsys/pkg/CREC-2004-06-25 /html/CREC-2004-06-25-pt1-PgS7507-2.htm.

5. Ibid.

6. Justice William O. Douglas, delivering the majority opinion, *Griswold v. Connecticut,* 381 U.S. 479 (1965), http://supreme.justia.com/cases/federal /us/381/479/case.html.

7. Justice Hugo Black, with whom Justice Potter Stewart joins, dissenting in *Griswold v. Connecticut,* 381 U.S. 479 (1965).

8. Justice William Rehnquist, dissenting opinion, *Roe v. Wade,* 410 U.S. 113 (1973), http://www.law.cornell.edu/supct/html/historics/USSC_CR _0410_0113_ZD.html.

9. Simon van Zuylen-Wood, "A Radical New Ploy to Destroy *Roe v. Wade*— Which Just Might Work," *New Republic,* September 2, 2011, http://www .tnr.com/article/politics/94470/personhood-abortion-mississippi-roe-wade.

10. Daniel C. Becker, *Personhood: A Pragmatic Guide to Prolife Victory in the 21st Century and the Return to First Principles in Politics* (Alpharetta, GA: TKS Publications, 2011), 25–26. See also "Personhood USA," http:// www.personhoodusa.com/.

11. Quoted in Y. M. Lichtenstein and T. Moskovits, "Justice Scalia: 'The American People Respect Religion,'" Hamodia, 2009, http://www .hamodia.com/inthepaper.cfm?ArticleID=370.

12. Submitted by Keith Ashley, a video, *The Key to Defeating Roe v. Wade Is Personhood*, PersonhoodUSA.com, September 15, 2011, http://www .personhoodusa.com/video/key-defeating-roe-v-wade-personhood.

13. Ibid.

14. *ACLU v. Mercer County, Kentucky,* 432 F.3d 624 (6th Cir. 2005).

15. *American Civil Liberties Union of Kentucky v. Mercer County, Kentucky,* US Court of Appeals for the Sixth Circuit, No. 03-5142, http://www .ca6.uscourts.gov/opinions.pdf/05a0477p-06.pdf.

16. Ibid.

17. Ibid.

18. Ibid.

19. Alan Keyes, "Separation of Morals and State," World Net Daily, December 30, 2000, http://www.wnd.com/news/article .asp?ARTICLE_ID=21149.

20. Ibid.

21. Joseph Farah, "The War on the Boy Scouts," World Net Daily, January 4, 2001, http://www.wnd.com/news/article.asp?ARTICLE_ID=21204.

22. Ibid.

ABOUT THE AUTHOR

J EROME CORSI has written and coauthored many books and articles,
including two #1 *New York Times* bestsellers: *Unfit for Command:
Swift Boat Veterans Speak Out Against John Kerry* (Washington
DC: Regnery, 2004) and *The Obama Nation: Leftist Politics and the Cult
of Personality* (New York: Simon & Schuster Threshold Editions, 2008).
Since 2004, Corsi has had six hardcover books appear on the *New York
Times* Bestseller List; they cover a wide range of topics, including presidential politics; foreign policy, with a special emphasis on Iran and Israel; and
various economic topics. Since 2004, he has appeared on Fox News, Fox
Business News, MSNBC, and CNBC, and he has given thousands of radio
interviews in local, state, regional, and national markets. Dr. Corsi received
his BA degree (1968) from Case Western Reserve University in Cleveland,
Ohio, and his PhD in political science (1972) from Harvard University
in Cambridge, Massachusetts. He is currently a senior staff reporter for
WND.com, and he lives with his family in New Jersey.

INDEX